CRIMES OF OMISSION

Distorted Justice: The Media's War on Truth

ROB ROSEN

A POST HILL PRESS BOOK
ISBN: 979-8-88845-974-4
ISBN (eBook): 979-8-88845-975-1

Crimes of Omission:
Distorted Justice: The Media's War on Truth

Cover design by Jim Villaflores

This is a work of nonfiction. All people, locations, events, and situations are portrayed to the best of the author's memory and knowledge. Although adequate research was undergone concerning criminal cases, real-life people and perceptions, and authentic situations and incidents, the author and publisher do not assume and hereby disclaim any liability concerning any legal or criminal details present in this book.

This book, as well as any other Post Hill Press publications, may be purchased in bulk quantities at a special discounted rate. Contact orders@posthillpress.com for more information.

Post Hill Press
New York • Nashville
posthillpress.com

Published in the United States of America
1 2 3 4 5 6 7 8 9 10

To the late Judi Paparelli
Thanks for believing in me well before I believed in myself.

Table of Contents

Part Three: Hellfire

Epilogue

Preface

When I was ten, if you had asked me what I wanted to be when I grew up, I would have said to become nothing like my father. Little did I know there was an actual job description for that: journalist.

From the outside looking in, my dad seemed to have it all: a dental practice, a depressed trophy wife, and a large Tudor house in the same Boston suburb that the Kennedys, Mike Wallace, and Conan O'Brien once called home. But none of that made him happy. He was a man possessed by impulsiveness and rage. These traits were on full display every weeknight when I obediently shuffled behind him to the den, where we would spend one hour of what was billed as bonding time. This mostly consisted of watching the local news at six, followed by the network news at six-thirty.

"Fuck you, you liberal shit!" my father would shout at the screen in his thick immigrant accent, spittle flying out of his mouth, his face purple with rage, eyes registering horror at the perceived injustice of it all. What exactly was this grave injustice?

It could have been anything, from a criminal getting a sentence—it was never enough—to an anchor reporting on the high unemployment rates for people of color. "Look at me. I'm a *shvartze*. I have it so bad! Poor me!" He would theatrically rub faux tears away from his eyes.

My father's political allegiances were head-spinningly inconsistent. He could go from Archie Bunker to Che Guevara in the blink of an eye. A handcuffed Black man doing a perp walk would prompt dramatic eye rolls and shouts of "Yeah, big surprise!" A handcuffed, balding White banker being led away in handcuffs would prompt him to raise his fist and shout, "*Revolución*!"

Any story involving women was sure to trigger him. A report about the gender pay gap would elicit shouts of "stupid American feminists!" Or maybe, "She is so ugly she has to work. Look at her. Who would fuck this horse?" He would laugh uproariously and look to me for approval. I always stared straight ahead impassively. Not because, as a child, I had some heightened sense of social justice—I didn't—but because I felt such disdain for him, his vulgarity, his overwrought behavior and his complete lack of forbearance. Truth had no place in this home.

Even fluff pieces could set my dad off. A nice, inoffensive story about a father volunteering to coach his son's baseball team would prompt shouts of "stupid Americans and their primitive sports. Children do what parent likes. Not other way."

During these so-called bonding sessions with my father, nothing caused my heart to drop as much as the following five words: *In the Middle East tonight.* My father's entrenched position was that Israel was infallible and that the only good Arab was a dead one. Any reporting more nuanced than this was denounced as anti-Semitic and proof that everyone hates Jews.

It was during these sessions that I developed habits that would serve me well professionally and quite poorly in my personal life. As my father screamed, spit, and threateningly waved his middle finger at the screen, I would become preternaturally calm and hyper-rational: "Dad, why are you upset that these Arab women are crying? Right or wrong, they lost their husbands and children."

"Fuck you!" My father would turn to me, face beet-red, shouting in his broken English, "You are a stupid child! You know nothing!"

If my mother happened to be in the room at the time, she would shake her head in disappointment and say, "Why do you upset your father like this? He works so hard for us."

I knew I was supposed to be more understanding of my broken parents—both of whom were war children. My mother was born in a Polish village in 1940 and then hidden by nuns during the German occupation. She emerged from the war an orphan; both her parents had been killed in the camps. My father's Russian family emerged from the war intact but traumatized. That's a hard concept for a child to grasp. It was the 1970s, but to me, World War II might as well have taken place in Jurassic times.

I saw journalists as everything I wished my father would be. Reporters had a sober demeanor. They never got swept away by the passions of the moment. Dan Rather, Tom Brokaw, Peter Jennings, the Boston local news anchors, all exuded calm. *Here's what happened today. Here's why it happened. Nothing to get excited about.*

But excitability was all I saw around me: my father shouting at a woman in the supermarket because he falsely believed she had more than fifteen items in the express line; my mom spending the day in bed, crying, begging me to go to law school, telling me that she didn't survive the war for me to become some sort of a TV person; or my dad making a scene on an airplane when told there was no bin space for his carry-on bag.

This was my home. A world where facts meant nothing. Truth was whatever my parents said it was, and asking questions was an act of insubordination. I was determined to leave this place, and journalism was going to be my "get out of jail free" card.

It may sound absurd, but TV news raised me. It's where I found role models and mentors. The elder statesmen of the business taught me how to work, how to think, how to reason, how to collaborate, how to lead, how to learn, and how to handle pressure. I entered the business as a child, and I'd like to think it made me a man.

But something happened along the way.

The business I love so much, the business that saved me—it changed.

It became full of distortions, dogma, snap judgments, and a stubborn refusal to question authority.

It became my father.

This book is my attempt to figure out how that happened, survey the damage, and find a path back home.

Prologue

Friday, May 29, 2020.

America was burning and seemed to be on the brink of civil war.

It was the third month of the pandemic, which, like seemingly everything else in America, had become highly politicized. Blue states were extending lockdowns, keeping schools and businesses closed, and mandating public masking. In contrast, red states were slowly reopening, despite hyperbolic—and, as it would turn out, false—warnings that this would lead to skyrocketing death rates.

But on this day, the pandemic would not lead any of the major TV newscasts. Instead, all the reporting was about a nation on fire. The United States, violently ripping itself in two.

That day, millions took to the streets demanding foundational societal changes. But when the sun went down, tens of thousands used the civil unrest as a pretense to burn, loot, destroy, and kill.

The incident that set off this latest round of violence had occurred just days earlier, when Minneapolis police officer Derek

Chauvin was caught on cellphone video, kneeling on the neck of George Floyd, a Black man suspected of trying to pass off a counterfeit twenty-dollar bill at a nearby convenience store.

Billions would watch in horror as Floyd repeatedly cried out, "I can't breathe."

Angry bystanders could be heard, off camera, berating Chauvin.

"You got him down. Let him breathe!"

"How long y'all going to hold him down?"

The answer to that last question was nine minutes and twenty-nine seconds. Many who watched and rewatched this reality snuff film would swear that Chauvin seemed to smirk as he kept his knee pressed on Floyd's neck, not letting up, even after the suspect had stopped resisting.

This video seemed to encapsulate everything anti-police activists had been claiming since the killing of Trayvon Martin sparked the Black Lives Matter (BLM) movement. Here was an arrogant and smug White police officer killing a Black suspect after casually ignoring his pleas for mercy.

The media seemed to believe it was on the right side of what many were calling a "racial reckoning" in America.

So, to many Fourth Estaters, it came as quite a shock when, that night, protesters in Atlanta began converging on CNN headquarters. Of all the institutions to be angry at, it seemed like the most unlikely target: Wasn't CNN an ally to the cause?

At first, the crowd was pretty tame.

As the day progressed, things slowly deteriorated. Some people took out spray cans and defaced the gawdy twelve-foot-high CNN letters proudly adorning the front of the building. Others managed to climb on top of the letters, triumphantly holding up BLM flags, as the crowd euphorically cheered and snapped photos, which were instantly uploaded to social media sites and spread across the globe.

As the sun went down, a few people in the crowd began hurling rocks and bottles at the glass entrance of CNN Center. The design made the building look cool and futuristic, but now, it was suddenly vulnerable to attack.

Inside, CNN employees were trapped and terrified. They called the police. Suddenly, they weren't reporting the story; they were the story.

A prominent sociologist once came up with a theory called the threshold model of collective behavior. It posits that riots don't happen because most people in a crowd are ready for violence—they happen when a few outliers start throwing rocks or setting fires, creating a permission structure for others to join in.

That's exactly what was happening at the CNN Center. The crowd began to feed off itself. No longer satisfied with throwing projectiles at the network's entrance, the most aggressive members of the mob were now determined to storm the gates. Emotions ran high, and the crowd cheered, as the leaders of the riot grabbed anything solid they could get their hands on—like street barricades and skateboards—and began smashing in the glass doors of the lobby.

Once they accomplished that mission, they were finally met with resistance: A wall of SWAT officers were fanned out inside the lobby, blocking the mob's access to the CNN studios and the frightened staff trapped inside.

The irony of this was lost on Nick Valencia, a CNN lifer who began his career as a teleprompter operator and improbably worked his way up to become an on-air correspondent. Now, here he was, in the lobby of his own workplace, reporting live on the standoff. As the crowd continued to throw rocks, firecrackers, and projectiles at the officers, Valencia, voice quivering, seemed unable to fathom why the protesters' rage would be directed towards him and his co-workers. "This is our home, you know. This is where we come to work every day. Journalists who are trying to tell the truth, trying to deliver information for the noble part of our society, and these demonstrators have decided to come here today to take out their frustrations and anger, not just on the police, but on our CNN Center as well."

Valencia may not have understood what was going on, but an influential Atlanta rapper certainly did. At a hastily called news conference begging for calm, Killer Mike said, "I love CNN.... But I'd like to say to CNN right now, karma's a mother. Stop feeding fear and anger every day. Stop making people so fearful. Give them hope."[1]

This book will illustrate how mainstream news coverage of law enforcement violence, from Trayvon Martin's death in 2012 to the killing of George Floyd in 2020, was not only highly incendiary but also dangerously misleading. It inflamed the public and brought racial tensions to a boiling point.

To prove this, I will contrast the media's reporting of these high-profile cases with a fact-based account of what actually happened. The truth is largely a matter of public record, but legacy media showed little interest in the complex realities of these killings. When you view the facts and the coverage side by side, it is difficult to believe that the disconnect was just an honest mistake.

1 Joseph Wulfsohn, "Rapper Killer Mike Pleads to CNN: 'Stop Feeding Fear and Anger Every Day,'" Fox News, May 29, 2020

The thesis of this book is not that the media lies to the American public. The vast majority of stories are factually correct. Every newsroom has risk-averse lawyers who do a pretty good job making sure overzealous reporters and producers avoid outright slander. Ideological watchdog groups and social media sleuths are ready to pounce whenever newscasters report something that is factually incorrect. The real bias in news come from crimes of omission. In other words, the distortions do not come from what is reported. They come from what is left out.

In the story of the anti-police movement of the 2010s, the crimes of omission were numerous. Most egregiously, legacy media almost exclusively reported on cases involving Black victims, even though two-thirds of unarmed suspects killed by police during that time period were *not* African American. Legacy media also sanctified each victim, refusing to portray them as the complex, and sometimes deeply flawed, individuals they truly were. Broadcast news minimized the violence associated with the protests, despite the heartbreaking destruction and loss of life that too often followed.

Legacy news also refused to take a critical look at the emerging BLM movement, even though there were clear signs from the outset that the group was steeped in radical, anti-Semitic, anti-capitalistic, and anti-Western beliefs. Any studies or data points that challenged the activists' narrative were either ignored or attacked. Journalists also failed to put American law enforcement in its proper context. They rarely mentioned that police shootings of unarmed suspects—while tragic—had become relatively rare. Nor did they mention that modern police methods were saving thousands of lives each year.

It is critical to remember that broadcast news is, first and foremost, a business, and many veteran decision-makers saw the protests, riots, and violence as an easy story to cover. It had all the ingredients of compelling television: a good vs. evil morality play, passion, race, and violence.

But the media has paid the ultimate price for the deceptive way it covered the most explosive story of the decade: It lost the confidence of the public. A 2024 Gallup poll reveals that the majority of Americans have more faith in Congress than in the media. Imagine that! People find Lauren Boebert and AOC (Alexandria Ocasio-Cortez) more believable than Anderson Cooper and David Muir.

Another poll shows 50 percent of Americans believe that journalists *purposely* try to mislead people and only 21 percent have 'high trust' in national news organizations.[2]

We have come a very long way from those halcyon days when families gathered around the television to watch newscasters like Walter Cronkite, the most trusted man in television, wrap each broadcast with his catchphrase, "And that's the way it is." We believed in him, and because we believed, we all shared a similar worldview. That's not to say everyone had the same political viewpoints in the 1970s and '80s; of course, they didn't. Disagreements are a healthy and normal part of a democracy. But we are at a frightening crossroads in our history—one where people can't even agree on the most basic facts. We are living in entirely separate realities, seeing the world through different, distorted lenses.

Imagine a house built entirely out of glass. Some of us are facing the front, looking out on a pleasant suburban street.

---

2 "American Views 2022: Part 2, Trust Media and Democracy," Knight Foundation, February 15, 2023

Others are facing the back, looking out on a beautiful backyard with a nice swimming pool. A third side of this metaphorical glass house faces a neighbor's dilapidated trailer, with a rusty old car and beat-up couches littering the lawn. The fourth side looks out on a depressing strip mall with boarded-up store windows.

America is like this glass house.

News outlets, which should be showing us a balanced view from all four vantage points, tend to show us only one. So, the person looking out on the beautiful backyard cannot understand why the person looking at the neighbor's trashy trailer is so pessimistic. And the person with a view of the decaying strip mall cannot fathom why the person facing the front of the house doesn't share her anxiety about the economy. We are all living in the same house, under the same roof, but our perceptions of reality are totally shaped by where we stand.

If you believe that we are facing imminent existential doom from climate change, that capitalism is destroying the planet, and that the country is systemically racist, you probably have very little in common with someone who believes that the country is going to hell because of stifling political correctness, creeping socialism, and a total breakdown in law and order.

These are not philosophical differences. These are differences in perceptions of reality.

The result: Politics has become America's bloodsport with families, couples, and friendships breaking up over irreconcilable differences in worldviews. Many who think they're cutting toxic loved ones out of their lives because of differences in values are actually breaking up with them because they're consuming their daily dose of "reality" from different, for-profit, corporate news organizations. Framed this way, these rifts seem ludicrous and utterly senseless. Yet, each side is convinced that *they're the ones* who have a firm grasp on reality, while it's the other person who's being lied to and misinformed.

This dynamic has plunged us into a national crisis. Talk of civil war has always seemed overwrought and sensationalistic, but it's now a very real threat. A stunning 2024 survey revealed that 47 percent of Americans believe it's likely or very likely that there will be another civil war in their lifetime.[3]

Real journalism requires a lot of hard work. There are no shortcuts. From 2016–2022, I created, directed, and served as showrunner for a series called *Reasonable Doubt*.[4] In every episode, a family, convinced that their loved one was wrongfully convicted of murder, would call our team in. We would reinvestigate the case, digging into all the fascinating twists and turns of a real-life murder mystery. At the end of each episode, in a highly emotional climax, we would let the families know whether we would get behind their case or whether we believed their loved one really was guilty. Thanks in part to our reporting, nine of the inmates we profiled were released—some were even exonerated. The justice system had failed those convicts, and I was proud to be leading a team dedicated to speaking truth to power.

However, in the vast majority of the cases we investigated, the justice system had done its job correctly, and we had to gently let the convict's family know that they were fighting a losing battle: Their loved one was guilty as charged. Delivering this heartbreaking news to a family took an emotional toll on many of the show's talented producers and researchers. Some were caught up in the burgeoning social justice movement and

---

3 "A Nation Divided?" Marist Poll, May 21, 2024

4 All fifty episodes of the series are available for streaming on Max.

had a strong predisposition to believe in the inmates' innocence regardless of what the facts revealed.

I had to break the staff off this impulse.

Every day, like a broken record, I reinforced the show's mantra: We were on a fearless pursuit of truth. We needed to let the facts lead us, not the other way around. Justice for the victims' families was just as important as justice for the inmates'. We would take each case, one by one, and do our very best to reach a fair and just decision—not based on what we wished to be true but based on what the facts revealed. It was an exercise in the radical acceptance of reality.

We also did our very best not to commit crimes of omission. There is a strong impulse in television, especially unscripted TV, to be reductionist, to erase all gray areas and make stories simple and clean with "likable" protagonists and irredeemable bad guys. Some of the cases we got behind featured inmates who were hard to root for: career criminals, drug dealers, gang members, or domestic abusers. We didn't try to soften their rough edges, to turn them into heroic Dr. Richard Kimble types. We presented them as they were and trusted the audience to be able to handle the messiness and gray areas of real life.

Correctly covering police violence in the 2010s would have required reporting *all* of the contradictory evidence in each high-profile case, allowing viewers to arrive at their own conclusions. It would have meant doing real investigative reporting, not just regurgitating the storylines provided by attorneys and civil rights activists. It would have meant refusing to amplify the unproven allegations that these incidents were racially motivated. Above all, it would have meant embracing the thing that makes journalism such an exciting, provocative, and intellectually stimulating profession: the relentless pursuit of truth.

Tragically, legacy news did not take this path, and this book will try to explain why. Dozens of high-profile reporters, anchors, producers, and managers spoke to me at length, providing vivid accounts of what went into the catastrophic newsroom decisions that corrupted the coverage of this critical, nearly decade-long story.

Legacy news' misleading coverage of police violence did serious damage to the health and stability of the country.

In a 2000 Gallup poll, only 4 percent of Americans believed race or racism was the most important problem in America.[5] Twenty years later, that number was up fivefold.

By 2020, largely due to the media's irresponsible reporting, most Americans were left with the indelible impression that US law enforcement was systemically racist. A very revealing poll asked respondents how many unarmed Black people they believed had been killed by the police in 2019.[6] Among those who self-identified as "very liberal," 53.5 percent guessed the number was at least one thousand. Another 39 percent of people who identified as "liberal" made the same guess. The actual number was just fourteen.[7]

This false narrative was so pervasive that even a majority of people who described themselves as "very conservative" believed that police had killed at least one hundred unarmed Black men that year—a figure off by a factor of seven.

---

5 Frank Newport, "Race Relations as the Nation's Most Important Problem," Gallup, June 19, 2020

6 "Estimate: How Many Unarmed Black People Were Killed by Police? (2019)," Skeptic Research Center

7 Heather Mac Donald, "There is No Epidemic of Fatal Police Shootings Against Unarmed Black Americans," Manhattan Institute, July 3, 2000

An important disclaimer: I am not a sociologist. I am not trying to provide a commentary on the history of policing in America, especially as it was enforced against Black communities. I am not casting judgment on the millions of Americans who took to the streets protesting police violence.

If we forget the sins of the past, we are doomed to repeat them. From slavery to the Holocaust, to countless bloody and needless wars, history is littered with examples of man's cruelty to man. It is critical for us to wrestle with our ghosts, but that work belongs to educators and historians—not journalists. Historical wrongs do not justify distorting present-day facts. The news is not a vehicle to settle old scores.

My intent in this book is simply to demonstrate that the media's coverage of the BLM-led movement between 2012–2020 was not only highly misleading, but often divorced from reality.

In the pre-digital age, the public relied on mainstream journalists to serve as their eyes and ears to the world. The reporting was never perfect—there was always some bias—but until the early 2010s, newsrooms tried to live up to The Journalist's Creed,[8] which states in part, "I believe that clear thinking and clear statement, accuracy and fairness are fundamental to good journalism."

It is my contention that if journalists had stayed true to their mission and had covered police violence with a healthy degree of balance, skepticism, and curiosity, America would not have burned in 2020, the nation would be more united today, and the public would still believe newscasters who say "and that's the way it is."

---

8 Walter Williams, "The Journalist's Creed," 1914

Part One
Slow Burn

"However much you deny the truth,
the truth goes on existing."

—GEORGE ORWELL

Chapter 1
Trayvon Martin: Birth of a Movement

Sometimes, small, seemingly insignificant events spark huge social movements that bend the arc of history.

In 1955, forty-two-year-old Rosa Parks, exhausted from a long day of work, refused to give up her seat on a Montgomery bus for a White passenger. This small act of defiance energized and kickstarted the civil rights movement.

In 2010, a Tunisian fruit vendor, enraged by police harassment, set himself on fire, sparking the Arab Spring.

And on February 26, 2012, a worldwide movement, which would ultimately bring the United States to the brink of civil war, was ignited when a troubled Florida teenager was walking home after getting snacks at a local 7-Eleven.

Trayvon Martin wasn't even supposed to have been in Sanford, Florida, on that fateful night. The high school junior lived with his mom, Sybrina Fulton, in the crime-ridden neighborhood of Miami Gardens, which is about a four-hour drive south. But he was spending the week with his dad—a punishment of sorts, after getting into trouble yet again.

Trayvon's family was worried about him. The seventeen-year-old was fascinated with guns, drugs, and violence. Online, he went by the handle "No Limit Nigga" and there were videos circulating on social media showing him openly and proudly smoking out.

Trayvon didn't have a criminal record, but he was constantly getting into trouble at school, which earned him three separate suspensions. The first offense was for being chronically late and skipping school. The second suspension happened in October 2011, when he was caught writing obscene graffiti on a school door.[9] In that incident, the school's police department did a routine check of Trayvon's backpack and found twelve pieces of women's jewelry, a watch, and a screwdriver, which they believed might have been a burglary tool.[10] Police searched their database but couldn't match the jewelry to any reported stolen items, so Trayvon wasn't charged with theft. His final suspension came in February 2012, when school administrators found trace amounts of marijuana in his book bag. As a repeat offender, Trayvon was kicked out of school for ten days.

As she did each time he got suspended, Sybrina Fulton packed her son's bags and sent him up north to spend some time with his birth dad, Tracy Martin, who would later say the purpose of the visit was to help Trayvon "disconnect and get priorities straight."[11]

---

9 "Police Investigated Trayvon Martin Over Jewelry," *Times Union*, March 27, 2012

10 Mark Memmott, "Trayvon Martin's Life Looking Much Like Many Teens,'" NPR, March 27, 2012

11 Karen Franklin and Ari Odzer, "Father Wants Man Who Shot His Son Arrested," NBC Miami, March 9, 2012

At the time, Martin, a truck driver, was living with his fiancé, Brandy Green, in a gated community called The Retreat at Twin Lakes. Despite the bougie-sounding name, the community was mostly working-class. It consisted of 260 townhomes and was racially diverse: roughly half White, 25 percent Latino, and 20 percent Black.

On the night of February 26, Tracy and his fiancée went out for dinner. Trayvon stayed home with Brandy's fourteen-year-old son, Chad. The two hung out together, playing video games. They were planning to watch the NBA All-Star Game. Chad would later tell police that just before tip-off he asked Trayvon to buy him some Skittles.

It was raining, with wind gusts of around thirteen miles per hour, but Trayvon zipped himself up in a dark grey hoodie and headed off to the nearby 7-Eleven, which was roughly a wet, ten-minute walk away. At the store, Trayvon bought a bag of Skittles and a watermelon fruit juice drink. As he left the store, he was talking on the phone with a female friend.

He never made it back home.

Twenty-eight-year-old George Zimmerman routinely patrolled the gated community in his dark silver 2008 Honda Ridgeline truck. The neighborhood watch leader was a familiar and comforting sight to residents, but that night he was off the clock, getting ready to go shopping at a nearby Target.

Like Trayvon, Zimmerman was no stranger to trouble. The third of four kids, he was raised in a strictly religious Catholic household in the well-off Virginia suburb of Manassas. His father was German, his mother Afro-Peruvian. Despite having African blood, Zimmerman considered himself Latino and checked that box on his voter registration forms. Zimmerman spoke fluent Spanish, which turned out to be a useful skill. His elementary school principal would often call him to his office to act as a translator between the administration and Spanish-speaking immigrant parents.[12]

In high school, Zimmerman showed flashes of ambition. He was so determined to buy himself a car that he juggled three part-time jobs while still going to school. It was grueling, but he kept at it until he had saved up enough to make his teenage dream come true.

As soon as George graduated from high school, his parents decided they had enough of the cold and moved to Sanford, Florida. George, who had no interest in attending college, tagged along.

Zimmerman got a job at an insurance agency and started taking night classes so he could get a license to sell policies on his own. A few years later, he opened his own Allstate insurance office with an African American friend.[13] It was a pretty impressive feat for a twenty-one-year-old, but the thrill was short-lived. For reasons that remain murky, the business was a failure, and the two closed up shop within a year. Zimmerman didn't take the setback well, and his life went into a tailspin. That summer, he was arrested for shoving an undercover cop. Zimmerman was charged with resisting arrest and violence and battery of an officer. The charges were ultimately dropped after he agreed to take anger-management classes, although those classes didn't seem to do him much good. The following month, his then fiancée filed for a restraining order, claiming she was the victim of domestic

12 Reuters, "George Zimmerman: Neighborhood Says It Was in Fear Before Trayvon Martin Shooting," *National Post*, April 26, 2012

13 "George Zimmerman: Prelude to the Shooting of Trayvon Martin," NBC News, April 25, 2012

violence. Zimmerman then went tit-for-tat, filing a restraining order of his own against her. The two wisely broke up.

In 2007, Zimmerman's personal life seemed to finally settle down when he married a cosmetologist named Shellie Dean. However, professionally, Zimmerman continued to flounder. He aimlessly bounced from one dead-end job to another and, during some rough stretches, didn't work at all, sitting at home collecting unemployment checks.

The year 2009 seemed to be a turning point for Zimmerman. He was always at his best when he was working towards a firm goal, and that year, he decided to pursue a career in law enforcement. He enrolled at a local state college, where he majored in criminal justice. He and his new wife also became active members of their local Catholic church. As part of the church's outreach program, Zimmerman volunteered to mentor two Black teenagers. The church would later discontinue the program, but Zimmerman continued to mentor the teens, paying whatever expenses came up out of his own pocket. Zimmerman made another fateful decision in 2009: He and Shellie rented a townhome in The Retreat at Twin Lakes.

Gated communities offer the promise of safety and security and usually charge a premium for it. The residents of The Retreat at Twin Lakes were not getting their money's worth. From New Year's Day, 2011, to the night of Trayvon's death roughly fourteen months later, police were called to the development 402 times, mostly for break-ins and thefts, and once, for a shooting.

In September 2011, Zimmerman, perhaps sensing an opportunity to make professional contacts with local law enforcement, formed a neighborhood watch group. A member of the Sanford police department, Wendy Dorival, came to meet with the volunteers. She gave them the standard spiel: You are there to be the eyes and ears of the community, but don't approach suspects on your own; call the police if you see anything suspicious; and most importantly, let the police do their job. Dorival was impressed with Zimmerman and would later testify in court, "He was very professional with me. He seemed a little meek to me. He seemed like he really wanted to make changes in his community to make it better."[14]

Zimmerman took his new job very seriously—maybe too seriously. He was like a grade school hall monitor, tirelessly patrolling the development. In his six months on the job, Zimmerman made forty-six calls to the police, mostly to report "suspicious" persons.

On the night of February 26, even though Zimmerman was planning to go shopping, he was still on high alert. There had been several burglaries in the development over the past few weeks, and most of the suspects in those cases were Black. We'll never know if that's why Zimmerman's eyes were suddenly drawn to Trayvon, as so many people assumed. It could also have been due to the fact that Martin was out in the rain and his face was obscured by his hoodie. Or it could have been that since Trayvon was just visiting, Zimmerman didn't know who he was and got suspicious. The only insights we have into Zimmerman's state of mind that night come from the four-minute-long call he made to the Sanford Police Department's non-emergency number at 7:09 p.m.

"Hey, we've had some break-ins in my neighborhood, and there's a real suspicious guy," Zimmerman calmly told the dispatcher. "The guy looks like he's up to no good, or he's on drugs

[14] Michael Muskal and Tina Susman, "Rules For Neighborhood Watch Discussed in George Zimmerman Trial," *LA Times*, June 25, 2013

or something. It's raining and he's just walking around, looking about."

The dispatcher immediately asked, "OK, and this guy, is he White, Black, or Hispanic?"

"He looks Black."

"Did you see what he was wearing?"

"Yeah, a dark hoodie, like a grey hoodie, and either jeans or sweatpants and white tennis shoes. He's here now. He's just staring."

At that same moment, Trayvon was on the phone with Rachel Jeantel. The two had known each other for a few years and had a very close, apparently platonic, relationship. Rachel would later testify that Trayvon told her he was being followed by a "creepy-ass cracker," and that he was trying to get away from him.

Zimmerman was telling the dispatcher a different story: "Now he's coming towards me. He's got his hand in his waistband.... Something's wrong with him." Zimmerman still sounded preternaturally calm. That confidence may have come from the fact that he was legally strapped with a licensed 9 mm handgun. "He's coming to check me out. He has something in his hands. I don't know what his deal is," he said.

The cop assured George that a patrol car was on the way, but that did not seem to placate Zimmerman. "These assholes," he complained, "they always get away."

Moments later, Zimmerman announced, "Shit, he's running."

In what would become one of the most critical parts of the call, the dispatcher asked Zimmerman, "Are you following him?"

"Yes," he replied.

"OK, we don't need you to do that."

"OK," he responded, sounding somewhat compliant.

The call ended at 7:13 p.m. Four minutes later, police arrived and found themselves in the middle of a crime scene. Trayvon Martin's motionless body was lying face down in the grass, just seventy yards from the front door of his dad's townhome. George Zimmerman was standing near the body. He immediately told officers that he had shot Martin and was still armed. Officer Timothy Smith handcuffed Zimmerman and confiscated his pistol. At 7:30 p.m., as Dwight Howard and Andrew Bynum squared off for the opening tip-off of the NBA All-Star Game, paramedics officially pronounced Trayvon Martin dead.

Sanford police brought Zimmerman in for questioning that night. He admitted he had been following Trayvon around the development but insisted that the teenager initiated the confrontation. In his telling, Martin came up to him and defiantly asked, "Do you have a problem?"

Zimmerman said he answered no, and that Trayvon responded, "You do now!" and punched him in the nose, knocking him to the ground. Zimmerman told police that Trayvon then got on top of him and began slamming his head against the ground. According to Zimmerman, Trayvon then reached for his gun, and it was only then, fearing for his life, that he pulled out his 9 mm and fatally shot Martin on the left side of his chest, just under his nipple.[15]

Christopher Serino, the lead investigator on the case, had his doubts about Zimmerman's story. In his report, he questioned whether George's injuries were consistent with his account of what happened. Sure, Zimmerman had a bloody nose, lacerations

---

15 Rene Stutzman, "Police: Zimmerman Says Trayvon Decked Him With One Blow Then Began Hammering His Head," *Orlando Sentinel*, August 23, 2019

on the back of his head, and some scratches, but Serino thought the injuries would have been more severe if Trayvon had beaten him up as badly as George claimed. He also believed that the whole situation could have been avoided if Zimmerman had just stayed in his car, like he was supposed to.

On the other hand, a couple of eyewitnesses seemed to back Zimmerman's account. One neighbor, Jonathan Good, told police he saw a man in dark clothing on top of a man wearing "red" or "light clothing"—Zimmerman was wearing a red jacket that night. Good told police the person on top was punching the person on the bottom, but it was raining and he couldn't tell if the blows were landing.

Good said he tried to call out to the two, but when they didn't respond and kept on fighting, he went inside to call 911, which is when he heard the gun go off.

Investigators may have had doubts about Zimmerman's story, but they didn't think they had nearly enough evidence to make an arrest. So, they sent him home for the evening.

The killing of Trayvon Martin had all the makings of a compelling story, but initially the media wasn't the least bit interested. For three weeks, it was completely ignored by network news and barely covered by the local stations. Even *The Sanford Herald,* which is dedicated to covering news in the small city of roughly sixty thousand residents, ran just one story on February 29 and then didn't run another piece until twelve days later.

During this period of relative quiet, the Sanford Police Department dragged its feet. Serino, suspicious of Zimmerman from the get-go, recommended that the district attorney charge him with manslaughter. But as he undoubtedly knew, it would be a difficult case to prosecute.

In 2005, Florida became the first state to pass a "Stand Your Ground" law, when then-Governor Jeb Bush signed the bill. Before that law was passed, individuals had a duty to retreat before using force, even in cases of self-defense. That meant if someone was being attacked, they couldn't just reach for their weapon and fire; they needed to first see if it was possible to run away. "Stand Your Ground" removed this requirement. Of course, if Zimmerman was telling the truth and he really was lying on his back getting pummeled by Martin, he would have been legally justified in pulling out his weapon and shooting, whether or not the new law had taken effect.

Trayvon's parents were grieving and outraged. This seemed like such a clear-cut case. A teenage boy walking home with nothing more than a bag of Skittles and a drink, shot and killed by a grown man. From the start, Tracy Martin believed this case was all about race. In his mind, that was the reason Zimmerman had confronted his son, and it was the reason the Sanford Police Department had yet to make an arrest. Martin told one reporter, "They will have to decide whether it's a hate crime or not.... I think my son was racially profiled, that that was the motive."[16]

Across the state, in Florida's capital city of Tallahassee, a forty-two-year-old lawyer was making a name for himself representing Black plaintiffs in racially charged cases. In 2002, Benjamin Crump had represented the family of a Black driver shot by a White state trooper. Five years later, he advocated for the family of a fourteen-year-old Black teenager beaten to death at a Florida detention center. So, when Trayvon's parents asked him to be their attorney, he readily agreed. This was the kind of case that

16 Corey Dade, "Father of Trayvon Martin: 'I Won't Rest' Until Son's Killer Is Prosecuted," NPR, March 28, 2012

could put him, and the anti-law enforcement movement, into the national spotlight.

Crump was a gifted attorney. Al Sharpton would later pay him the highest of compliments, calling him "Black America's attorney general."[17] If you had to boil down what made the dapper Benjamin Crump so successful, you could point to his passion, work ethic, or the way he calmly but resolutely articulated his positions. But his most critical asset—his secret sauce—might be that he had a unique understanding of how to manipulate the media. He intuitively knew how journalists think, what ingredients they need to get a story on the air, and most importantly, he understood how to help shape those stories so that they benefited his clients.

Crump recognized that a lot of TV news coverage is driven by emotionally resonant video or audio clips. For example, it's doubtful that anyone would have ever heard the name Rodney King if a Los Angeles plumber, George Holliday, hadn't woken up to a huge commotion in front of his house, grabbed his new video camera, and started taping the infamous beating. And that was Crump's challenge with his new case: The media wasn't covering Trayvon's shooting because all they had were talking heads and dry police reports. As people in the business would flippantly say, it made for bad TV. But Crump immediately zeroed in on the one way he could make Trayvon's shooting a very compelling news story: Somehow, he had to pressure the Sanford Police Department to release the 911 tapes. There were seven in all. The one from Zimmerman, and six others made by terrified

17 Aaron Morrison and John Seewer, "'Black America's Attorney General' Seems to be Everywhere," AP, May 2, 2021

neighbors. Crump understood that those tapes would give the story the emotional resonance it needed to merit airtime.

Crump's strategic pressure campaign began on March 8, 2012, when he called his first news conference. He framed Trayvon Martin's death as part of what he claimed was a much larger pattern of racial profiling and systemic racism. He simplified the story, laying out the narrative that the media would obediently follow—Trayvon was targeted because he was Black and wearing a hoodie. Crump said the Sanford Police Department owed it not just to the Martin family, but to the entire world, to release those 911 tapes. Crump argued that since the police hadn't arrested Zimmerman, the least they could do was release the tapes in the name of transparency.

Eight days later, Crump and Trayvon's parents met with city officials. Whatever they said behind closed doors worked. Hours later, Sanford officials relented and released the 911 tapes. City officials probably hoped this move would ease the growing scrutiny on how they were handling the investigation. They were wrong. They had been outsmarted and outmaneuvered. Trayvon Martin's death was about to become the biggest story in the world.

On March 17, 2012, ABC News's David Muir looked gravely into the camera and pronounced, "We're going to turn to the anger and anguish in Orlando, Florida, tonight. Police have just released the 911 calls in the shooting death of a teenage boy who went out to buy some Skittles and then was shot and killed by a man who was leading a neighborhood watch."

He then threw to the telegenic Matt Gutman, a thirty-four-year-old reporter, who would be at the forefront of the network's social justice coverage for the next eight years. Gutman's report was, for the most part, factually correct, but it followed a Crump-approved narrative; all the grey areas of the case—any information that might cast doubt on the "Trayvon as a victim" storyline—were either minimized or ignored.

At one point in his report, Gutman crossed the line, saying, "In a series of jarring 911 tapes, you hear seventeen-year-old Trayvon Martin fighting for his life." He was referring to screams heard in the background of some of the neighbors' calls to police. Martin's family would later insist the voice belonged to Trayvon, while Zimmerman's family said they were sure it was George's. Audio experts were never able to come to a firm conclusion.[18] By stating, without a shred of evidence, that Trayvon was the victim "fighting for his life," Gutman completely dismissed the very real possibility that he had been the aggressor in the confrontation.

The following night, ABC gave the story a more prominent spot in the newscast. Again, Matt Gutman's reporting seemed shaped by Benjamin Crump's narrative. Citing unnamed "law enforcement experts," Gutman speculated that Zimmerman was drunk when he called the police that night—something that was never substantiated and would not be brought up in his trial.

By Monday, March 19, thanks to the 911 tapes, Trayvon Martin's shooting was the biggest story in the country. That night, Matt Gutman continued his credulous, incendiary reporting. He juxtaposed a tearful bite from Trayvon's mom with the sound of the gunshot from one of the 911 tapes and then solemnly intoned, "But for now, police are still calling this self-defense." The implication was clear: The police department's position was

---

18 Colette Bennett, "Experts in Zimmerman Case: Can't Tell Who Is Screaming in 911 Calls," CNN, June 8, 2013

untenable, and sooner or later, they would have to do the right thing and arrest Zimmerman.

CBS News also interviewed Trayvon's mom, Sybrina Fulton, who made the provocative accusation that "if he had pulled the trigger and he was an African American and he shot a Caucasian man—White man—yes, he would be in jail." The ethics of running a sound bite like this land in a gray area. On the one hand, she was a central part of the story, and she was making an emotionally charged claim. On the other, it's a volatile accusation and running the bite without contextualizing it—just letting it dangle there as some sort of obvious truth—creates a powerful emotional response in the audience: It is prejudicial and inflammatory without technically being a lie.

CNN's Anderson Cooper opened his coverage with a smiling picture of a young Trayvon holding a baby. And if there was any doubt where the photo came from, he then introduced Tracy Martin and Benjamin Crump, who were joining him as live in-studio guests. It had all the trappings of a real news interview, except for any actual probing questions.

Cooper made no attempt to challenge his guests, tossing them underhand pitches like, "You have no doubt that if it was Trayvon Martin who had shot a White person, that Trayvon would be in jail. That if it was any African American who had shot a White person, that suspect would be in jail."

Crump nodded eagerly and said, "Absolutely, Anderson. They could say self-defense, but they would still be arrested and put in jail."

Cooper blithely ignored any of the complexities of the case. Instead, at one point, he turned to Tracy Martin and asked the following pseudo-question, which made it abundantly clear that he had already rendered his judgment: "The idea that Mr.

Zimmerman thought there was something suspicious about your son. Your son was wearing white sneakers, jeans, and a hoodie, which I got to tell you—I wear every single day of my life when I'm not on camera. And I don't think anybody, even if they didn't recognize me, would have said, well, I look suspicious.... To you, is that just a matter of race?"

Even a lawyer questioning his own client at a trial might make more of a pretense of asking tough questions than Cooper did during that interview.

Not surprisingly, when ABC's Matt Gutman interviewed George Zimmerman's first attorney, Craig Sonner, there were no lollipop questions—just a hostile cross-examination.

Gutman started the interview by showing grainy surveillance footage of Zimmerman being led into the police department on the night of the shooting. The video then zoomed in on the back of Zimmerman's head. Even though the image was too low in resolution to make out any meaningful details, Gutman still confidently concluded, "The back of his head shows no gash." We would later find out this was untrue, and ABC News would have to "clarify" its reporting, stating that enhanced video did indeed show there were gashes on the back of Zimmerman's head. But during this interview, Gutman projected nothing but absolute certainty. He turned to Sonner and demanded, "Does he look injured to you?"

The entire interview was testy and adversarial. Gutman kept cutting Sonner off, unsuccessfully trying to get him to walk into a "gotcha" moment.

"Did Mr. Zimmerman seek medical treatment?"

Sonner calmly replied, "That evidence is all going to come out—"

"That's evidence?"

"When the case is litigated."

"But earlier you said that at some point he did seek medical attention."

"Then I've already answered your question—"

"But it was vague, so I'm following up on it."

"Well, then I've already answered your question—"

"So he did seek medical attention."

"Well, I'm not going to continue to litigate the case here."

According to researchers at Pew,[19] in the first month after the 911 tapes were released, MSNBC dedicated a striking 49 percent of its prime-time coverage to the story. CNN followed with 40 percent, but Fox News only gave it 15 percent. There were also stark differences in emphasis. For MSNBC, it was Sanford's racial history and Florida's "Stand Your Ground" law. CNN's coverage of the story was more straightforward, but with an obvious Trayvon bias. And Fox News spent most of its time reporting on how the other networks were reporting the story.

This is one of the most underappreciated parts of news bias—deciding which stories to cover and which to ignore, which parts of a story to highlight and which to leave out. Clearly, viewers of MSNBC and CNN were seeing the Trayvon Martin story through a very different lens than were viewers of Fox News. It was as if all the networks were handing out different pieces of the same jigsaw puzzle, but unless a viewer watched all the coverage, on all the networks, they would never be able to complete the puzzle.

[19] Pew Research Center Staff, "How Blogs, Twitter and Mainstream Media Have Handled the Trayvon Martin Case," Pew Research Center, March 30, 2012

To be fair, this was a highly sensitive story, and many network producers and reporters had a hard time not personalizing it. As CNN's Don Lemon said, "On this story, there is a certain understanding that comes from minorities, and particularly African Americans, just because we've lived it."[20] Lemon also revealed that at a planning meeting, one of his producers, a Black mother of two boys, "was almost in tears saying, 'We've got to do something on this story.'"

If the Sanford Police Department thought they were under pressure before releasing the 911 tapes, they must have felt under siege afterward. The story had struck a raw nerve in the American psyche. And unlike most ephemeral stories that come and go with each news cycle, the Trayvon Martin case was an A-block story on most newscasts for weeks.

A big reason for this was the clever maneuvering of Benjamin Crump. He had played the police department, and now, in phase two of his plan, he was making himself and Trayvon's parents available to anyone with a microphone and a camera. His messaging was consistent: This was not an isolated incident. Trayvon Martin's death was part of a much larger story about systemic racism in the American justice system.

This framing was cemented on March 23, 2012, when President Obama, at a press conference in the White House Rose Garden, was asked about the case. "My main message is to the parents of Trayvon—if I had a son, he'd look like Trayvon," said the president, swallowing hard and pausing for a moment before continuing, "I think they are right to expect that all of us as Americans

---

20 Brian Stelter, "In Slain Teenager's Case, a Long Route to National Attention," *New York Times,* March 25, 2012

will take this with the seriousness it deserves and we're going to get to the bottom of what's happening."

Mitt Romney, who was well on his way to winning the GOP presidential nomination, also made it clear that he wasn't entertaining the possibility that the real victim in this case might have been George Zimmerman: "What happened to Trayvon Martin is a tragedy. There needs to be a thorough investigation that reassures the public that justice is carried out with impartiality and integrity."

LeBron James and Dwyane Wade, the megastar leaders of the soon-to-be NBA champion Miami Heat, got their teammates to pose for a protest photo. The players all stood together against a generic backdrop, heads bowed, wearing matching hoodies. The implication was clear: Trayvon Martin was murdered for being Black and wearing a piece of "street clothing" that White America did not approve of. Ironically, at the time, the NBA prohibited its players from wearing hoodies at league events.

Trayvon's case soon became a cause célèbre. Flea and Anthony Kiedis of the Red Hot Chili Peppers wore hoodies on stage during a concert in Tampa. Not to be outdone, other celebrities like Sean "Diddy" Combs, Jamie Foxx, and Will Smith posted photos of themselves wearing hoodies.

Film director Spike Lee took things a step too far, irresponsibly retweeting a post that purported to reveal George Zimmerman's home address. However, it turned out to be the address of a Florida couple who had absolutely nothing to do with the case. Fearing for their lives, they went into hiding, and Lee issued a public apology.

A foundational principle of the United States is the presumption of innocence, but when it came to George Zimmerman, everyone seemed to have conveniently forgotten this basic rule. It's one thing for celebrities and politicians to jump to conclusions, but journalists are supposed to serve as a check on those impulses. Their job is to be fair and impartial—like referees in an NFL game. But all of a sudden, the refs didn't want to blow the whistle anymore. They wanted to play, and they were all on Team Trayvon.

The most egregious example of this came on the morning of March 29, 2012, on NBC's highly rated *Today* show. In a stunning breach of ethics, the network aired an edited version of Zimmerman's call to the police, which was deliberately doctored to make him look like he had racially profiled Trayvon. In the original call, the conversation went like this:

> Zimmerman: "The guy looks like he's up to no good, or he's on drugs or something. It's raining and he's just walking around, looking about."
>
> Dispatcher: "OK, and this guy, is he White, Black or Hispanic?"
>
> Zimmerman: "He looks Black."

But on the *Today* show, the call was cut up so that Zimmerman was made to say, "This guy looks like he's up to no good. He looks Black." The dispatcher's question—inquiring about the suspect's race—was completely cut out. This clearly distorted the conversation, making it seem like Zimmerman volunteered the information.

NBC eventually conducted an internal investigation and fired the producer who made the deceitful edit. Zimmerman would later file a $100 million lawsuit against NBC, but a judge would toss it out, ruling he had failed to show actual malice.

CNN was also guilty of peddling falsehoods. Reporter Gary Tuchman did an entire piece speculating that Zimmerman might have uttered a racial slur when he called the police. As audio experts later confirmed, Zimmerman said, "These fucking punks," when he complained about young thieves who were committing crimes in his gated community. But Tuchman was pretty convinced he heard him say, "These fucking coons." As part of his news package, the reporter took the tape into an edit bay and listened to it over and over, concluding, "It sounds like this allegation could be accurate, but I wouldn't swear to it in court." After this hit piece ran, CNN's senior legal analyst Jeffrey Toobin, who would be suspended years later for exposing himself on a work Zoom call, opined that the slur was huge, because it could allow the Department of Justice to charge Zimmerman under The Hate Crimes Act. But of course, the report wasn't accurate, and the DOJ later declined to press charges, saying there was insufficient evidence that Zimmerman acted with any racial bias.

The biggest crime of omission was in the reporting of Trayvon Martin himself. If you close your eyes and try to conjure up an image of him, chances are you will see a young, innocent, and harmless child. That's because the media consistently used his grade school photos, which were at least four to five years old. When these were juxtaposed with pictures of the stocky and older George Zimmerman, viewers were left with the indelible impression that the neighborhood watch leader killed a small, defenseless child. The truth was far more nuanced. Trayvon

Martin was actually taller than Zimmerman—5'11" to 5'8"—although Zimmerman outweighed the teenager by forty pounds.

The media also showed little interest in investigating Trayvon's troubled past, and on the rare times that they did, Benjamin Crump was there to shame them, claiming that bringing up Trayvon's flaws was really an attempt to sweep his death under the rug. That argument would only have had merit if it was obvious that Trayvon was the victim. But at that point, any objective journalist should have known that the case remained a mystery and there was a very real possibility Zimmerman had fired his gun in self-defense.

With film titles like *Paul McCartney Really Is Dead* and *Elvis Found Alive*, documentary director Joel Gilbert is nobody's idea of a true journalist. He is openly right-wing, prone to peddling conspiracy theories, and his movies—to be generous—have a homemade quality to them. He is the kind of citizen journalist who can easily be dismissed by the elites. But he does have two qualities they seem to lack: curiosity and resourcefulness.

In 2019, Gilbert, then fifty-four, released *The Trayvon Hoax*. In it, he did something none of the traditional outlets bothered to do; he got his hands on seven hundred pages of transcripts containing all of Trayvon Martin's text messages before his death.

Gilbert, disheveled in a Steve Bannon kind of way, says Florida is an open-records case, so he was amazed that it never occurred to legacy journalists to request the documents.[21]

"The media creates a narrative," he says. "They are disinterested in any storylines that do not support the narrative."

---

21 Whenever a quote is presented in the present tense, it indicates that this was told directly to the author, on the record.

Trayvon's texts definitely do not fit the narrative of an innocent child. A lot of them are sexually explicit. Others reveal that he loved to fight. In one, Trayvon brags about "knocking someone out." In another text, he says that he had been involved in his share of street fights and that his strategy was to "swing first."

What's even more damaging is that Trayvon wrote about drugs a lot, even admitting that he smoked pot almost every day. He texts to a friend about the street drug "purple lean," which is made with hard candy, soft drinks, and cough syrup, leading Gilbert to speculate that this might have been the real motivation for Trayvon's late-night Skittles run.

There is no doubt that Gilbert has a spotty record as a journalist—but this was good, old-school reporting. The texts, after all, came straight from Trayvon's phone. It is our best look into the mind of the troubled seventeen-year-old. But this aspect of the story was simply too hot for most legacy outlets to touch.

"Everyone was terrified," Gilbert theorizes. "It was an emotional narrative that could not be penetrated. It's a taboo. They did not want to hear any fact that might disrupt the public's emotional bond with Trayvon."

On April 11, 2012, there was a major break in the case, making it the lead story on every network and cable newscast, including Fox.

On ABC, Diane Sawyer stared into the lens and told her audience, "After forty-five days of inflamed argument and rising tensions in America, the prosecutor has announced that George Zimmerman will be charged with second-degree murder. A charge that could put him behind bars for life. His crime: shooting an unarmed seventeen-year-old while Zimmerman was patrolling the neighborhood."

Tellingly, Sawyer slipped and didn't say "his alleged crime," but by this point, any regular consumer of legacy newscasts was probably convinced that Zimmerman's conviction was nothing more than a formality.

What they weren't told is that prosecutors had their work cut out for them. To get a second-degree murder conviction in Florida, prosecutors would have to prove beyond a reasonable doubt that George Zimmerman's shooting of Martin was a criminal act "demonstrating a depraved mind without regard for human life."

Over the next fourteen months, as lawyers prepared for trial, the story slowly faded away, and the public turned its attention to other matters. In September, the US consulate in Benghazi, Libya, was attacked, resulting in the deaths of four Americans. In November, President Obama won reelection. The mass shooting at Sandy Hook Elementary School, which killed twenty-six people, including twenty children, dominated the news in December. The following April, the deadly Boston Marathon bombing captured the nation's attention.

On June 24, 2013, George Zimmerman's murder trial began and the country turned its attention back to the case.

The jury, as allowed by Florida law, consisted of just six people. Six women, five of them White, would decide George Zimmerman's fate.

But the thing that initially caught everyone's eye was the defendant himself. Over the previous months, George Zimmerman had gained well over one hundred pounds. Not a helpful visual for someone trying to prove he had been physically overpowered by a seventeen-year-old.

In opening arguments, prosecutor John Guy declared that Zimmerman was a vigilante who profiled Trayvon Martin because he looked like he "was up to no good." Guy concluded his argument with a flourish, "We are confident at the end of this trial, you will know in your head, in your heart, and your stomach that George Zimmerman did not shoot Trayvon Martin because he had to. He shot him for the worst of all possible reasons: because he wanted to."

It's worth noting that unlike many of the news reporters covering the story, the prosecutors avoided any overt references to race. They did make a coded reference to it when they argued that Zimmerman profiled Trayvon, but they stopped short of claiming that was his motivation for confronting Martin.

In the opening defense arguments, lead defense attorney Mark O'Mara let his partner take center stage.

Don West, a bald and athletic-looking attorney, amplified what Zimmerman had been saying from day one: This was a case of self-defense. "Trayvon Martin armed himself with the concrete sidewalk and used it to smash George Zimmerman's head," he proclaimed, pacing the courtroom. "It's no different than if he picked up a brick or bashed him against a wall, and the law is very specific as to when you can defend yourself if the other person has a deadly weapon."

West's statement was powerful and set the tone for the trial, but much of the media coverage that night fixated on an ill-conceived and punchline-free joke he used to start his opening statement: "Knock, knock. Who's there? George Zimmerman. George Zimmerman who? Congratulations, you're on the jury." No one laughed, and an embarrassed West promised to leave the joke-telling to the professionals.

The prosecution's case started falling apart on June 26, when Rachel Jeantel, the teenager Trayvon was talking to on his way back to his dad's townhouse, took the stand. She was combative, hard to understand, seemed uninterested in the proceedings, and got defiant whenever her testimony was challenged.

Jeantel said that she heard Trayvon on the phone asking a man, "Why are you following me for?"

She said she could hear the man breathing hard before replying, "What are you doing around here?"

She testified that she then heard Trayvon yelling, "Get off! Get off!"

Right after that, she claimed the phone went dead.

Under cross-examination, she was asked why she hadn't told police the part about Trayvon yelling "Get off! Get off!" until five weeks after his death. She said she withheld that crucial information because she didn't want to get involved.

She was asked why she lied to police about her age, telling them she was sixteen when she was really nineteen. Again, she said it was because she didn't want anything to do with the case.

Why hadn't she called police after she heard Trayvon yelling and the call got disconnected? She replied that she didn't think she needed to. She'd watched a lot of *The First 48*, and on that true-crime show, the cops usually tracked down witnesses, not the other way around.

She was an abysmal witness and became the fodder for some late-night comedy punchlines. But much of the news coverage minimized the damage she had done to the prosecution's case, suggesting that she was probably just too traumatized to be a good witness.

On June 28, there was more trouble for the prosecution. John Good, Zimmerman's neighbor, and the only truly objective witness in the case, took the stand.

Good was well prepared and meticulous. He estimated that he was standing about twenty to thirty feet away from the fight, but since it was raining, it was hard for him to make out details. He testified he could see someone in dark clothes straddling someone wearing red or white, who was lying on the ground. He told the court the person on top was "using arm motions going down, not just once but multiple times." He described it as "ground and pound."[22] Good also said it sounded like the person on the bottom was crying for help, but he wasn't 100 percent sure about that.

Veteran reporter Ashleigh Banfield was in the courtroom every day, covering the trial for CNN. She is an old-school reporter, who has won a bunch of prestigious awards: everything from an Emmy to something called a Telly. It was during the Zimmerman trial that she realized the ground had shifted in broadcast journalism: "One hundred percent—I saw a problem in the reporting of Trayvon Martin," she says, clearly still upset. "I pride myself on covering crime based on court records—not public opinion. I was mystified and angry. There were lies being told."

In Banfield's opinion, part of the problem was political, "There were facts that weren't deemed appropriate. The narrative was a little boy with Skittles and iced tea is violently murdered by an adult. The photographs used supported that. A lot of Trayvon's background was ignored. I could not understand how this tornado of misinformation was traveling at warped speed."

---

[22] Lizette Alvarez, "Neighbors Describe Witnessing Confrontation in Florida Murder Case," *New York Times,* June 28, 2013

Activist journalism wasn't the only thing clouding the narrative. Banfield believes another major factor was laziness: "Reading headlines doesn't make you an expert. Sitting through the trial—reading transcripts—gets you closer. People weren't doing the work."

If they had been doing the work, reporters covering the trial would have understood the significance of what happened in court on July 9. That day, well-respected forensic pathologist Dr. Vincent Di Maio testified that the physical evidence clearly showed that Trayvon Martin had been on top of Zimmerman when the fatal shot was fired. He also testified that Zimmerman's injuries did seem consistent with his account of what happened. When the prosecution cross-examined him, looking to cast doubt on his findings, Di Maio fired back, "This is not exactly a complicated case forensically."[23]

This testimony was a game changer, making it painfully obvious to any fair-minded observer that the prosecution would never be able to clear the high bar they needed to get a conviction. But in that night's news coverage, only CNN gave Di Maio's testimony much airtime.

The trial came to a merciful close on Friday, July 12. In his closing arguments, prosecutor John Guy was now forced to concede that there was a fight and that Trayvon might have been on top of Zimmerman after all: "My point is there was a fight, there was a struggle. At some point it appears, based on the evidence, at some points the defendant was on top, at some points the victim was on top. But why did it occur? If you believe he is an innocent man, the victim just came up and decided to smack him?"

---

23 Lizette Alvarez, "Martin Was Shot as He Leaned Over Zimmerman, Court Is Told," *New York Times*, July 9, 2013

Zimmerman's attorney, Mark O'Mara, told the jury that the prosecution had provided little evidence and that he wished the verdict contained three choices: "Guilty, not guilty, and completely innocent, because I would ask you to check that one."

After sixteen hours of deliberation, the jury checked the "not guilty" box.

George Zimmerman was a free man. Or was he? Even after a jury of his peers found him not guilty, broadcast news just rolled merrily along with its predetermined narrative. On the night the verdict was announced, ABC News led with a seven-minute Matt Gutman package. Instead of trying to calmly explain how the jury reached its decision, he used his time to inflame passions even further.

At one point, he interviewed someone who claimed Rachel Jeantel had been "mammified" in court.

He interviewed an attorney who argued, "Saying this case was not about race is ignoring the pink elephant in the room. This case is about race."

He interviewed a Sanford church parishioner who declared unchallenged, "I can assure you unequivocally, if I had been a Black man who killed a seventeen-year-old White boy under the condition that the boy was murdered, I would be in jail—probably doing time now."

No mention of the fact that the prosecution's case had fallen apart in court.

No mention of the compelling evidence that led the jury to acquit.

No mention of the fact that the preponderance of the evidence indicated that, yes, George Zimmerman was probably telling the truth; he likely had acted in self-defense.

"How could everyone ignore the facts that came out?" Ashleigh Banfield wonders. "There are cases that highlight racism and biases. This was not one of them."

But the damage was done. The American people trusted mainstream journalists to give them a clear picture of the trial, and they were being told every night that a racist, gun-toting, wannabe cop had blown away a child walking home with juice and candy. Over the next week, there were massive street protests in more than one hundred American cities. Some even turned violent, as people struggled to express their grief and outrage over what they thought was a grave injustice.

Atlanta Falcons receiver Roddy White tweeted, "Fucking Zimmerman got away with murder today wow what kind of world do we live in. All them jurors should go home tonight and kill themselves for letting a grown man get away with killing a kid."

Not to be outdone, Giants receiver Victor Cruz called for vigilante justice, telling a reporter, "Zimmerman doesn't last a year before the hood catches up to him."[24]

Despite the acquittal, George Zimmerman's life was destroyed. His marriage fell apart and he never got to pursue a career in law enforcement.

His attorney angrily blamed the media for destroying his client's life: "He was like a patient on an operating table, where a mad scientist was performing experiments on him with no anesthesia. He didn't know why he was turned into this monster, but quite honestly you guys had a lot to do with it. You took a

---

[24] "Zimmerman Verdict Sparks Strong Reactions from Some NFL Players," NBC Sports, July 13, 2013

story that was fed to you, and you ran with it and you ran right over him."[25]

Despite O'Mara's admonishment, as far as news executives were concerned, the Trayvon Martin story was a winner.

It had all the elements of great television: passion, good vs. evil, violence, and race.

And best of all, journalists could tell themselves they were on the right side of a historical movement for social justice.

The fact that an innocent man's life was ruined, that there was now unrest in American streets, that racial tensions were simmering—none of that seemed to concern the people running legacy newsrooms.

After all, they were just getting started.

---

[25] Greg Allen, "Zimmerman Not Guilty of All Charges," NPR, July 14, 2013.

Chapter 2
The Death of Eric Garner

Eric Garner was the type of guy most people would cross the street to avoid. A massive man, standing 6'3" and weighing in at about 395 pounds, he was a garrulous street hustler, who would approach just about anybody who happened to be walking by. The forty-three-year-old mostly worked in Tompkinsville Park, just a short walk from the Staten Island Ferry terminal. He would go up to strangers, many of them white-collar types on their way to work in Manhattan, and offer to sell them "loosies"—local slang for single cigarettes. Garner would try to get anywhere from fifty cents to two bucks for a single smoke. Between this side hustle and his disability checks, he managed to scrape by.

Garner wasn't always one of America's forgotten people. In the past, he'd held some promising jobs, having worked as a mechanic, a bouncer, and even a horticulturist for the New York

Department of Parks and Recreation.[26] But Garner had demons he could never shake. His first run-in with the law came when he was just ten years old, and over the course of his short life, he would be arrested more than thirty times. Some of the collars were for small-time offenses like selling "loosies," marijuana possession, and petty larceny. Others were more serious, like assault, resisting arrest, and grand larceny.[27]

In 2007, Garner sued the NYPD, claiming they conducted a humiliating strip search of him in public. It's unclear whether the complaint had merit, but the city reportedly settled for $30,000, and the case never went to trial.

Garner's problems extended beyond his inability to stay on the right side of the law. You just had to take a quick glance his way to see that he had serious health issues. The man, whom some called "a gentle giant," was morbidly obese. As a result, he also suffered from asthma, diabetes, and high blood pressure; most alarmingly, his heart had swollen to about twice its normal size.[28]

Despite all this, Garner managed to have a stable family life. He had been married to his high school sweetheart, Esaw, for twenty-seven years. The two lived in a Staten Island housing project, where they raised six children and were the proud grandparents of three babies.

Officer Daniel Pantaleo, just twenty-nine at the time of the incident, was already an NYPD veteran. Eight years on the job, he was part of a Staten Island street patrol that focused on small

---

26 Daudi Abe, "Eric Garner (1970–2014)," BlackPast, July 21, 2016

27 Rebecca Davis O'Brien, Michael Howard Saul, and Pervaiz Shallwani, "New York City Police Officer Won't Face Criminal Charges in Eric Garner Death," *Wall Street Journal*, December 4, 2014,

28 "Officer's Chokehold Triggered Eric Garner's Death, Medical Examiner Testifies," CBS News, May 15, 2019

quality-of-life issues—part of the "broken windows" philosophy of policing.

Pantaleo's record suggests that he was an aggressive, maybe even abusive, cop. Seventeen complaints had been filed against him, which works out to about two a year—roughly double the rate of the typical NYPD officer.

Two of those complaints ended up in lawsuits.

In one suit, two men claimed that Pantaleo publicly strip-searched them. The city paid $30,000 to settle the matter out of court.

In the other, he was accused of pushing and falsely arresting a man. The city settled that one as well.[29]

Like most American big cities, New York is a tangled mess of confusing, sometimes even contradictory, laws and regulations. There is so much red tape that no one even knows the precise number of laws citizens are expected to obey; the best guess is somewhere in the tens of thousands. So, in 2007, it went mostly unnoticed when New York City made the sale of cigarettes illegal unless they were in sealed packages of at least twenty. Purportedly, this law was passed for health reasons. The politicians who voted for it claimed that if people had to buy expensive, heavily taxed packs of cigarettes, they would be more likely to quit. A more plausible explanation is that store owners lobbied to make "loosies" illegal, because they believed it undercut their business.

It was a hot and humid summer day on July 17, 2014. Eric Garner, wearing yellow shorts and a white T-shirt, was out of breath after having just broken up a fight on a sidewalk in front

29 Dareh Gregorian, Larry McShane, and Rocco Parascandola, "NYPD Officer Daniel Pantaleo Faces Other Lawsuits After Dodging Charges in Eric Garner Chokehold Death," NY Daily News, January 9, 2019

of Tompkinsville Park. Daniel Pantaleo and three other officers noticed the commotion and approached him, but instead of asking about the fight, they immediately accused him of selling "loosies." Garner's friend, twenty-two-year-old Ramsey Orta, pulled out his cellphone and began recording the confrontation. Little did he know, he was about to document Eric Garner's death.

"Every time you see me, you want to mess with me. I'm tired of it! It stops today!" Garner shouted at the officers. He seemed upset but not unhinged. Defiant, but not a threat. "I'm minding my business, officer. I'm minding my business. Please just leave me alone!"

This went on for a while until one of the officers grabbed Garner's arms in an attempt to cuff him. He pulled away, yelling, "Don't touch me!"

At that point Pantaleo snuck up behind Garner, wrapped his arms around the big man's neck, and wrestled him down to the ground. As the other officers tried to put Garner in handcuffs, Pantaleo removed his arms from Garner's neck and pushed his face into the pavement. In total, he had his arms pressed over Garner's neck for approximately twelve to fifteen seconds.[30]

Still struggling, Garner called out, "I can't breathe!" eleven times, before he lost consciousness. He was lying on the sidewalk, motionless, for about seven minutes before an ambulance finally arrived. Less than an hour later, Eric Garner was officially declared dead.

Thanks to Orta's video, the story was an immediate media sensation.

On ABC News, anchor Dan Harris stared soberly into the camera and announced, "Tonight, America's largest police force

---

30 "Appeals Court Upholds NYPD's Firing of Daniel Pantaleo in Eric Garner's Death," CBS News, March 26, 2021

is facing serious controversy over a video that's gone viral, showing officers arresting a suspect who later died. The video is wrenching."

Days later, on the ABC News show *Nightline*, mainstream journalism crossed a new line. Viewers, who had gotten a steady diet of biased, one-sided reporting from the network during the Trayvon Martin case, were now fed straight-up propaganda.

The reporter who fronted this piece was not some new upstart trying to make a name for himself but sixty-year-old Ron Claiborne, a usually careful, circumspect, old-school, Ivy League–educated newsman. But you wouldn't know it on this night.

"This case has already taken on racial overtones," he solemnly told viewers, even though there was zero evidence that it played any role in Eric Garner's death. But to prove his point, he got a sound bite from the late Reverend Calvin O. Butts, who declared, "This happens every day in Detroit, in Chicago, in Los Angeles, in Atlanta. This happens all across areas where there are large populations of color." The camera then cut away to Claiborne nodding along to this sage, received wisdom, "It is ugly and it is mean.... I do not believe a White person would have been treated that way on Staten Island by the police."

This points to one of the fundamental mistakes mainstream news made covering stories of police violence in the 2010s. Historically, Black suspects in the US were treated very differently than White ones. But was this still true in 2014? And if so, to what degree? Getting answers to these critical questions would have required courage, tenacity, and a willingness to do the hard work of digging for relevant data. Reporters were clearly not interested in doing that kind of heavy lifting.

Instead, Claiborne took the easy route. In his quest to pack his piece with maximum emotional punch, he then took us out to the streets, where protesters angrily declared that Garner was killed because of his race. Again, no balance, no contextualization, no reminder that there was no evidence to suggest this was true.

The package ended with scenes from Garner's funeral in which, once again, Claiborne chose to run the most inflammatory sound bites. In one, Al Sharpton screamed, "You think we're not going to fight this one? You can get ready for the long haul! We are not going to stop until we get justice!" Claiborne then ran a bite from another reverend who came close to making an outright call for violence, telling the congregation, "We have every right to want revenge!"

Other than a quick, perfunctory comment from an ex-cop, Claiborne made no attempt to balance his story.

In fact, he was so busy exploiting the speculative racial angle of the case that he didn't even address its most critical question: Was Pantaleo's takedown of Garner a legal move under NYPD guidelines? This, after all, was going to determine whether the officer might be disciplined, fired, or even face criminal charges. Getting to the bottom of this would not have been a particularly difficult feat to pull off. All Claiborne needed to do was take the cell phone video of Garner's arrest to several legal and police experts to get their take on it.

Chokeholds have always been a hot button issue. In 1993, right in the middle of the crack epidemic, at a time when cops were overwhelmed by rampant, out-of-control crime, NYPD Commissioner Raymond Kelly surprised the rank and file by completely banning their use. There were zero exceptions to this new edict; officers could not put their arms around the necks of suspects even if they felt their lives were in danger.

As Chief John Timoney told *The New York Times*, "Basically, stay the hell away from the neck. That's what it says." [31]

Despite the new edict, some cops routinely defied the ban, and the use of chokeholds quietly continued. It wasn't something that was talked about in the open, but the blue wall of silence protected rogue cops who wrapped their arms around the necks of suspects. In the rare cases when officers got busted for using chokeholds, they rarely faced meaningful consequences.

In one highly publicized 1994 case, a security guard named Anthony Baez was throwing a football around with his brothers in the Bronx. One of the balls got away from the men and hit a police car. The cops who were sitting inside the squad car seemed to believe it was intentional. They got out and arrested the brothers, but Anthony resisted. The case was similar to Garner's in that Baez was in poor health and chronically obese—he stood 5'6" and weighed 270 pounds. Officers used a chokehold to bring him down, but the move triggered an asthmatic attack. Baez ended up dying later that night. The case got some publicity and the cop who used the chokehold was charged with manslaughter. He was later acquitted in a bench trial.

So, did Pantaleo actually use a chokehold when he tried to subdue and arrest Eric Garner? The officer denied it, claiming he brought Garner down using a method called a "seatbelt hold," which is perfectly legal. This argument is tough to swallow since seatbelt holds, by definition, mean no direct pressure to the neck and the video clearly shows otherwise. The medical examiner

---

31 Ian Fisher, "Kelly Bans Chokes by Officers," *New York Times*, November 24, 1993

confirmed this when she listed Garner's manner of death as a homicide caused by neck compressions.[32]

NYPD Commissioner Bill Bratton knew he had a crisis on his hands with the Eric Garner case. It required him to walk a very delicate and fine line. On the one hand, he needed to soothe and reassure the public, which was growing increasingly concerned about reports of police abuse. On the other hand, Bratton also needed to protect his rank and file, assuring them he had their backs.

Appearing on *CBS This Morning*, he conceded that, based on the tape, "What we see is certainly disturbing," but couched it by adding, "Police, unfortunately, when force is used, is never good to look at. This particular scene, which has been repeated thousands upon thousands of times, really has struck a chord with the public."

Bratton's word salad did little to appease anyone.

NYPD officers felt they were being unjustly criticized for just doing their job—a dangerous job at that.

Meanwhile, the Reverend Al Sharpton led angry demonstrators through the streets of New York, demanding serious law enforcement reform.

The temperature went down just a bit on August 19, 2014, when the Staten Island district attorney announced that he would seek a criminal indictment against Officer Pantaleo, who, by that point, had been demoted to desk duty.

32 Josiah Bates, Sanya Mansoor, and Mahita Gajanan, "'The Correct Decision.' NYPD Fires Daniel Pantaleo, Officer Involved in Eric Garner Chokehold Death," *Time*, August 19, 2019

In New York, grand jury proceedings are completely closed to the public and the media. To this day, we don't know what criminal charges the DA tried to get the grand jury to indict Pantaleo on.

What we do know is that during grand jury proceedings, the prosecution gets to lay out its case, but the defense doesn't. It's like watching a boxer throw combinations against a heavy bag, and then, without ever seeing his opponent spar, trying to predict who will win their fight.

The legal standard prosecutors must meet to get an indictment is called "probable cause," which means there's no need to prove the defendant is guilty of anything, just that it wouldn't be a complete waste of taxpayer time and money to move forward with a trial. Also, unlike a criminal case, the verdict doesn't need to be unanimous. In New York, a simple majority will do.

It's a pretty low bar to clear.

The clichéd joke is that a grand jury would indict a ham sandwich, and it's not far from the truth. Hard data is difficult to come by, but it's estimated that more than 99 percent of grand juries return an indictment. According to the Bureau of Justice, in 2010, 162,000 federal cases were prosecuted and grand juries failed to return an indictment in only eleven of them.[33]

On September 29, 2014, the grand jury in the Eric Garner case convened for what most expected to be a slam-dunk indictment. Twenty-three jurors were selected: Reportedly, fourteen

[33] Ben Casselman, "It's Incredibly Rare for a Grand Jury to Do What Ferguson's Just Did," *New York Times*, November 24, 2014

were White and nine were people of color, of which at least five were Black.[34]

The prosecution laid out an extensive case, calling fifty witnesses to the stand, including Officer Pantaleo, who reportedly spent two hours testifying. He must have been very likeable and persuasive, because on December 3, 2014, after less than a day of deliberations, the grand jury decided that the prosecution had failed to even meet the weak "probable cause" standard. Daniel Pantaleo would not be facing any criminal charges.

The stunning news led every major network and cable newscast. On CBS, Scott Pelley, who seems to have perfected his stuffy, on-air delivery by watching old episodes of *Masterpiece Theatre*, somberly led his newscast by framing it in purely racial terms: "Today, a grand jury in New York City declined to bring charges against a White police officer in the death of an unarmed Black man."

Of course, Ron Claiborne of ABC News did the same.

Surprisingly, CNN's Anderson Cooper did not accentuate the racial angle when he kicked off team coverage. But after the lead packages ran, he assembled a panel of outraged pundits. Not one of them could bring themselves to consider the possibility that the grand jury had executed its civic duties in good faith and that there might have been a reason, other than racism, which led them to their controversial decision.

It's estimated that only 25 percent of Americans who get a jury summons end up reporting for service, and it's easy to see why. In addition to doing a thankless job for roughly fifty dollars a

---

34 Andrew Siff, "NYC Grand Jury Expected to Vote in Eric Garner Case," NBC New York, December 1, 2014

day, they open themselves up to threats and abuse if they reach an unpopular verdict. That's exactly what was happening to the twenty-three members of the Eric Garner grand jury, who were being publicly excoriated and second-guessed.

President Obama made his feelings about the decision clear: "It is incumbent upon all of us as Americans regardless of race, region, faith—that we recognize this is an American problem and not just a Black problem, or a brown problem, or a Native American problem—this is an American problem, when anybody in this country is not being treated equally under the law that's a problem and it's my job as president to help solve it."

New York Mayor Bill de Blasio was more succinct, calling the decision "a national moment of grief."

New York Senator Kirsten Gillibrand piled on: "Nobody unarmed should die on a New York street corner for suspected low-level offenses. I'm shocked by this grand jury decision and will be calling on the Department of Justice to investigate."[35]

Celebrities also got in on the act.

Ice-T tweeted, "This Eric Garner s**t is making me sick to my stomach. We all watched a snuff FILM! No indictment!"

That same day, Alicia Keys released a song titled "We Gotta Pray," a protest against the grand jury decision.

Derrick Rose of the Chicago Bulls posted pictures of himself wearing an "I can't breathe" shirt. Reggie Bush of the NFL Detroit Lions did the same.

But the real energy and passion were out on the streets, where there were more than fifty demonstrations nationwide. Most were peaceful, as reporters dutifully and repetitively kept

---

35 Maya Rhodan, "Lawmakers Call For Federal Investigation Into Chokehold Death," *Time*, December 3, 2014

pointing out, but some were not. In New York City, three hundred people were arrested. And in Berkeley, California, things got way out of hand when protesters began damaging property and throwing bricks and rocks at police officers.

There was legitimate cause for anger. It's fair to conclude that Pantaleo used a chokehold on Eric Garner, a clear violation of NYPD policy. This would later be confirmed during a disciplinary hearing in 2019, which would lead to Pantaleo's firing from the department.

But the media ignored other factors that might have swayed the grand jury. For one, it does seem likely that Garner's health was so poor, he likely would have died no matter what method officers used to subdue him. The same medical examiner who ruled the manner of death a homicide admitted under oath that because Garner's health was so bad, even a "bear hug" could have killed him.[36] The NYPD's top in-house doctor also testified that Garner's death was brought on by a heated argument followed by a physical struggle.

Another angle the media failed to consider in their one-sided indignation at the grand jury's decision is that the DA may have overcharged Pantaleo. This is a common tactic used by prosecutors who, assuming the grand jury will just rubber-stamp whatever is brought to them, try to gain maximum leverage for possible future plea deals. Since the records are sealed, we'll never know what charges the prosecutor brought against Pantaleo. But if it was something severe, like second-degree murder, it's possible the jury might have refused to indict on those grounds.

---

36 Michael R. Sisak, "Medical Examiner: Chokehold Triggered Eric Garner's Death," AP News, May 15, 2019

More likely, the grand jury just didn't want to indict a law enforcement officer. This is common throughout the country, especially in more conservative areas. Staten Island, while not exactly red, might as well be Alabama when compared with its neighboring boroughs. In the 2012 presidential election, it voted for Barack Obama over Mitt Romney by a couple of percentage points. In contrast, Obama got a nearly unanimous 83 percent of the vote in Manhattan.

The way people responded to the Eric Garner case was a kind of Rorschach test. Some saw his killing as a blatant example of systemic police brutality, which, they argued, was common in poor and minority neighborhoods. To others, it was just an isolated example of a rogue cop breaking the rules and revealed nothing about the state of policing in America. There was a third camp that was completely unsympathetic to Garner. They believed all the fuss was just misplaced empathy for criminals and that cops were being held to unreasonably high standards.

These are all strong currents of thought in America, and journalists should have been agnostic to those differing points of view. It was not the job of reporters to hold viewers' hands and lead them to a "correct" opinion. Their job was to present all of the messy, contradictory facts relevant to Eric Garner's case. They needed to walk viewers through the entire glass house, show them all the rooms, all the views, and then allow them to reach their own conclusions.

The biggest journalistic sin in this case was the way reporters lazily framed it in racial terms. There never was one iota of proof that Officer Pantaleo was motivated by Eric Garner's skin color when he applied that banned chokehold. There is also no reason to believe that the diverse grand jury based its decision on racial bias. But the media continuously framed this story through that lens, amplifying radical voices making irresponsible claims while refusing to ask tough, skeptical questions.

The media's message was clear: American police were hunting down Black men, and White America was perfectly happy to let them get away with it.

It wasn't apparent at the time, but something had shifted in America after the killing of Trayvon Martin. From NFL fields to Hollywood movie sets, from the White House to the streets of big American cities, it suddenly became chic to voice some of the most radical ideas many thought had been left behind in the late 1960s. Broadcast journalists, who were supposed to be neutral regarding these kinds of culture-war issues, were now openly sympathetic to the activists and aggressively amplifying their messaging.

Some journalists were seeing themselves in a new light. No longer willing to simply report the news in an even-handed way, they began to voice doubts about the foundational principles of their craft.

A fight was brewing between the old school of journalists and a new generation of reporters who had an entirely different vision for their profession: Instead of being in the business of truth-telling, they saw journalism as a means to fight for a more just and equitable world.

Journalism was suddenly under attack from within.

Chapter 3
The War on Truth

In November of 1991, I started my first full-time news job, in the idyllic city of San Diego, California. The station that hired me, KFMB-TV, a CBS affiliate, was far from glamorous. It sat in a depressing warehouse, in an out-of-the-way part of the city called Kearny Mesa. I don't think many people actually lived there, and certainly no one chose to. Kearny Mesa's main raison d'être seemed to be to host every industrial business and payday loan center in the county, so they would remain safely out of the sight of tourists. The pay was meager even by 1991 standards—$21,000 a year—barely enough to keep the lights on and sustain me on a steady diet of Kraft Macaroni & Cheese and fast food.

But I wasn't complaining. After a soul-sucking year selling cars near the Mexican border, desperately trying to get someone interested in my thin resume, which basically consisted of filler jobs and the promise to work *really, really hard*, I got a bite from KFMB's legendary iconoclastic news director, Jim Holtzman.

Little did I know, he would have a huge influence on the rest of my career.

I was part of a new wave of Generation X kids flooding newsrooms at that time. We had grown up on MTV, and because of that, the old-timers seemed convinced that we were going to destroy whatever credibility TV news had left. But even though Holtzman was an old-school journalist, he wasn't anchored to the "that's the way things have always been done" kind of thinking; he constantly took risks—like hiring me. Some of his other ideas didn't work out quite as well, like the time he tried to turn the 11 p.m. news into a single-themed show called *This Day*.

Holtzman understood that television was a medium geared more towards conveying emotions than dry facts, so he tended to shy away from covering things like school board hearings or city council meetings. He believed that if people wanted those kinds of stories, they should read newspapers. Holtzman was also allergic to flowery, stilted TV news language and banned words like blaze, eatery, and all double-hyphenated adjectives from his newscasts. He wanted us to be conversational. To write the way people actually talked.

TV news is a relatively new form of journalism. The first nightly half-hour network newscast, the *CBS Evening News* with Walter Cronkite, didn't debut until the fall of 1963. Those pioneering reporters and producers were definitely not elitists. They were mostly working-class, and very few of them had advanced degrees. Even Cronkite himself was a college drop-out. These guys may not have had much formal education, but they were tough, tenacious, relentless reporters who understood the interests and concerns of their viewers. That's because they lived in the same neighborhoods, sent their kids to the same public schools, ate at the same restaurants, rooted for the same teams, and shared the same anxieties as their viewers. They didn't need to *try* to understand the audience. They *were* the audience.

This first wave of TV news journalists was getting close to retirement when I started my career. I had the good fortune to be mentored by some of these giants. They taught me what it meant to be a journalist, what our north star should always be, and what our obligation was to the public.

I have distilled their lessons into five foundational laws of journalism. I think it's critical to go over them, as it will vividly illustrate just how far the profession has strayed from its core mission.

Law #1: Objectivity

"When I started, there was no sense that you tried to influence people by the way you tell a story."

—JIM HOLTZMAN
FORMER KFMB NEWS DIRECTOR

"The foundation of journalism is to provide as much factual information as possible from all perspectives. To give people enough information so they can choose if it's time to buy a house, or who to vote for. I never wanted to teach people what to think."

—PAT LALAMA
INVESTIGATIVE JOURNALIST

Here's a thought exercise.

Let's say you asked a friend who just took his daughter to a Taylor Swift concert to tell you about it. "Oh my God! The music is just so horrible," he complained. "One song sounds like the next. The girl can't dance. She looks like a big Muppet out there. What do these teenage girls see in her? It's not like the music when we were kids—now that was the real deal! And the price tag for the tickets—Jesus, we could have gone on vacation for what I spent on that show. But my daughter had a good time, so I guess that's all that matters." You had asked your friend to play reporter, to be your eyes and ears at an event you didn't attend. But he actually told you very little about the concert. Instead, he was trying to convince you to see Taylor Swift in the same negative light that he does. He was being an advocate.

But let's say that friend had the soul of a true journalist. His report might sound more like this: "The stadium was completely sold out, not an empty seat in sight. I would say the vast majority of the fans were teenage girls but there were some boys in the crowd too. And of course, lots of adults like me, who came to chaperone and bond with their kids. The second Taylor Swift came out, accompanied by a huge troupe of dancers, the entire audience went wild. Everyone stood up and never sat down again. Swift seems to have gone through a few different musical stages—from country to pop to dance—and she transitioned between the genres seamlessly. Admittedly, the tickets were pricey. Our seats were five hundred dollars a pop, and some of the ones close to the stage were going for as much as four grand. But Taylor worked hard for the money, putting on a spirited three-hour show."

Obviously, there are an infinite number of ways to tell this story, but in the first example, there is a clear subjective agenda:

This person hates T Swift and resented having to shell out good money to take his daughter to the show. In the second example, you learned a lot more about the concert, the artist, and the mood of the fans in attendance. Best of all, it's unclear whether the narrator even likes Taylor Swift—which is a fairly good litmus test: If you don't know what a reporter personally thinks about a topic, chances are they've done a pretty good job being objective.

Another basic component of objectivity is getting both sides of a story.

Of course, not every story demands balanced viewpoints. So, which ones do? Where is the magical line in the sand? Like most things in journalism, the answer requires a little bit of subjectivity and a lot of good faith.

Let's start with the easy examples. There are things in this world that are just empirically true: The earth is round; the Eagles won Super Bowl 59 by a score of 40–22; the Dow Jones rose just over 13 percent in 2024; and Taylor Swift's Eras Tour grossed approximately $2 billion—the highest in history.[37] These are all examples of things that are factual and easily verifiable. Just because some outliers want to argue that the earth is flat or that the moon landing was staged does not mean that a reporter must reach out to them for balanced coverage.

There are also certain moral lines that do not require balanced viewpoints. As veteran LA news anchor Terry Anzur says, "If I was doing a story about child molestation, I don't have to get the other side. There is no other side." Ditto for murder, rape, famine, and disease.

---

[37] Chris Willman, "It's Official: Taylor Swift's Eras Tour Is History's First $2 Billion Tour," *Variety*, December 9, 2024

Of course, a journalist needs to be very judicious about where to apply this standard because it can easily slide into bias or even activism.

I reminded Holtzman of an incident in his newsroom that had a big impact on me. One of his reporters, Gina Lew, had done a story about abortion but failed to get a pro-life perspective on it. I didn't know it at the time, but Holtzman is pro-choice and identifies as liberal; yet he berated Lew in front of the entire newsroom and refused to air her package until she got a quality soundbite from a credible anti-abortion advocate.

"Reporters are people," says Holtzman. "They come in with their own experiences. I had a reporter, John Culea, who would say, 'I'm a born-again Christian. I'm right-to-life.' He knew himself. He knew he couldn't do those stories."

Holtzman says self-awareness is an essential attribute of a great journalist. "People who gravitate towards reporting want to tell stories about people. You need a lot of empathy for that. I think people who want to tell stories about people tend to be liberal. They tend to have a bleeding heart. I recognized that in me."

Unfortunately, some of the most venerated reporters in the world lack this critical self-awareness gene.

Award-winning war correspondent Christiane Amanpour is a prime example. At an event where, ironically, she was being honored for her work in advancing press freedom, she made the following statement: "It appeared much of the media got itself into knots trying to differentiate between balance, objectivity, neutrality, and crucially, truth. We cannot continue the old paradigm—let's say like over global warming, where 99.9 percent of the empirical scientific evidence is given equal play with the tiny minorities of deniers.... So, I believe in being truthful, not neutral."[38]

Amanpour has done some amazing work in her career, but this was pure nonsense. She made the bizarre claim that the media gives "equal play" to fringe deniers, which is completely untrue. Legacy news reports overwhelmingly treat climate change as settled science.

Her argument is also flawed from a first-principles standpoint. Here's what we know to be true: The earth's surface temperature has risen about two degrees Fahrenheit since 1850. So, how many scientists believe this is mainly caused by the burning of fossil fuels? Amanpour says 99.9 percent, but that number is wildly inflated. The real number, while impossible to precisely gage, is closer to 80 percent.[39] Since 20 percent of scientists believe the earth's warming is mostly caused by factors other than the burning of fossil fuel, journalists—who are generally not experts on the subject—shouldn't completely dismiss this minority point of view. After all, at one point, the overwhelming majority of scientists believed that the earth was at the center of the universe, that intelligence could be measured by the shape and size of someone's skull, and that babies were born without any innate traits or abilities.

Amanpour was engaging in level one thinking. Even if the 80 percent of scientists prove to be correct and the burning of fossil fuels has warmed the planet by a couple of degrees, there are some critical follow-up questions that require serious debate and

---

38 Marc Morano, "CNN's Christiane Amanpour Equates Climate 'Deniers' with Proponents of 'Ethnic Cleansing and Genocide,'" Climatedepot.com, November 25, 2016

39 Earl J. Ritchie, "Fact Checking the Claim of 97% Consensus on Anthropogenic Climate Change," Forbes, December 10, 2021

consideration: Can we do anything about it? Is it reversable? Is it actually a crisis? Fossil fuels have extended lifespans and lifted billions out of poverty. Are we certain that climate change is such an existential threat that we would be willing to trade in much of that progress in order to reduce CO_2 emissions? Amanpour twisted herself into a knot. While claiming to be fighting for truth in reporting, she was actually trying to shut down public debate on an issue about which she held an entrenched opinion.

Amanpour was not being subtle in her argument. She was calling for journalists to completely dismiss the possibility that climate change comes from anything other than manmade activity. She was equating the minority viewpoint of esteemed scientists with crackpots and flat-earthers. This is nothing more than naked activism masquerading as journalism.

Most news bias comes in much more nuanced forms. A reporter or producer has many subtle ways to shape the way viewers feel about a story.

As an example, let's say it's 2020. A local news reporter is assigned a story about the owner of a small family-run grocery store who got fined for keeping his business open in defiance of COVID lockdowns. This reporter might have very strong feelings about the pandemic. Maybe she knows a family member who died from the virus, or maybe she is scared of getting COVID herself. If she does not have the self-awareness to see that bias in herself, she might feel justified in distorting the story and turning it into a morality play about a greedy business owner who puts profits over the well-being of the community.

There are many small ways in which she can turn viewers against this business owner.

For example, the visual composition of an interview subject influences how they are perceived. In the unspoken language of TV, high-angle shots tend to convey confusion and doubt, while a low angle shot makes a subject appear heroic. The store owner might be framed *60 Minutes* style—in an extreme close-up with every drop of sweat visible and every facial expression exaggerated. This tends to make subjects look guilty and uncomfortable.

Lighting also has a subliminal effect on how we feel about an interview subject. Warm lighting can help make someone look sympathetic; cold lighting can make them seem clinical and uncaring.

The way a story is written is critical. Will the reporter make a good faith effort to present the store owner's best argument, or will she intentionally choose sound bites where he stumbles or where she scores a contrived *gotcha* moment? The audience will never know which minute of a thirty-minute interview makes it to air, so this decision, which is almost solely at the discretion of the reporter, is probably the most crucial one in the process.

As the script is being written, word choices become important. Is he "upset" about being shut down or "defiant"? Is he "worried" about the safety of his employees or "indifferent"?

After a news package is written, it goes off to a video editor, who also has power to shape the piece. Will she choose cutaway shots of the store owner that are representative of the interview, or will she cherry-pick shots that make the owner look angry, mean, or annoyed?

Clearly, reporting is an art. You could take the raw footage from just about any story and cut it in countless different ways. Every single one of them might be factually correct and get approved for air by a corporate attorney. But each version could also leave viewers with entirely different opinions and feelings about the story.

So ultimately, objectivity is about intent. Is the journalist trying her best, through every single step of the process, to be balanced and fair? Or is she hoping that her story will shape the way viewers think?

As Walter Cronkite said, "Our job is only to hold up the mirror." [40]

Law #2: The North Star: Truth

> "The notion of journalism for social change is the rot that changes the north star from truth."
>
> —BILL APPLEGATE
>
> LEGENDARY TV GENERAL MANAGER

> "Seek the truth, find the truth, tell the truth."
>
> —SHEPARD SMITH
>
> FORMER FOX NEWS ANCHOR

The journalist has one mission: the fearless pursuit of the truth. Every other consideration is a distraction.

This means that when working on a story, journalists must let go of any desired outcomes. A reporter may want a candidate to win, a law to be passed, or a movement to succeed, but those desires are nothing more than traps, which can easily take them off the path of truth-telling and onto the road of advocacy.

---

[40] Richard Nelson, "A Journalist Defines His Role," Commonwealth Policy Center, July 6, 2017

In an infamous 2022 TED Talk, Katherine Maher, then-CEO of Wikipedia, made a shocking admission: "Our reverence for the truth might be a distraction that is getting in the way of finding common ground and getting things done."[41] You would think this would disqualify Maher from ever working in a truth-seeking news operation again, but sadly, you'd be wrong. In 2024, Maher was hired to run NPR.

From MSNBC to Fox News Channel (FNC), television news is largely out of the "hard truths" business. Management has trained its audiences to expect a predictable mix of distorted stories that affirm their worldviews. The bean counters are terrified of upsetting their ever-shrinking audience.

The biggest losers in this dynamic are the viewers. Most mainstream newscasts squashed the Hunter Biden laptop story, because, after all, defeating Donald Trump to "save democracy" was a desired outcome. At the same time, Fox News seemed open to Donald Trump's stolen election claims, despite the fact that there was little to no evidence that "steal the vote" was based on much more than an unwillingness to accept the outcome of an election. As a result, 69 percent of registered Republicans polled in 2023 still believed Trump beat Biden in 2020.[42]

Uncompromising truth-telling can be tricky, as people who covered the O. J. Simpson trial found out firsthand. The "trial of the century" was racially charged, especially since it came right

---

[41] Tim Hains, "NPR CEO Katherine Maher: A Reverence for the Truth Might Be Getting in the Way of Getting Things Done," Real Clear Politics, April 17, 2024

[42] Jennifer Agiesta and Ariel Edwards-Levy, "CNN Poll: Percentage of Republicans Who Think Biden's 2020 Win Was Illegitimate Ticks Back Up Near 70%," CNN.com, August 3, 2023

on the heels of the LA riots. Simpson's lawyers exploited this dynamic, leaning into race, deflecting attention from their guilty celebrity client by putting the LAPD and its unsavory history with communities of color on trial.

On March 15, 1995, prosecutor Christopher Darden was questioning limo driver Alan Park, who had been in his car, waiting to take Simpson to the airport the night of the murders. He testified that he heard a voice on O. J.'s property.

Darden asked if the voice sounded like it belonged to a Black person.

Johnnie Cochran, the lead defense attorney, pounced, theatrically accusing Darden of leaning into racial stereotypes. As millions watched on live TV, Cochran, who had once mentored Darden, said he was personally disappointed and offended that a Black man would stoop to this level.

Investigative reporter Pat Lalama was covering the trial for KCBS-TV, and as she watched these theatrics play out, a couple of conflicting thoughts crossed her mind. On the one hand, it seemed obvious to her that Cochran's objections were insincere. On the other, she knew that a lot of people would want her to condemn Darden's line of questioning as inappropriate, or maybe even racist.

She decided to ignore both those impulses and simply report on exactly what she knew to be true: "It's not my job to determine whether there's such a thing as a 'Black dialect,' so I just reported on what Darden asked the witness. Johnnie Cochran was just doing what a defense attorney does. So, I just ended up reporting what he said. My job is to tell the viewers what was said in the courtroom and how the jury reacted. It is not my job to lecture."

When truth is a reporter's north star, the facts lead them, not the other way around. This, inevitably, can lead to disappointment.

Over our five-season run, *Reasonable Doubt* investigated fifty separate murder cases involving claims of wrongful convictions.[43]

Every day, like a broken record, I cautioned the producers and researchers not to fall in love with the convicts and their families—not to let themselves *want* someone to be innocent. I would tirelessly remind them that desired outcomes are traps—traps that can cause minds to close and corrupt a fearless search for truth.

The staff loved producing the episodes where we concluded that a convict was wrongfully convicted of murder. But in the great majority of cases, the convicts were right where they belonged: behind bars. Those episodes depressed the team, and I had to consistently remind them that we are not advocates: We are truth-tellers. And as long as we did everything possible to reach the right conclusion, we could hold our heads high.

There were a few producers who couldn't separate their inner social justice warriors from the work. Some even withheld or minimized important evidence, hoping to manipulate the outcome of our investigations. Obviously, they were not asked back.

Truth as a north star can be a lonely hill to die on. It can make you seem sanctimonious, out of touch with the times, heartless, or even cruel. But as longtime USC journalism professor Joe Saltzman tells me, "When a student says, 'I want to be an activist,' I say, 'Do that. Go change the world. Just don't use journalism to do it.'"

---

43 All episodes stream on Max.

Law #3: Truth to Power

"We're just about the least trusted people in America, and it's our own damn fault."

—DIANE DIMOND
INVESTIGATIVE JOURNALIST

It may sound a bit high-minded, but at its best, journalism has an essential role to play in a democracy. It serves as a check on the power of government, big business, the famous, and the wealthy. Journalists exposed the Watergate scandal and brought down a corrupt presidency. *The New York Times* and *The Washington Post* courageously published the Pentagon Papers, which revealed that the government lied to the public about the Vietnam War. *The Boston Globe* uncovered the Catholic Church's sex abuse scandal, as portrayed in the 2016 Academy Award–winning movie *Spotlight*.

Old-school journalists were aggressive, persistent, and not intimidated by the rich and powerful. They were competitive and ambitious and wanted to be the ones to break impactful stories.

Today's broadcast journalists are a different breed. Take the media's irresponsible coverage of COVID, in which lockdowns, vaccine mandates, and extended school closings were covered from an entirely institutional point of view. Government mandates were treated as obvious and necessary emergency measures, which required no skepticism. Absolutely no tough questions were asked of the bureaucrats who were mandating that working-class families sacrifice their businesses and their children's education in the name of public health. On the rare occasion that someone did get airtime for challenging these draconian measures, they were portrayed as right-wing kooks, conspiracy theorists, science-deniers, or purveyors of "disinformation."

Disinformation, by the way, is code for anything people in power don't like.

The mRNA COVID vaccines were billed as a miracle of science. We were told they were safe and extremely effective. As President Biden said in a 2021 CNN townhall, "You're not going to get COVID if you have these vaccinations." This turned out, of course, to be completely untrue. But even as reports of such "breakthrough infections" emerged, the media showed zero interest in investigating the phenomena. Instead, they doubled down, amplifying the government's messaging, and dismissed any concerns about the safety or effectiveness of the shots as the "disinformation" of conspiracy theorists and anti-vaxxers. In fact, we now know that the government strongly pressured social media sites to shadow-ban posts from citizen journalists who questioned the administration's vaccine policy. Some of these alternative news sites got in trouble for doing nothing more than reposting the CDC's own data. In an Orwellian twist, the government claimed that while these posts might have been factually true, the information could have led to "vaccine hesitancy."

This was a frightening turn of events. Only in authoritarian countries do those in power get to decide what is labeled "misinformation."

Old-school journalists would have taken a radically different approach to covering the pandemic. Those reporters would have seen it as their professional responsibility to speak truth to power and ask tough, skeptical questions of the politicians, who after all, work for us. Yet, the legacy news was too timid to push elected leaders to explain why they locked us in our homes, shut down small businesses, closed schools, mandated that people cover their faces, and forced citizens to take untested vaccines.

To be clear, reporters should not have taken an opinionated stance against these controversial decisions—they should have simply been skeptical. Asking tough questions of elected officials would have forced those in power to explain and justify their orders.

COVID is just one of countless examples of modern journalists failing to hold those in power accountable.

Old-school reporters would have been all over Tara Reade's 2020 accusations of sexual assault against then-candidate Joe Biden. They would have aggressively questioned Jussie Smollett's dubious claim of getting assaulted by two White supremacists in the middle of a freezing cold night in the heart of a bougie, deep-blue Chicago neighborhood. Undoubtedly, they would have demanded to know whether President Biden was able to perform his duties when he clearly appeared enfeebled. The list goes on.

This unwillingness to challenge the power structure reminds me of my time in entertainment "journalism"—air quotes intended.

I was part of that machine for about six years, working at *Extra*, standing on red carpets, asking inane questions of celebrities ("What are you wearing?" and "How excited are you to be here tonight?" are what pass as probing questions at a movie premiere). The pay was decent, but the work was soul-sucking. In Hollywood, the publicists run the show. If you dare ask one of their clients a real question—like about a recent arrest for domestic assault or why their last three movies bombed—you will find yourself completely cut off: not just from that one star, but the publicist's entire roster of celebrities.

Shows like *Extra* and *Entertainment Tonight* have basically been co-opted by the machine. As long as they run fawning, superficial pieces about celebrities, they will continue to get access to them. The only time a star becomes fair game is when they do something so egregious that they are dropped by their agencies and are no longer protected by the Hollywood cabal. If the nightly entertainment shows want to do pieces bashing Mel Gibson, Roseanne Barr, Kevin Spacey, Armie Hammer, or Mo'Nique, they have a bright green light. Anyone with a decent agent or publicist is off limits.

Winona Ryder was always in the machine's good graces. In 2001, the actress was caught red-handed shoplifting at Saks Fifth Avenue in Beverly Hills. I wrote and cut what I thought was a fair piece on the story but was then instructed by a mid-level manager to recut it, minimizing the more damning parts of the footage where the actress is clearly seen cutting price tags off the stolen items and then placing them in her bag. Furious and full of self-righteous indignation, I made a stink, demanding to know why we were in the business of altering reality to help a star get away with shoplifting. I was told that her publicist was powerful and we could not afford to piss her off. Besides, Winona might give us an interview if we played ball. I wish I could tell you I stood my ground and refused the assignment, but after a lot of fruitless arguing, I did what I was told. Winona Ryder never did give us the interview, but justice prevailed: She was convicted of felony grand theft.

The only show that dared to treat the entertainment industry with the skepticism of a truly free press was the renegade tabloid newsmagazine *Hard Copy*. In its 1990s heyday, it was a thorn in the side of the Dream Machine.[44] It was loathed by entitled stars—most notably George Clooney, who was unable to accept that he actually had to answer any questions tougher than "How does it feel to be *People* magazine's most handsome man of the year?" Ironically, the show was owned by Paramount, proving the golden rule of Hollywood: You can get away with almost anything as long as you're making people money.

In 1993, no entertainer was making people more money than Michael Jackson. At that point, he was considered untouchable. Soft-spoken, preternaturally talented, a singer, dancer, and Top 40 hit machine, he had rarely gotten bad press, other than being mocked for his eccentricities.

Investigative journalist Diane Dimond had the courage to break the story that brought down the legend. In 1993, while working at *Hard Copy*, she got tipped off that he had been accused of sexually abusing a thirteen-year-old boy.[45]

"I was like, 'How do we prove it?'" Dimond says she took her time getting the story together before reporting the explosive allegations. She refused to go on the air until she was 100 percent convinced that the facts lined up: "People came forward and said to me that they worked at Neverland and that they saw Jackson bringing young boys through there. But I wouldn't accept that at face value. I would say to them, 'Prove that you're who you say you are. How do I know you actually worked at Neverland?'"

Dimond believes one of the biggest flaws with today's breed of journalists is an unwillingness to do the heavy lifting it takes to break huge stories. They also often lack the inner fortitude to withstand the hate that comes their way after reporting hard

44 I worked there as a director for its final season. I missed the show's glory days.

45 Full disclosure: I befriended the family of Jackson's accuser many years later, but we never discussed the case in any depth.

truths. As Dimond puts it, "People would say Diane Dimond doesn't like Michael Jackson, which was ridiculous. My work took me to where the truth was."

Law #4: Separation of News and Opinion

"As a journalist, I felt successful when
I got attacked by both sides."

—TERRY ANZUR

FORMER LOS ANGELES NEWS ANCHOR

When I was starting out, some old-school journalists advised me not to register to vote. They felt that even participating in elections could compromise a reporter's credibility and neutrality. That's how committed they were to maintaining a wall between news and opinion.

What we're seeing today is the polar opposite of that ethos. Many journalists routinely go on social media and post wildly provocative and partisan opinions.

For example, in 2020, Joy Reid of MSNBC sent out this gem: "Republicans are the party of voter suppression, hypocrisy, and the politics of racial division. Period." Not to be outdone, Reid's co-worker, Keith Olbermann, tweeted, "Trump is killing us. He is killing us by the thousands. He is killing us by ignoring science. He is killing us by political calculation. And now he's killing us by not leading, by not even pretending to care." Soledad O'Brien is a highly decorated journalist, the winner of three Emmy Awards, a Peabody, and a DuPont. You'd think she would know better, but she made this credibility-killing post about Trump supporters: "LOL. If you have to have the handful of Black people at your rally hold up t-shirts that say you're not a racist...chances are overwhelming that you are a racist."[46]

When reporters rip off their masks of neutrality and show themselves to be emotional, opinionated, even unhinged, they damage the credibility of the business and themselves. How are we supposed to trust Joy Reid to objectively tell us about President Trump's latest tax proposal when we know how she feels about Republicans?

In my discussions with well-placed network sources, many complained about the ubiquitous use of panelists to comment on stories in the middle of newscasts. This problem is especially acute on cable, where the networks have hours of airtime to fill. Getting a bunch of people to sit around a long table and give hot takes on the stories of the day is a very cost-effective way to fill time—certainly cheaper than giving investigative reporters the time they need to break stories. The biggest problem with these panels is that the average viewer doesn't know where the objective reporting stops and the subjective commentary begins. The lines are fuzzy. Making things worse, the legacy cable networks tend to stack their panels with people who conform to their audience's worldview. So, Fox News, on a good day, might have one liberal on a panel of mostly conservative commentators. It's kind of a kangaroo court, with all the trappings of a fair and impartial discussion, but clearly the goal is for the audience to walk away with their biases affirmed.

In contrast, the old school was dead serious about maintaining a big, impenetrable wall between news and opinion. In 1994, I was a young producer at KCBS-TV in Los Angeles. That year,

---

[46] Soledad O'Brien, Twitter (now X), August 1, 2019.

California voters passed Proposition 187, a very controversial initiative that denied all social services and health care to illegal immigrants. One of our reporters, Bob Jimenez, filed a report about it that would barely raise an eyebrow today. It was slanted, and it was obvious that he disapproved of the new law; but overall, it was not hysterical. Our anchor, the late, hard-living, well-coiffed Michael Tuck, was not about to let this blurring of news and commentary go without a fight. As soon as the newscast ended, he charged right up into Jimenez's face.

"That piece was bullshit!" he shouted menacingly.

The entire newsroom stopped what they were doing. Tuck had once punched a news director during a heated argument, earning himself the nickname "Jock-O." There was no telling where this would go.

Jimenez tried to defend himself, "I was just reporting..."

"That was not reporting. That was opinion."

"The prop is a sham!" Jimenez argued back. "I'm just reporting on that."

"You want to do the piece—fine, but make sure it's clearly marked as an editorial!"

Tuck slammed his fist on Jimenez's desk and stormed off. Score one for the old school.

Law #5: Crimes of Omission

> "Omission has always been the
> great sin of journalism."
>
> —JOE SALTZMAN
>
> USC JOURNALISM PROFESSOR

Almost every newsroom in the country has some sort of a morning meeting where managers, reporters, producers, and members of the assignment desk gather to decide what stories they'll cover that day. The work is fluid. News is always breaking, and reporters are routinely pulled from one story and assigned to another as things develop. But the morning meeting is critical. In almost every newsroom, the staff is encouraged to speak up and pitch stories they believe in. It is here that bias and groupthink sets in.

At one Los Angeles station, I worked for a news director who routinely shot down, and even scoffed at, any stories that might have a tinge of conservative sensibility. Without issuing a memo, or openly admitting to a bias, this boss made it clear that those kinds of stories were not going to be part of his newscast.

As the late great investor Charlie Munger famously said, "Show me the incentive and I'll show you the outcome." People who work in newsrooms tend to be aggressive and ambitious. They are angling for career advancement. So, they end up pitching the kind of stories their bosses want. I doubt that during the Fox News meetings, anyone would pitch a story about how climate change is responsible for an increase in hurricanes along the Gulf coast. Likewise, any reasonably ambitious young reporter at ABC News is not going to pitch a story about how President Trump's economic policies are lowering unemployment rates in Black and Latino communities.

What you end up with is an unspoken consensus. Everyone wants to pitch the kind of stories that elicit a slap on the back and approving smiles from the boss. Pitch too many stories that run counter to the unspoken ideology of the newsroom, and you are likely to find yourself marginalized and written off as someone who "just doesn't get it."

This dynamic is not new. Monolithic thinking has always been a huge problem for TV news.

Joe Saltzman worked at KCBS-TV in the 1960s. He says that in that era, newsrooms were almost entirely populated by working-class White men: "No news stations had a Black reporter. So, during the 1965 riots, everyone was shocked that the Black community could riot." He recalls, "Back then, if you read the *LA Times*, Black people didn't even exist. Journalists were so White and that created an inherent bias."

The racist bias of the 1960s has been replaced by a completely different set of biases today. In 2020, four out of five newsroom employees have a college degree, more than twice the national average.[47] And 77 percent of those diplomas are in the arts and humanities. Is it any surprise then, that by 2022, only 3.4 percent of American journalists were Republicans?[48]

So even though legacy newsrooms have spent the past thirty years crowing about their efforts to diversify, that only applies to immutable traits. It clearly has not produced diversity of thought, religious beliefs, or economic background. Newsrooms now consist of employees who mostly come from comfortable backgrounds, received a great education at the finest liberal arts schools, and work in big blue cities. They think alike because they are alike.

As the five foundational laws of journalism came under attack in the early 2010s, the management teams of the most esteemed

---

[47] Elizabeth Grieco, "10 Charts About America's Newsrooms," Pew Research Center, April 28, 2020

[48] Kerry Picket, "Only 3.4 Percent of U.S. Journalists Are Republicans: Survey," *Washington Times*, December 30, 2023

institutions of the profession offered very little in the way of resistance.

As Daniel Okrent, a former *New York Times* editor, said, "Just watching this collapse in this series of concessions that news management has been making over the past several years is really dispiriting.... The new way makes the case that even fairness, in our old definition, no longer matters. What matters, it seems to be, more and more, is, 'Are you on the right side or the wrong side?'"[49]

By the mid-2010s, newsrooms across the country were in open revolt, with young, fervent ideologues taking on the old guard, demanding that news assume a new mission: fighting for social justice.

How did they defend the radical notion of wiping out the foundational principles of the fourth estate?

Wesley Lowery, of *The Washington Post*, put it this way in an infamous tweet: "American view-from-nowhere, 'objectivity'-obsessed, both-sides journalism is a failed experiment.... The old way must go."[50]

Emilio Garcia-Ruiz, editor in chief of the *San Francisco Chronicle* agreed, telling a reporter, "The consensus among younger journalists is that we got it all wrong. We are the problem. Objectivity has got to go."[51]

Nikole Hannah-Jones, the author of the error-riddled work *The 1619 Project*, has proudly declared, "All journalism is activism."

49 Jack Shafer, "What the Uprising Against Ronna McDaniel Really Means," Politico, March 28, 2024

50 Zadie Winthrop, "Should Journalists Rethink Objectivity? Stanford Professors Weigh In," *Stanford Daily*, August 20, 2020

51 Andrew Heyward, "Opinion: Journalistic 'Objectivity' Has Lost Its Relevance. Maybe That's a Good Thing," Local Media Association, January 31, 2023

Stanford journalism professor Ted Glasser says that journalism needs to "free itself from this notion of objectivity to develop a sense of social justice."[52]

As newsrooms grew more strident and sanctimonious, the few remaining moderates or conservatives were pushed out or frightened into submission.

A doom loop ensued. New hires were vetted for proper ideological leanings. Dissenting voices were silenced. The news became more activist-driven, more self-assured that it was fulfilling its self-declared mission of making the world a more just and equitable place.

Journalist Bari Weiss, who describes herself as left-of-center, couldn't stomach this new dynamic and resigned from *The New York Times* in 2020. She would go on to launch The Free Press, which embraces the principles of old-school journalism.

In her resignation letter, she beautifully summed up how the tenets of journalism had been destroyed by the new guard:

> *...A new consensus has emerged in the press, but perhaps especially at this paper: that truth isn't a process of collective discovery, but an orthodoxy already known to an enlightened few whose job it is to inform everyone else.*
>
> *All this bodes ill, especially for independent-minded young writers and editors paying close attention to what they'll have to do to advance their careers. Rule One: Speak your mind at your own peril. Rule*

52 Jonathan Turley, "Hannah-Jones: 'All Journalism Is Activism,'" jonathanturley.org, July 20, 2021

> *Two: Never risk commissioning a story that goes against the narrative. Rule Three: Never believe an editor or publisher who urges you to go against the grain. Eventually, the editor will cave to the mob, the editor will get fired or reassigned, and you'll be hung out to dry.*[53]

Ultimately, the Trayvon Martin and Eric Garner cases did not prompt journalists to engage in sober self-reflection. In fact, they were the canary in the coal mine.

In the summer of 2014, an eighteen-year-old kid who seemed to be in the middle of a psychotic break was about to become a martyr. From the outset, the circumstances of his shooting were murky. Yet, legacy news showed little interest in uncovering the hard truths of the case.

Michael Brown's death would become the symbol of the anti-law enforcement movement. His story, despite being embellished and fictionalized, would become part of an orthodoxy immune to challenge or critique.

The nation was already simmering, and this teenager's death ignited the spark that fueled a raging wildfire.

---

[53] Bari Weiss, "Bari Weiss on Why She Left *The New York Times,*" *New York Post,* July 14, 2020

Part Two
Wildfire

"In a time of deceit, telling the truth is a revolutionary act."

—GEORGE ORWELL

Chapter 4
Ferguson

Michael Brown seemed to have woken up on the morning of August 9, 2014, with a death wish. Every single action he would take over the next few hours—every self-destructive decision—would bring him a step closer to where he ultimately ended up: face down and motionless in a pool of his own blood.

It was the summer after his high school graduation, and Brown was living with his grandmother in the Canfield Green apartment complex, a run-down, low-income property located in a rough part of town. Despite poor grades and the unfortunate habit of sleeping in and missing morning classes, he had managed to get a diploma. This was not entirely surprising since his high school consistently ranked among the very worst in Missouri.

His parents would claim Brown was just days away from going to a for-profit technical school, Vatterott College, to become a heating and cooling technician.[54] But, like many things about this case, that might have been apocryphal. The school refused to confirm or deny that he had enrolled.

It was a lazy Saturday morning when Michael Brown got dressed for the last time. The eighteen-year-old put on a simple uniform: long khaki shorts, a white T-shirt, yellow socks, shower sandals, and a red St. Louis Cardinals hat.

He was a familiar figure in his neighborhood. Standing 6'4", friends nicknamed him "The Bodyguard." Brown was usually seen wearing headsets, bopping along to his favorite rap artists like Migos and Kendrick Lamar. Although he was uninterested in schoolwork, he did seem motivated to make a name for himself in rap. In the weeks before his death, Brown recorded a bunch of tracks under the moniker "Big Mike" and posted them online.

The songs aren't awful or embarrassing but show little promise. His lyrics occasionally revealed flashes of sensitivity, especially when he vividly described his bleak living conditions. But most of the time, he comes across as an insecure teenager, trying to project the image of a hardened gangster. In one track, he even claimed to enjoy watching people get gunned down in the streets. Other songs are cumbersome and derivative odes to the joys of smoking pot.

Brown was the child of unwed teenage parents. His mother was just thirteen when she gave birth to him. The two seemed to have had a complicated relationship. In the song "My Pain," he raps, "Feel my pain, feel my pain, my own momma don't give a damn." In a Facebook post, he wrote how it was wrong "...how yo' own family don't wanna see you do good."

---

[54] Julia Bosman, John Schwartz, and Serge F. Kovaleski, "A Youth, an Officer and 2 Paths to a Fatal Encounter," *New York Times*, August 15, 2014

A possible reason for the tension between Brown and his mom was that he had started hanging out with gang members. His mother watched in horror as Michael got drunk and smoked out with his new friends, even though he stopped short of joining a gang himself.

It's unclear whether this is what led Brown to move out of his mother's house in St. Louis and into his grandmother's in Ferguson.

Depending on how you choose to view it, at the time of his death, Brown was either having a religious awakening or a psychotic break. His grandmother was in poor health, and he had told his parents he believed he could heal her through prayer. He also told them he had literally seen Satan chasing an angel in the sky.[55] His parents had laughed at him, but he insisted that what he'd seen was real.

The month before Brown died, his father remarried. Michael called him a few weeks later and told him his new wife was going to die. His father couldn't believe what he was hearing and hung up on him. Brown then called up another family member and said, "Pop's mad at me. Tell him I said what I said because I've been having these visions and images of death. Tell him I keep seeing bloody sheets."[56]

The night before his death, Brown posted a cryptic message on Facebook: "Everything happens for a reason. Just start putting 2 n 2 together. You'll see it."

---

55 John Eligon, "Michael Brown Spent Last Weeks Grappling With Problems and Promise," *New York Times*, August 24, 2014

56 TheGrio Staff, "Michael Brown Sr. Pens Emotional Letter for Father's Day: 'Your Kids Need You,' TheGrio, June 19, 2015

It was a typically warm Missouri morning when Brown walked out of his apartment complex, and ran into Dorian Johnson. The two men made an odd pair. Johnson was in a completely different phase of life: He was twenty-two, had a job cleaning train platforms, and was raising his baby daughter with his girlfriend. The two had met when Johnson invited some neighbors over to play video games. Brown showed up, and the two bonded after some deep and intense conversations.

As the two set off for the Ferguson Market & Liquor store, Johnson grew concerned about his new friend's state of the mind. Brown was telling him that strange, spiritual things were happening all around him. To prove his point, Brown walked straight into the middle of traffic on a busy street. Johnson watched as cars swerved out of the way, barely avoiding colliding with his reckless friend.

"He had a look like, 'I told you,'" Johnson would later tell The Washington Post, adding, "I had an eerie thing the whole time we were walking."[57]

When they got to the store, Brown leaned over the counter, grabbed a box of Swisher Sweets, and handed them to Johnson. The co-owner of the store, Andy Patel, who was manning the register that day, would later say he told Brown he needed to pay for the cigars before taking them. This seemed to infuriate Brown, who then grabbed more boxes of the cigarillos, which are commonly used to roll joints. As an anxious mother and child looked on, Patel came around the counter and stood by the door, trying to block Brown's exit. He had no chance of stopping "Big Mike," who had a huge size and weight advantage. The

---

[57] Wesley Lowery, "Dorian Johnson, Witness to the Ferguson Shooting, Sticks By His Story," *Washington Post*, August 9, 2019

eighteen-year-old roughly shoved Patel out of his way and then took a couple of menacing steps in his direction before the store owner backed off. The moment Brown and Johnson walked out the front door, Patel called the police to report the robbery.

As the two walked home, Johnson was feeling unsettled by what his young friend had just done. "He wasn't in a mind state of not knowing what he was doing. He was in a mind state of trying to figure out what was happening to him," Johnson would later say. "He was just trying to find understanding."[58]

When the two got to Canfield Drive, Brown started walking in the middle of the road again, and Johnson stayed by his side. For someone who had just committed a robbery, and who was easily identifiable because of his size, it was an irrational choice. If he believed he was being guided and protected by spirits, he would soon find out that was not the case.

At that exact moment, twenty-eight-year-old Darren Wilson was in a Ferguson Police Department SUV, patrolling the neighborhood by himself. As he pulled onto Canfield Drive, he spotted Brown and Johnson walking down the middle of the street, forcing cars to awkwardly maneuver around them. Wilson rolled down his window and told them to get off the road. He then angled his car on the street to block the two men's forward progress and force them onto the sidewalk.

It was right around this time that a police radio call came through describing the robbery suspects. Darren Wilson looked up and realized that the teenager who was recklessly walking down the middle of the street matched the description.

---

58 Wesley Lowery, "Dorian Johnson, Witness to the Ferguson Shooting, Sticks By His Story," *Washington Post*, August 9, 2019

Darren Wilson knew all about the mindset of small-time thieves, and that's because he had been raised by one. Wilson's mom was a troubled soul: a small-time grifter who habitually wrote bad checks and got arrested for it several times. She had no shame and once even stole money that young Darren had raised for his Boy Scout troop.[59]

In 2002, when Wilson was just sixteen, his mom died under murky circumstances. This sent him into a tailspin. He started hanging out with a bad crowd, aimlessly drifting from one dead-end construction job to another. After the 2008 real estate crash, those construction jobs dried up and Wilson realized that he needed to do something else to survive. That's when he decided to join the police academy.

In 2009, Wilson got his first job in law enforcement with the Jennings Police Department in Missouri. The following year, he moved to nearby Ferguson. It was there that Wilson met his first wife, a twenty-one-year-old college student named Ashley Brown. The two were married for only two years before filing for divorce because, as they said in their court papers, their marriage was "irretrievably broken." This might have been a euphemistic way of saying Wilson was having an affair. He had fallen in love with his field officer, a woman named Barbara Spradling, who was nine years his senior. The two had bonded when Wilson started confiding in her about his troubled marriage.

"I was, like, 'Wow, this guy has been through a lot,'" Barbara told *The New Yorker*. "And it seemed like he handled it all pretty gracefully."[60]

---

[59] Jake Halpern, "The Cop," *New Yorker*, August 3, 2015

[60] Jake Halpern, "The Cop," *New Yorker*, August 3, 2015

In the fall of 2013—the same year he filed for divorce—Wilson and Spradling bought a suburban home together.

Despite all this turbulence in his personal life, Wilson had an exemplary work record. Just six months before the Michael Brown shooting, he had received a commendation for "extraordinary effort in the line of duty."

But his professionalism was about to be put to the ultimate test.

As Wilson sat in his car, Brown marched up to him, screaming profanities. According to Wilson, and several witnesses, Brown then leaned in through the window and punched the officer twice in the face. Wilson would later testify before a grand jury that he tried to grab Brown's arm, but "felt like a five-year-old holding onto Hulk Hogan."

It was at this point that Wilson said he feared for his life.

"I felt that another one of those punches in my face could knock me out or worse," Wilson recalled. "I mean it was—he's obviously bigger than I was and stronger.... I've already taken two to the face.... The third one could be fatal if he hit me right."

According to Wilson, Brown was trying to grab his gun. The two struggled for the weapon, and Wilson finally gained control of it.

Brown then allegedly taunted him, "You are too much of a fucking pussy to shoot me."

It was at this exact moment that, for the first time in his law enforcement career, Wilson fired shots at a suspect. The first bullet grazed Brown's thumb; the next one missed and ended up in the driver's side door. At that point, Brown and Johnson realized that Wilson meant business and started running. Wilson got out of his car and pursued them.

Brown then made the final suicidal decision of his life.

When he got about 150 feet from the police car, he abruptly stopped running, turned around, faced Wilson, who had his gun drawn, and started charging towards the officer.

As Wilson later recounted, "He turns, and when he looked at me, he made like a grunting, like aggravated sound and he starts, he turns and he's coming back towards me. His first step is coming towards me, he kind of does like a stutter step to start running. When he does that, his left hand goes in a fist and goes to his side, his right one goes under his shirt in his waistband and he starts running at me.... And when he gets about that 8 to 10 feet away, I look down. I remember looking at my sites and firing, all I see is his head and that's what I shot."

Wilson fired ten rounds at Brown; five bullets hit, all entering the front of his torso.

An eighteen-year-old was now lying in his own pool of blood, dead. If this had happened at a different time in history, it probably would have been a short-lived local news story: a tragic, cautionary tale about mental illness. But in the post-Trayvon world, Brown's death became an international scandal. A killing that purportedly provided irrefutable proof that the American law enforcement system was racist and corrupt.

About twenty-five people witnessed the shooting, and, as is common in these kinds of cases, there were numerous discrepancies in the details. But when it came to the big picture, most witnesses largely backed up Officer Wilson's version of events.

Dorian Johnson, though, had a completely different story to tell, and his version would have an outsized influence on the way this case would be covered. Johnson claimed that the confrontation started when Wilson, still seated in his squad car, reached out and grabbed Michael Brown by his neck.

Johnson also made a claim that, though discredited, remains burned in the minds of many people to this day. He said that during the foot chase, Brown stopped, turned around, raised his hands, and said something to the effect of "I don't have a gun," but that Officer Wilson ignored him and fired off ten rounds, killing the teenager in cold blood.

The following day, thousands took to the streets of Ferguson, chanting "No justice, no peace."

ABC News was the first to cover the story, with Byron Pitts leading off the coverage: "We return next to Missouri where tensions are high after an unarmed teenager was shot dead by a police officer. Details of the incident are in question, but what is certain tonight—there is heartbreak left behind."

He then threw to Bazi Kanani, who fronted a package strongly tilted against the police narrative. Kanani interviewed Dorian Johnson, whose statements should have been taken with a huge grain of salt since he was Brown's friend and an accomplice to the robbery. But there was no skepticism, no tough questions.

Kanani also gave airtime to Piaget Crenshaw, another witness, who told the reporter, "I saw him turn around with his arms up in the air and they shot him in the face and chest and he went down unarmed." Her testimony would later be discredited when it turned out she had run inside her house to call 911 after the first shots were fired and couldn't have possibly seen what happened next.

In 1991, when the Rodney King beating video was first released, there was outrage, but no violence. Los Angeles didn't go up in flames until a year later when the four officers caught on tape were acquitted by a Simi Valley jury. But in Ferguson, there was no grace period, no time to gather facts. It just seemed like everyone, including the media, jumped to a knee-jerk conclusion: Racist White cop murders innocent Black teenager. No further analysis needed.

For sixteen straight nights, the city of Ferguson would burn. The brunt of the suffering would fall on the innocent small-business owners and hardworking residents who had the misfortune of calling Ferguson home. These sacrifices, we were told, were not in vain.

On Monday, August 11, Michael Brown's parents hired none other than Benjamin Crump to represent them. Hoping to quell the violence, the FBI announced that it was opening a civil rights inquiry into the shooting.

But on CNN, that night's coverage was dominated by a completely different story: the shocking suicide of beloved comedian Robin Williams.

The other major newscasts all still led with the unrest in Ferguson. ABC News ran one of its typical emotionally unbalanced stories, leaning into the grief of Michael Brown's mom and the rage of protesters: "They're killing our young people and it's gotta stop!"

Only NBC gave some airtime to the devastated business owners trying to pick up the pieces after another night of looting and destruction.

With the predictable exception of Fox News, the police account of the shooting was never given equal weight to claims that Brown had been murdered. It was as if the word of Dorian Johnson, who had just participated in a robbery, was more credible than that of Wilson, who had an exemplary record of serving the community.

In fact, two nights later, CNN's Wolf Blitzer interviewed Johnson, who was given the floor to tell "his truth"—a polite, modern euphemism for lying.

Johnson embellished his original tall tale, now claiming that Wilson had reached out of the car window, grabbed Brown by the throat, and tried to pull him inside. He told Blitzer that he and Brown then started running away, but Wilson pointed a gun at them and fired, hitting Brown from behind. In Dorian's telling, a bleeding Brown heroically implored him to "keep running bro." Brown then turned around, his arms up in surrender, only to be gunned down by Officer Wilson.

To be fair, Blitzer had no way of knowing this story was largely made up, but he should have interjected, asked follow-up questions, and shown some curiosity and skepticism. After all, this was Brown's friend and accomplice—not exactly an impartial witness.

On August 14, after another night of violence, President Obama spoke from the White House, saying, "It's important to remember how this started—we lost a young man, Michael Brown, in heartbreaking and tragic circumstances. He was eighteen years old. His family will never hold Michael in their arms again." The statement was fairly anodyne, but it showed that even the president seemed unaware of the evidence suggesting Darren Wilson may have been justified in his use of deadly force.

While President Obama characteristically chose his words carefully, many celebrities did not.

John Legend posted, "I'm heartbroken over what's happening in Ferguson. This is not the America I want to live in. We need justice for Michael Brown and peace for his family."

Justin Timberlake tweeted, "We're all human beings and we all deserve respect & equal treatment. #MikeBrown."

NBA legend Kareem Abdul-Jabbar, normally a thoughtful progressive voice, also rushed to judgment, writing an opinion piece for *Time* magazine called "The Coming Race War Won't Be About Race." In it, he argues, "...unless we want the Ferguson atrocity to also be swallowed and become nothing more than an intestinal irritant to history, we have to address the situation not just as another act of systemic racism, but as what else it is: class warfare."[61]

It was at this time that the nascent Black Lives Matter movement began to hit the mainstream. In the weeks after the shooting of Michael Brown, the use of the hashtag exploded on Twitter, appearing more than fifty-eight thousand times a day.[62]

Jeff Zucker was in his second year as president of CNN Worldwide when the Michael Brown story broke. Forty-nine years old, bald, bespectacled, and only standing 5'7", he looked more like an accountant or insurance actuary than a TV legend.

Zucker got his start in 1986, after graduating from Harvard. NBC hired him, first as a researcher for the Olympics and then as a field producer for the *Today* show. In 1992, at the age of twenty-six, when most people in the news business are desperately trying to get out of undesirable small markets and move to big-city TV stations, Zucker was named executive producer of *Today*. The boy wonder killed it, and thanks to a lot of his innovative ideas, the morning show became number one. In 2000, at

---

61 Kareem Abdul-Jabbar, "The Coming Race War Won't Be About Race," *Time*, August 17, 2014

62 Monica Anderson, "The Hashtag #BlackLivesMatter Emerges: Social Activism on Twitter," Pew Research Center, August 15, 2016

the age of thirty-five, he received the keys to the kingdom and was named president of NBC Entertainment. That's when he hit his ceiling. His ideas, which had worked so well in morning television, did not translate to prime time, and NBC's ratings tanked. By the time he left in 2010, NBC was in last place.

CNN was a chance for the former wunderkind to redeem himself. He was determined to do whatever it took to make the most out of the opportunity.

Zucker held daily staff meetings with his reporters, managers, and producers. His style was forceful and direct. He knew exactly what he wanted, and he expected his staff to deliver. There were no rules forbidding employees from speaking up or questioning the boss, but most understood it wasn't a wise thing to do. There was an unspoken understanding that he was the king—the Bill Belichick of TV news. Challenging him was a sign of hubris and would probably do little to enhance a producer's or reporter's career prospects.

Zucker had a simple philosophy when it came to covering news: Find the three biggest stories of the day and then go all-in and completely dominate them. With Ferguson on fire for sixteen straight nights, Zucker didn't need three stories; he put all his chips in the middle of the table and bet that if he flooded the zone with wall-to-wall coverage of the rioting, it would be a ratings winner. Turned out, the boy wonder hadn't lost his touch after all. He was absolutely right.

Between August 10–25, 2014, Americans comfortably settled into their easy chairs and were treated to a safe, front-row seat to witness a poor American city burning itself down. It had every ingredient of a must-see TV news story: race, conflict, passion, and violence. Best of all for CNN, it was relatively easy to cover. Send a bunch of crews and reporters to the front lines, and let them fill the airtime with continuous live shots.

It was here that Don Lemon, then a forty-eight-year-old news anchor, raised his profile, making a big show of "courageously" putting on a gas mask on live TV, even though he was safely ensconced far from the front lines.

Some reporters were frustrated by the wall-to-wall coverage, complaining that they couldn't get on the air when they had interviews with civic leaders or thoughtful protesters. The only time the control booth would throw to them was when they were standing in front of something visual and dramatic, like a store getting looted or being set on fire.

CNN's coverage of the Ferguson riots illustrates the marriage of convenience between the old-school newsroom managers and the new breed of idealistic journalists. The executives were interested in what they have always been interested in: ratings. Higher ratings lead to more ad revenue. More ad revenue leads to more profits. More profits lead to fat bonuses and promotions. But no news manager could ever admit to such rapacious motivations. Conveniently, the newsroom social justice warriors provided them with cover. Networks could now show sixteen straight nights of violence porn and justify the coverage by claiming they were providing a public service: shining the spotlight on a generational social justice movement.

On August 18, the governor of Missouri, Jay Nixon, called in the National Guard to try and stop the violence. It didn't work. On August 20, a grand jury consisting of nine White and three Black members began hearing evidence in the case against Darren Wilson. That didn't stop the riots either.

On August 25, more than four thousand people turned out for Michael Brown's funeral. Many walked into the church holding up their hands in mock surrender.[63] Huge photos of Michael Brown wearing his ubiquitous headsets were mounted on each side of his casket.

The funeral was a star-studded affair. Jesse Jackson, Sean "Diddy" Combs, and Spike Lee were in attendance. President Obama even sent three White House aides to represent the administration.

And, of course, Al Sharpton showed up to stir the pot. Even though the grand jury was only a few days into hearing the evidence in the case, Sharpton had already made up his mind; Wilson, and the entire system, was guilty as charged: "Michael Brown wants to be remembered for making America deal with how we are going to police the United States. We are required in his name to change the country!"[64]

That night, the violence continued. But the next day, for reasons nobody ever understood, things suddenly got quiet. It would remain that way for three full months, but this respite was a mirage—the calm before the storm. Ferguson, as well as the rest of the country, was about to erupt.

It's hard to think of any other story in modern memory where there was such an extreme divergence between the facts of the case and the way the media reported them. Anyone watching CNN's wall-to-wall live broadcasts, or the legacy networks'

---

63 CBS New York/AP, "Rev. Sharpton Speaks to Thousands at Funeral for Michael Brown in Missouri," CBS News, August 25, 2014

64 Bill Hoffmann, "PJ Media's Klavan: Sharpton Rhetoric Poisons Black Lives," Newsmax, August 26, 2014

Crump-influenced coverage, couldn't be blamed for believing a grand jury indictment was nothing more than a formality.

It wasn't.

On the Monday night before Thanksgiving, the St. Louis district attorney called a news conference to announce that the grand jury had decided not to indict Darren Wilson.

Over the next eight nights, Ferguson—already reeling from the summer's violence—would essentially be destroyed.

After the grand jury's decision, the media followed the same playbook it had used after George Zimmerman was found not guilty of murdering Trayvon Martin. Instead of taking a moment of self-reflection to consider whether they might have gotten the story wrong, they simply doubled down on the narrative.

ABC News correspondent Steve Osunsami stoked the fires, declaring, "Michael Brown's family says their son is crying back from the grave and they want to know just how much evidence does it take to indict a White police officer for killing a young Black man in this country." If that wasn't enough to incite the public, Osunsami then reported on an irresponsible and completely unfounded conspiracy theory that the grand jury's decision was announced late on Monday evening so that there'd be more looting and destruction.

The one-sided reporting of the Michael Brown case poisoned public opinion. After months of being told only part of the story, the only way people could wrap their heads around the grand jury's decision was to declare that it was just further proof of an irredeemably racist and corrupt power structure.

From coast to coast, in more than 150 different American cities, tens of thousands took to the streets. Protests even spread to Canada and London.

Emotions ran high. In New York City, protesters blocked major bridges and staged die-ins, stopping traffic on busy streets. In Los Angeles, demonstrators closed down the gridlocked 101 Freeway. In Oakland, more than ninety people were arrested for looting, vandalism, and arson.

Instead of using their platforms to call for calm, many celebrities quite literally stoked the flames, adding to the uninformed chorus of voices insisting that the decision was unjust.

Serena Williams posted, "Wow. Just wow. Shameful. What will it take???"

Magic Johnson tweeted, "We must work together to stop the unnecessary loss of young men of color. Justice was not served in Ferguson."

Reggie Bush, then of the Detroit Lions, took things a step further on Instagram with a highly inflammatory post: "The Palestinian people know what it means to be shot while unarmed because of your ethnicity #Ferguson #Justice."

Dozens of stars, including Samuel Jackson, Mark Ruffalo, Danny DeVito, and Stephen King, slammed the decision.

Chris Rock summed up mainstream Hollywood's feelings when he posted the following: "Doesn't take 100 days to decide if murder is a crime, it takes 100 days to figure out how to tell people it isn't."

President Obama may have been one of the few public officials who understood there was something off about this narrative. He couldn't come out and say it, but in a tacit acknowledgment that perhaps Michael Brown wasn't the right case to build a movement around, the president said, "The frustrations we've seen are not just about a particular incident. They have deep roots in many communities of color who have the sense that our laws are not being applied uniformly.... That's an impression folks have and it's not just made up. It's rooted in realities that have existed in this country for a long time."

This last line from the president is important. It is critical to stress that America has an undeniably shameful history in the way it has mistreated its Black citizens. However, these historical injustices do not provide justification for the media's one-sided, biased reporting of the police brutality cases of the 2010s. It is precisely because of this shameful history that the media had an obligation to get the story right—to present tough, balanced coverage that explored whether there really was a present-day crisis in policing. Instead, it ripped open old wounds and recklessly inflamed resentments rooted in the past.

It was during the winter riots in Ferguson that the myth of the "mostly peaceful protest" was born.

Instead of simply reporting on the destruction taking place right in front of their faces, reporters were bending over backwards to contextualize the violence, claiming that all this mayhem was being caused by just a tiny minority of outliers. While it is true that there were mostly peaceful protests during the day, led by people who were sincerely committed to the fight for police reform, the nights were mostly dominated by lawbreakers who were using Michael Brown's memory as a thinly veiled excuse to attack cops, loot, vandalize, and burn things down. As St. Louis County Chief Jon Belmar said, "I don't have any hesitation in telling you that I don't see a lot of peaceful protests out here tonight." But the media, in a pattern that would continue through the riots of 2020, constantly minimized the damage and kept insisting that the protests were "mostly peaceful."

Sometimes this created unintentional comedy, like during the riots in Kenosha, Wisconsin, when a reporter did a live shot in front of a raging fire, as a lower-third banner read "*Fiery but mostly peaceful protests.*"

It is worth noting that while legacy news was going to absurd lengths to contextualize the violence on the streets, it was showing zero interest in contextualizing the actual police shootings. Had they done so—had the public understood how rare these incidents had become—a lot of jobs, businesses, and ultimately lives could have been saved.

Instead, during the second round of rioting in Ferguson, eighty buildings were badly damaged and twelve burned to the ground. There were hundreds of shots fired, dozens of people suffered serious injuries, and hundreds more were arrested. One young man was found dead in his car, but it remains unclear whether it was directly related to the unrest.

If there was any doubt that Darren Wilson was justified in shooting Michael Brown, it was laid to rest when Eric Holder's Department of Justice released a devastating report on March 4, 2015. Just like the grand jury, it cleared Wilson of any wrongdoing in the case.

The report, coming from President Obama's progressive attorney general, should have been yet another sobering come-to-Jesus moment for the media. Point by point, it rebuked almost every single distortion that had been peddled by Benjamin Crump and obediently amplified by legacy news.

On the initial struggle in the car, the DOJ report stated, "The evidence supports Wilson's account that Brown reached into the SUV through the open window and punched and grabbed Wilson.... This is corroborated by bruising on Wilson's jaw and scratches on his neck, the presence of Brown's DNA on Wilson's collar, shirt, and pants, and Wilson's DNA on Brown's palm."[65]

On the fatal shots fired outside of Wilson's police car, the DOJ concluded, "The evidence supports Wilson's account that he fired several shots because he believed Brown was charging at him."

The DOJ even weighed in on the "hands up, don't shoot" narrative that was now an apocryphal part of American culture: "Multiple credible witnesses corroborate virtually every material aspect of Wilson's account and are consistent with the physical evidence.... There are no credible witness accounts that state that Brown was clearly attempting to surrender when Wilson shot him."

So much for the stories peddled by Piaget Crenshaw and Dorian Johnson, which were eagerly platformed by credulous reporters.

That night, none of the networks led with the DOJ's conclusive findings. When they did get to the report later in their newscasts, they minimized Wilson's exoneration, focusing instead on another part of the report, which found systemic problems within the Ferguson Police Department.

NBC's Lester Holt's distorted lead-in typified the coverage: "Today, we got the full and damning report from the feds. It alleges a pattern of racial bias among authorities in Ferguson, Missouri. But the DOJ, which released the report, found no such evidence in the case that launched this investigation—the police shooting of Michael Brown."

---

[65] "Department of Justice Report Regarding the Criminal Investigation Into the Shooting Death of Michael Brown by Ferguson, Missouri Police Officer Darren Wilson," Department of Justice, March 4, 2015

Darren Wilson was in hiding when the DOJ report came out. He had faced so many death threats that he had his new wife check into the hospital anonymously for the birth of their first child.[66]

Eric Holder's report should have been his moment of redemption. Proof that there had been a rush to judgment, that he was a good cop—an innocent man caught up in an unfortunate, tragic situation. But the message never got out.

The DOJ report also should have alarmed legacy journalists, who had gotten the story completely wrong from day one. Their irresponsible coverage had destroyed one man's life and left an impoverished city in smoldering ruins.

But there would be no course correction.

That became glaringly obvious when a radical new social movement emerged from the wreckage of Ferguson, and the media instantly sanctified it.

66 John Halpern, "The Cop," *New Yorker*, August 3, 2015

Chapter 5
BLM

Thirty-one-year-old community activist Alicia Garza had an emotional reaction to the news of George Zimmerman's acquittal. The jury's verdict felt like a personal attack, and she was struggling to process her feelings.

"It felt like a gut punch, you know?" she said.[67]

Feeling powerless, she did what many millennials do when they're experiencing a surge of strong emotions. She posted on Facebook:

> *I continue to be surprised at how little Black lives matter. And I will continue that. Stop giving up on*

[67] Jamilah King, "#blacklivesmatter How Three Friends Turned a Spontaneous Facebook Post Into a Global Phenomenon," *California Sunday Magazine*, December 12, 2015

> *Black life. Black people, I love you. I love us. Our lives matter.*[68]

Little did Garza know that by sharing her pain with the world, she had just given birth to one of the biggest and most polarizing movements in American history.

Alicia Garza was born in the heart of Oakland to a single mom who ran an antiques business. She left home to go to college at UCSD, in San Diego County. The school sits adjacent to La Jolla, a mostly White, uber-wealthy, idyllic beachside neighborhood. While many of her classmates were surfing or strolling the tony streets of the Spanish-styled town, Garza was fully engaged in activism. In one of her more successful efforts, she helped the university's custodial staff get a modest pay raise. In 2004, she came out as queer and married Malachi Garza, a trans-male activist, four years later.

Alicia Garza had a bestie in the world of activism: a woman named Patrisse Cullors. The two met at a Black leadership conference and bonded right from the get-go.

"There's a long story to tell about that," Garza recalled, "but the best part is that basically we danced together all night long, until four in the morning. I thought, 'Wow, this is my soulmate right here.'"[69]

Their bond was so powerful, they immediately nicknamed each other "twin." And for good reason: They were almost carbon

---

[68] Jordan Zakarin, "How Patrisse Cullors, Alicia Garza and Opal Tometi Created the Black Lives Matter Movement," Biography, January 27, 2021

[69] Jamilah King, "#blacklivesmatter How Three Friends Turned a Spontaneous Facebook Post Into a Global Phenomenon," *California Sunday Magazine*, December 12, 2015

copies of each other. Both were roughly the same age, openly queer, and steeped in left-wing activism.

The only real difference was that Patrisse had a much more difficult and traumatic childhood.

Cullors was born in Van Nuys, a bleak city north of Los Angeles, best known as the porn capital of the US. She was raised in a housing project by her single mom, who was a devout Jehovah's Witness. Cullors went to a mostly White middle school and felt a deep sense of shame whenever her mom dropped her off in her beat-up car.

But her biggest source of pain was watching her brother's life unravel. Monte Cullors was bipolar and diagnosed with schizophrenia.[70] In 1999, he got arrested for stealing their mother's car. Cullors claims that her brother was physically abused by prison guards and emerged from the experience "a brutalized man."

Cullors didn't meet her biological father until she was eleven. He, too, could never get his life together. A repeat drug offender, he spent his days in and out of prison, ultimately dying in a homeless shelter in 2009.

When Cullors turned sixteen, she got thrown out of the house after coming out to her God-fearing mother. Despite all these setbacks, she went on to get a diploma from UCLA with a degree in religion and philosophy.

Extreme left-wing activism animated Cullors, who proudly wore her radicalism on her sleeve. She was a protégé of Eric Mann, an alumnus of the Weather Underground, a domestic terrorist group. Angela Davis, a self-declared communist, was also an inspiration and a mentor. Cullors is openly hostile to capitalism

---

70 Patrisse Cullors, "My Brother's Abuse in Jail Is a Reason I Co-Founded Black Lives Matter. We Need Reform in L.A.," *LA Times*, April 13, 2008

and has repeatedly told interviewers, "I think that reading Marx, Lenin, and Mao has really influenced the way I think about economies."

This brand of revolutionary radicalism would lay the foundation for BLM. As Cullors would later tell a reporter, "We are trained Marxists. We are super-versed on, sort of, ideological theories. And I think what we really tried to do is build a movement that could be utilized by many, many Black folk."[71]

When Cullors read her "twin's" Facebook post, she loved the phrase "Black Lives Matter" and started using it as a hashtag on her own posts on Twitter and Tumblr.

The words were simple and powerful, and it started getting Cullors thinking—maybe "Black Lives Matter" could become the name of a new movement. She logged onto Facebook and wrote on Garza's wall, "twin, #blacklivesmatter campaign? Can we discuss this? I have ideas. I am thinking we can do a whole social media/ all out in the streets organizing effort. Let me know."[72]

The two got on the phone, and the idea excited them, but they were self-aware enough to know that they couldn't make it happen alone. They needed to bring in a third person—someone who understood how to create social media campaigns.

That's how Ayọ Tometi (then known as Opal), who was making a name for herself as an advocate for illegal immigrants, joined the team.

Tometi was born and raised in Phoenix. Her stable childhood was shattered in middle school when the law caught up

---

71 Yaron Steinbuch, "Black Lives Matter Co-Founder Describes Herself as 'Trained Marxist,'" *New York Post*, June 25, 2020

72 Jamilah King, "#blacklivesmatter How Three Friends Turned a Spontaneous Facebook Post Into a Global Phenomenon," *California Sunday Magazine*, December 12, 2015

with her undocumented Nigerian parents. For a few tense years, it looked like her family might have to leave the country. Watching her parents go through the heartache and fear of possible deportation made a deep impression on Tometi. Eventually, her family was put on a path to citizenship, but Tometi, shaken by those insecure years, decided to dedicate her life to helping other immigrant families.

Fueled by this aspiration, she became an academic overachiever, getting a bachelor's degree from the University of Arizona in 2005, and then a master's in communication from Arizona State University in 2010.

This last degree would turn out to be critical for BLM. Tometi understood the brand-new world of social media. She knew how to build viral online campaigns.

Once approached, she eagerly agreed to join Cullors and Garza's fledgling movement. Within days, she bought the Blacklivesmatter.com domain name and designed its now ubiquitous logo.

At first, it seemed like BLM would end up becoming just another of the countless social justice movements that come and go without garnering much mainstream attention. In the six months after Cullors's first tweet, the hashtag only averaged a paltry thirty mentions a day.[73] But the following year, after the Michael Brown shooting, the hashtag went viral, averaging about fifty-eight thousand daily mentions. By the spring of 2023, the hashtag had been used forty-four million times on Twitter/X alone.[74]

---

73 Monica Anderson, "The Hashtag #BlackLivesMatter Emerges: Social Activism on Twitter," Pew Research Center, August 15, 2016

74 Samuel Bestvater, Risa Gelles-Watnick, Meltem Odabas, Monica Anderson, and Aaron Smith, "#BlackLivesMatter Turns 10," Pew Research Center, June 29, 2023

Even though BLM signs were ubiquitous during the Ferguson protests, the news media didn't seem to know what to make of the movement and barely reported on it. That began to change in the fall of 2015, when ten BLM protesters made themselves impossible to ignore, disrupting an event for presidential candidate Hillary Clinton. As security guards escorted the BLM activists out of the rally, they collectively raised their fists in defiance.

After running a story on the incident, CNN cut to its opinion panel. Nobody called out the group for disrupting the campaign event or questioned its motives. Van Jones summed up the groupthink when he said, "It's remarkable to have a group—a slogan—take up this much mind share. A year ago, you never heard the slogan."

As the BLM movement grew, prominent conservatives began speaking out against it. On July 11, 2016, the man once known as America's mayor, Rudy Giuliani, had this to say: "Black Lives Matter never protests when every 14 hours someone is killed in Chicago, probably 70–80% of the time by a Black person. That means they don't believe Black lives matter. They mean—let's agitate against the police matters.... Black Lives Matter therefore puts a target on the back of police."

That night, Anderson Cooper addressed the growing BLM backlash: "With all these demonstrations over the past few days, some critics, including Mayor Rudy Giuliani, are once again accusing Black Lives Matter of inciting violence against police officers. Over the weekend, Giuliani called the activist movement, quote, 'Inherently racist.'"

Cooper's tone and intonation made it clear that he didn't think much of the former New York mayor's critique.

He then tossed to reporter Randi Kaye, who began her package by saying, "What started as a hashtag has turned into a rallying cry. The goal—to shine a light on racial injustice."

But was that really BLM's goal? Just a little digging, a little curiosity on the part of the news media, would have revealed that this surging movement, started by three radical women, was not what it seemed to be.

A constant refrain from journalists is that it's easy to cast aspersions on BLM now, with the benefit of hindsight. But this is a deflection. The truth about the movement was always hiding in plain sight. To their credit, the leaders of BLM never tried to moderate their views or fool the public into thinking they were anything other than a radical, far-left organization. It is legacy media that gaslit the public and presented BLM as a well-meaning grassroots movement, earnestly fighting for equality and justice. Had the public known the *entire truth* about BLM, it is highly unlikely it would have gained such broad, mainstream acceptance, or that it would ultimately have been able to defraud the public out of tens of millions of dollars.

So, what was this evidence hiding in plain sight?

It wouldn't have taken Edward R. Murrow to sus the story out. Had a reporter simply logged onto the group's website in 2015, they would have seen a list of BLM's "guiding principles." One of them was, "We are committed to disrupting the Western-prescribed nuclear family structure requirement."

Or they could have found an *SF Weekly* article where Garza said, "Black lives can't matter under capitalism. They're like oil and water."[75]

[75] SF Weekly Staff, "The Bay Area Roots of Black Lives Matter," *SF Weekly*, November 11, 2015

BLM splintered into numerous regional chapters and subgroups. They, too, were transparent about their beliefs. One such group, Movement for Black Lives, actually called for abolishing not only the police but also all prisons.

Like many radical leftist organizations, BLM flirted with murderous overseas authoritarians. Tometi spent time with Venezuela's Marxist dictator, Nicolás Maduro, whose oppressive rule created a humanitarian catastrophe, causing eight million of his desperate citizens to flee the country. But Tometi did not see it that way: "In the last 17 years we have seen the Bolivarian Revolution champion participatory democracy and construct a fair, transparent election system recognized as among the best in the world."

As a couple of Heritage Foundation members quipped, "Millions of Venezuelans suffering under Maduro's murderous misrule presumably couldn't be reached for comment."[76]

But perhaps the most alarming unreported red flag about BLM was its ties to radical anti-Semitic movements. From the very start, Palestinian flags could be seen at BLM rallies in Ferguson, even though this was never mentioned by legacy reporters.

In 2015, Patrisse Cullors led a delegation to the West Bank. "This is an apartheid state," she told reporters. "We can't deny that and if we do deny it we are a part of the Zionist violence."[77]

Joining her was an activist named Ahmad Abuznaid, a member of Dream Defenders, which has ties to known terrorist groups. His take on the trip: "The goals were primarily for group members to experience and see firsthand the occupation, ethnic

---

[76] Mike Gonzalez and Andrew Olivastro, "The Agenda of Black Lives Matter Is Far Different From the Slogan," Heritage, July 3, 2020

[77] Team Ebony, "Dream Defenders, Black Lives Matter & Ferguson Reps Take Historic Trip to Palestine," *Ebony*, January 9, 2015

cleansing and brutality Israel has levied against Palestinians, but also to build real relationships with those on the ground leading the fight for liberation."

After the October 7 massacre in Israel, many American Jews were horrified to learn that BLM chapters were celebrating the brutal slaughter of 1,200 innocent victims, which included babies and young women attending a concert. BLM Grassroots posted a statement saying, "As a radical Black organization grounded in abolitionist ideals, we see clear parallels between Black and Palestinian people."[78] Other BLM chapters posted memes with paragliders—an obvious reference to how the terrorists infiltrated Israeli territory.

For legacy media, any criticism of BLM was a third-rail issue. Even when that criticism was coming from a Black celebrity.

On June 30, 2020, at the height of BLM's influence over mainstream American thought, actor Terry Crews tweeted, "We must ensure #blacklivesmatter doesn't morph into #blacklivesbetter."

The backlash was swift, but Crews stood firm. On July 4, he tweeted a response to the online mob calling for his cancellation: "Are all white people bad? No. Are all black people good? No. Knowing this reality I stand on my position to unite with good people, no matter the race, creed or ideology. Given the number of threats against this decision—I also decide to die on this hill."

Smelling a chance to virtue signal, a smirking Don Lemon invited Crews to appear on his CNN show.

"Terry maaannnnnnnn, you stepped in it," Lemon said by way of introduction.

---

[78] Matthew Impelli, "Black Lives Matter Org Praises Hamas, Sparks Backlash," *Newsweek*, October 10, 2023

Crews then attempted to explain himself: "There are some very militant type forces in Black Lives Matter. What I was issuing was a warning. You can see how extremes can go far, can go wild."

CNN cut to a split screen: Crews on one side, Lemon on the other. And as Crews continued to speak, Lemon mugged for the camera in faux horror. His nose crinkled up, like he had just smelled rancid milk.

"You think Black Lives Matter is an extreme movement?" Lemon asked indignantly.

"No, it's a great mantra. It's a true mantra. Black lives do matter but when you're talking about an organization—you're talking about the leaders. You're talking about the people responsible—"

"I got you. I got you," Lemon interjected, not wanting to open the Overton window wide enough to actually engage with Crews's point.

The actor then brought up the fact that nine Black kids had been murdered in Chicago over the previous two weeks, but BLM remained silent.

"I know. But that's not what the Black lives movement is about, Terry," Lemon intoned condescendingly. "It's about police brutality and criminal justice."

It was a telling exchange. A former NFL player best known for starring in Everybody Hates Chris and hosting America's Got Talent was actually reporting hard truths, while the man whose job it was to deliver unbiased information was gaslighting his audience.

Brian McGrory was the editor of *The Boston Globe* from 2012–22—a very challenging time for big-city newspapers. He not only had to face the existential threat that social media posed to traditional print but also had to figure out how to cover the polarizing Trump presidency and the BLM-led anti-law enforcement movement. But no one ever heard McGrory complain about it. For the native Bostonian, the job was the fulfilment of a lifelong dream that started when he launched a neighborhood newsletter as an eight-year-old.

McGrory invites me into his utilitarian office. With his shock of red hair and piercing eyes, Brian looks the part of a veteran newsman. He is a world-weary and reserved New Englander through and through. But occasionally, he will spark to something you say and burst into a surprisingly warm peal of laughter.

In 2020, McGrory made the extraordinary decision to allow *Globe* staff members to participate in BLM rallies, which, up until that point, had been explicitly forbidden. And for good reason: How could readers trust reporters to be objective if they were actively participating in polarizing social movements?

"I made a decision at the *Globe*," McGrory explains, "where reporters, journalists were allowed to participate in public displays that reflected their identity but didn't reflect politics. And I acknowledged that this was a fuzzy, hazy area.... We would sort of assess it on a case-by-case basis."

McGrory decided that BLM rallies met that standard: "If it's a Black Lives Matter march in your community and you're Black, and you want to be in it, it's who you are. It's what you do. Journalism can't take away the fact that this is who you are. March. If it's an abortion rights rally that has political repercussions, we don't want you in that march."

I look at McGrory skeptically and ask, "Can I challenge you on this?"

"Yes," he says, welcoming the pushback, "I get it. It's worth challenging."

"Let's say I'm a Southern Baptist and a big part of my identity is my religion, and being pro-life feels as much a part of my identity as someone's race. Why would I be exempted? Isn't there a double standard there?"

"Because what you're doing, if you wanted to march in a pro-life march or participate in a pro-life rally, that actually leads to a political conclusion."

"Yes, but BLM's focus was beyond simply policing. It has roots in Marxism and anti-Semitism," I fire back. "So the slogan 'Black Lives Matter' is very benign—who could be against it—but yet the actual organization was very political. I mean everyone is pro-life, right? But you don't have any trouble separating the slogan from that movement."

McGrory sighs, and I get the sense he isn't enjoying this back-and-forth exchange anymore. "First of all, you have the advantage of years of hindsight," he says. "I wasn't probing, nor were many people in that moment probing, what's the leadership of the Black Lives Matter group. I mean, a lot of people didn't know there was a Black Lives Matter group at that point. It was the spirit, not the organization, that we were allowing people to participate in."

"If I was in your newsroom back then—I don't know if you would have wanted me around—but I would have said very early on, 'Hey, I just went on the BLM website. I don't know who these people are, but they seem very extreme, and they're not just concerned with police brutality. Can we look into it?'"

McGrory, like most reporters, prefers to ask tough questions instead of answering them. His body language shifts, and he looks down at his watch, the universal signal of *let's wrap this up*. "It's a much bigger picture, and I think you're being too literal," he argues. "I don't think most people marching in the streets are marching because of a BLM organization. I think they are marching because of the words *Black Lives Matter*."

McGrory is a journalist's journalist, but he clearly has a blind spot when it comes to BLM. He is conflating the sentiments of the words *Black lives matter* with the actual organization. This position was the norm in legacy media.

During the summer of 2020, in the midst of the George Floyd riots, BLM hit peak influence. According to a Pew Research survey, an astounding 67 percent of all Americans supported the group during the unrest.[79]

The New York Times ran a fawning piece entitled "Black Lives Matter May Be the Largest Movement in U.S. History."

The NBA had the words "Black Lives Matter" stenciled in large letters right in the middle of its courts during games.

And in a surreal development, some of the most prominent capitalist corporations made huge donations to BLM, empowering a group whose stated mission was the destruction of the free market.

Here's just a sample of some of the eyebrow-raising donations:

DoorDash: $500,000
Deckers: $500,000
Amazon: $10 million
Gatorade: $500,000
Microsoft: $250,000
Nabisco: $500,000

---

[79] Kim Parker, Juliana Menasce Horowitz and Monica Anderson, "Amid Protests, Majorities Across Racial and Ethnic Groups Express Support for the Black Lives Matter Movement," Pew Research Center, June 12, 2020

Dropbox: $500,000[80]

But BLM wasn't just raking it in from Fortune 500 companies. It collected $90 million in 2020, and the vast majority came from individuals making small contributions averaging about thirty dollars.[81]

By that turbulent summer of 2020, Tometi and Garza had left BLM, and Cullors was running the organization by herself.

She took full advantage of her unchecked power.

The formerly anonymous grassroots activist signed with the prestigious CAA talent agency and, in October 2020, got a sweetheart overall deal with Warner Bros. Television Studios. In a splashy, self-congratulatory press release, it announced that Cullors would be creating scripted, unscripted, animated, and digital content.[82]

She never ended up making anything.

Cullors was generous about spreading all her newfound wealth among friends and family. She gave $778,000 to an arts group run by the father of her son.

Her brother, Paul, a graffiti artist, got $840,000 for "consulting" and "security services."

Cullors moved millions of dollars in donations to a charity in Canada run by her wife. That charity then bought a ten-thousand-square-foot mansion in Toronto, which used to belong

---

80 Fred Lucas, "These 18 Corporations Gave Money to Radical Black Lives Matter Group," The Daily Signal, July 7, 2020

81 Zoe Christen Jones, "Black Lives Matter Foundation Raised $90 Million in 2020," CBS News, February 24, 2021

82 Will Thorne, "Black Lives Matter Co-Founder Patrisse Cullors Signs Overall Deal with Warner Bros, Television Group," *Variety*, October 15, 2020

to the Communist Party of Canada, for a very capitalist-friendly $6.3 million.[83]

Back in the States, Cullors admitted to using donations to buy a $6 million Los Angeles mansion, which featured a swimming pool, an office space, and a soundstage.[84] She would later use the mansion for personal events.

"I look back at that and think, that probably wasn't the best idea," she said in a rare moment of self-reflection.

But Cullors wasn't done there. She personally bought four separate homes, including one for $1.4 million in the mostly White enclave of Topanga Canyon, near Malibu, California.

Another one in Georgia featured a private airplane hangar and a 2,500-foot paved runway.

This outraged Hawk Newsome, the head of BLM New York, who called for an investigation, saying, "If you go around calling yourself a socialist, you have to ask how much of her own personal money is going to charitable causes."[85]

After word of the mansions leaked out, Cullors stepped down from the organization she co-founded. But instead of being contrite, she was defiant, claiming she had PTSD from the controversy.

BLM Global put out a statement, trying to portray Cullors as a victim of racism: "The narratives being spread about Patrisse have been generated by right-wing forces intent on reducing the support and influence of a movement that is larger than any one organization. This right-wing offensive not only puts Patrisse, her

---

83 Jon Brown, "BLM Transferred Millions to Canadian Charity to Buy Mansion Formerly Owned by Communist Party: Report," Fox News, January 29, 2022

84 Rashad Grove, "Black Lives Matter Co-Founder Patrisse Cullors Admits to Using BLM Mansion for Personal Use," *Ebony*, May 11, 2022

85 Isabel Vincent, "Inside BLM Co-Founder Patrisse Khan-Cullors' Million-Dollar Real Estate Buying Binge," *New York Post*, April 10, 2021

child, and her loved ones in harm's way, it also continues a tradition of terror by White supremacists against Black activists."[86]

Cullors wasn't the only BLM leader caught with their hands in the cookie jar. Tyree Conyers-Page, the former head of BLM Atlanta, was sentenced to forty-two months in federal prison for money laundering and wire fraud. He was convicted of taking $450,000 in donations and spending it on bespoke suits, an evening with a prostitute, and a home in Ohio. As he texted to a friend, he "won the lottery" and ended up with "a big-ass cribo."[87]

When it was all said and done, public filings show that only one-third of the $90 million in donations went to charitable foundations. A total of $8.7 million went completely missing. BLM has been embroiled in a series of lawsuits and government investigations and, as of this writing, is in danger of losing its tax-exempt status.[88]

All of this blatant corruption did not cause Cullors to engage in sober self-reflection. In 2022, she appeared on a podcast called *Into America*. When asked about the way tens of millions of dollars in donations were being misspent, she flippantly replied that BLM was awash in "a lot of White guilt money."

Legacy media's coverage of BLM is one of its greatest crimes of omission. It refused to do even the most basic reporting about what the group stood for, who the founders were, and whom they counted amongst their allies and mentors. It refused to portray

---

86

87 Sean Patrick Cooper, "BLM Collected Over $90 Million in Donations. Where Did It Go?" The Free Press, October 22, 2024

88 Isabel Vincent, "Only 33 Percent of BLM's $90m in Donations Helped Charitable Foundations," *New York Post*, March 27, 2023

BLM the way the organization was openly portraying itself, choosing instead to sanitize all of BLM's prickly edges so that it would be more palatable to the public. It's impossible to think of any other movement in American history that was as radical, as opposed to all the basic liberal values of the West, as corrupt—and yet barely received any critical or skeptical reporting.

BLM—the organization—was a grift. And when it was all said and done, everybody lost: Cities lay in ruins, the country was torn apart, the homicide rate for Black people skyrocketed, and many well-meaning people threw away their hard-earned money supporting a group whose practices did not match the promise implicit in its name. The only winners in this madness seemed to be the leaders of BLM, who ultimately achieved the capitalistic rewards they claimed to abhor: power, influence, and wealth.

Chapter 6
Broken Windows

It all started with a social experiment.

In 1969, a Stanford psychologist named Philip Zimbardo ran a study that would change the face of modern policing. He abandoned a car in a poor, high-crime area of the Bronx, New York. It had no license plates, and the hood was propped open. Within ten minutes, thieves started stripping it for parts. Once everything of value was taken, vandals began destroying the car, smashing in the windows, and ripping out the upholstery. Within hours, the car was reduced to an urban piece of playground equipment, as neighborhood kids began jumping around inside its hollow shell.

Zimbardo then repeated the experiment in the affluent neighborhood of Palo Alto, California. He abandoned the exact same type of car, in the same condition, with no license plates and the hood propped open. But unlike in the Bronx, nothing happened. For days, people just walked right on by.

No big surprise. It's what you would expect from a wealthy community. But Zimbardo made one adjustment to the abandoned car, and that's when things got interesting.

He took a sledgehammer and smashed in its windows. Suddenly, the car attracted the attention of thieves. Within hours, the car was stripped of all its valuable parts, just like in the Bronx experiment.

From this test, Zimbardo concluded that the root cause of crime is not poverty, but disorder and neglect. The shattered windshield of the Palo Alto car sent a clear signal to would-be thieves: Nobody in authority was paying attention. And suddenly, the car that had sat there untouched for days was fair game for criminals.

Thirteen years later, in 1982, two criminologists, George Kelling and James Wilson, wrote a groundbreaking article for *The Atlantic.* Inspired by Zimbardo's experiment, they argued that signs of urban decay—anything from broken glass to graffiti—are triggers for crime: "Vandalism can occur anywhere once communal barriers—the sense of mutual regard and the obligations of civility—are lowered by actions that seem to signal that 'no one cares.'"[89]

And with that article, the theory of broken windows policing was born. Essentially, the two criminologists argued that if you cracked down on small crimes, there would be far fewer big ones. They urged police departments to get tough on so-called quality-of-life infractions. That meant no longer looking the other way at things like panhandling, littering, jumping turnstiles, prostitution, or public drinking. They also urged police departments

[89] George L. Kelling and James Q. Wilson, "Broken Windows," *The Atlantic*, March 1982

to have a strong visual presence, with lots of officers out on foot patrol.

It all sounded good in theory, but in the 1980s, police departments were stretched thin and didn't have the time or resources to deal with smaller quality-of-life issues. The crack epidemic was exploding, and America's biggest cities were turning into war zones. As gangs and drug dealers battled over turf, the homicide rate skyrocketed to third-world levels. In 1990, a record 2,245 people were murdered in New York City alone. It is estimated that 60–70 percent of the victims were Black.

The bloodbath was a nationwide phenomenon. In 1990, a thousand people were killed in Los Angeles. The following year, there were 928 murders in Chicago and 479 in Washington, DC—a milestone so shocking for a city with a relatively small population that it became known as The Murder Capital. Overall, roughly 120,000 people were murdered in the US in the first half of the 1990s. The crime epidemic wasn't limited to homicides. Desperate drug addicts were committing record numbers of thefts, robberies, and aggravated assaults to maintain their habit. Those crime stats also skyrocketed to record levels.[90]

The trend towards a breakdown in law and order began to take hold in the mid-1970s. The graph of violent crime in the US is shaped like a hockey stick, with the numbers starting to slowly rise around 1975 and then accelerating at an alarming rate in the early '90s. Crack didn't start the American murder epidemic, but it was a huge accelerant.

Since these kinds of statistics have been recorded, one thing remains consistent—African Americans have been disproportionately victimized by crime. Dating back to the early 1960s,

---

90 "United States Crime Rates 1960 – 2019," Disastercenter.com

Black men are roughly seven times more likely to be murdered than White men, and Black women are roughly four to five times more likely to be homicide victims than their White counterparts.[91]

Broken windows policing was a popular topic in academic settings, but it wouldn't be tried out in the real world until 1994, when William Bratton became the New York City police commissioner.

Nothing about Bratton's childhood would suggest he was destined to become a seminal figure in law enforcement. The man who would change the face of American policing was born in 1947, in the Boston neighborhood of Dorchester, which was then mostly Irish. If you've seen the Ben Affleck movie *Gone Baby Gone*, you get the idea. Bratton's childhood home was barebones; it didn't even have running hot water until William was in high school. His father had to work two jobs just to make meager ends meet.[92]

But Bratton was driven to make his mark in law enforcement. By the time he turned thirty-two, he was already second in command at the Boston Police Department. One of the things that made him rise so quickly was that, unlike a lot of other cops, he was open to new ideas. During those formative days, Bratton used to spend time with academics at Harvard Kennedy School. It was there that he was first exposed to the philosophy of broken windows policing.

When Mayor Rudy Giuliani made Bratton the city's thirty-eighth police commissioner, New York was in a state of despair.

---

91 "Trends in Homicide: What You Need to Know," Council on Criminal Justice, December 2023

92 James Lardner, "The Commish," *New York Times*, February 1, 1998

The city had a $2.3 billion budget deficit, the unemployment rate was in the double digits, and, of course, crime was ubiquitous.

Bratton, then forty-seven, moved swiftly. First, he weakened the bureaucracy in the department by giving precinct commanders much more authority and autonomy.[93] Then he modernized the force, introducing a computerized system called CompStat, which kept tabs on every crime committed in every precinct. And finally, he implemented the broken windows theory, instructing his officers to go out and aggressively police quality-of-life infractions. This included expanding the use of stop-and-frisk.

"I loved it!" Angel Maysonet gushes. "The community wanted us to be out there."

Maysonet is a larger-than-life Bronx native who spent thirty-two years on the job for the NYPD, working his way up from patrol cop to detective to a member of the Joint Terrorism Task Force.

He says one of the biggest advantages of Bratton's policing techniques was that officers spent a lot more time interacting with people in the neighborhoods they patrolled: "It fostered a better relationship with the community because they knew you. It built trust."

It also worked. Better than anyone could have imagined.

Misdemeanor arrests targeting quality-of-life crimes went up 70 percent during the Bratton years. And just as George Kelling and James Wilson had predicted in their *Atlantic* article, this caused serious crimes to fall. Between 1990 and 1999, homicides

93 Andrea R. Nagy and Joel Podolny, "William Bratton and the NYPD," Yale SOM Case 07-015, February 23, 2007

in New York City plummeted 73 percent. Burglaries went down 66 percent; assault, 40 percent; and robbery, 66 percent.[94]

In a 1998 news conference, Rudy Guiliani took a victory lap for broken windows policing. "Obviously murder and graffiti are two vastly different crimes," he said. "But they are part of the same continuum, and a climate that supports one is more likely to tolerate the other."

Bratton's success was dramatic, and his techniques were quickly copied by police departments throughout the country. It even made waves overseas as departments in the UK, France, and Australia adopted some of his methods.

"We enforce the law. We enforce behavior and we don't go after any class of people," Bratton said of his department's mission statement.

America has declared a lot of wars—on terrorism, drugs, COVID—and few, if any, have provided us with much in the way of concrete victories.

But this was different.

Within a few short years, Bratton's policing techniques completely reversed decades of spiraling crime. In fact, by 1999, the national homicide rate was the lowest it had been since the early 1960s.

And it stayed that way.

Until 2015—the year after the Michael Brown shooting.

American newsrooms have historically had a pro-police bias. Sensational "if it bleeds, it leads" stories are easy to cover and usually perform well in the all-important ratings scorecard. So,

---

[94] Hope Corman and Naci H. Mocan, "What Reduced Crime in New York City," National Bureau of Economic Research, July 2002

reporters have always been well served by having law enforcement contacts who can tip them off to juicy true crime stories.

Sal LaBarbera was one of those media-friendly cops.

The now retired LAPD detective spent twenty-eight years working homicide. Tall and lean with intense eyes that have seen way too much, he looks like a character out of a Scorsese movie. He's an old-school cop—most comfortable taking a drag from a cigarette, while gazing out into the night, lost in thought.

For years, he worked in Los Angeles's high-crime South Bureau.

"We weren't getting any news coverage," he recalls. "If someone got killed in Beverly Hills, it was the lead story, but if a kid got killed getting off a school bus—there would be nothing. No attention at all."

LaBarbera decided to do something about it. He began feeding stories to the *Los Angeles Times* and local TV news stations. He learned what he had to bring to reporters in order to get them interested in a story.

"I started putting out press releases. I promised reporters all the elements they needed to get a story on the air: family photos, the crying mom. Suddenly, these forgotten victims were getting airtime."

Great sources are a goldmine for reporters, but they can also be a trap. There is a quiet bias when someone is feeding you exclusives. If you dig a little too hard, if you fight to get "the other side of the story," you risk alienating that source, who might then start feeding all those great stories to one of your competitors. For that reason, TV news bias historically leaned too far in the direction of law enforcement.

However, by the time of the Ferguson riots, the media had done a complete one-eighty. Many journalists lost interest in their police contacts. Suddenly, it was the activists, and lawyers like Benjamin Crump, who were cultivating media contacts and manipulating the coverage.

"People in the media started unfriending me," LaBarbera recalls. "No one even took a minute to talk it out. A lot of them just flipped. People on the side of law enforcement didn't have a voice anymore."

On April 22, 2015, Don Lemon invited Bratton, then serving his second stint as NYPD police commissioner, for a one-on-one CNN interview. On the heels of all the civil unrest, tough questions about policing were expected and appropriate. But Lemon, who had bent over backwards to contextualize the violence in Ferguson, was not willing to do the same for the police. He did not mention that Bratton's policies had literally saved tens of thousands of lives in the US. Nor did he mention that with safer cities, the country had undergone a transformative urban revival.

Instead, Lemon spent the entire extended interview grilling Bratton about the alleged shortcomings of American law enforcement.

"Every week, we seem to show video that appears to show questionable behavior by police. What's going on?"

Lemon leaned in and fixed Bratton with his best *serious reporter* expression.

Bratton, unflappable, responded with his thick Boston-townie accent, "I think you're seeing the fact that cameras are becoming ever present in our lives. And you'll see those videos with increasing frequency going forward."

Don Lemon seemed disappointed. "So you don't think it's happening more. Just the proliferation of cameras. More people with cameras to capture it."

"That's right," Bratton responded.

Lemon asked several more follow-up questions in the same vein, but he wasn't getting much of a reaction from Bratton, who answered him in his trademark matter-of-fact, almost intentionally dull public speaking style.

Lemon then moved on to the explosive topic of race: "Do you think people of color, especially men of color—Black men—are targeted by police?"

"I don't think so. People go where the calls are," Bratton explained. "Another reality is that those neighborhoods, oftentimes, are minority neighborhoods—Black neighborhoods, Hispanic neighborhoods. So, the chance of police encountering individuals is more significant because we have more police in those areas. You'd expect we'd have more police where there's more crime—where there's more disorder."

Bratton was diplomatically expressing what a lot of cops told me in a more direct way. If you're going to police smartly, you're going to deploy officers to high-crime areas. Those high-crime areas, statistically, tend to be poor and, oftentimes, minority neighborhoods. This strategy can pose a huge political risk. Since troops are being moved from safe and affluent communities to poorer ones, cops will disproportionately be stopping and arresting people of color, opening themselves up to accusations of profiling and racism.

And that's exactly the line of questioning Don Lemon was relentlessly pursuing during the interview: "Where does the mistrust come from? Surely, all of it is not perception. You have to admit there's a disconnect between communities of color and police officers."

Bratton is not a typical cop's cop, and his answer showed sensitivity and nuance: "Some of it is based on the history of our country—the legacy—particularly as it relates to Blacks—African

Americans. The history of slavery and the use of police throughout much of our history to, in effect, enforce slavery laws. Up until the 1960s with the civil rights laws, enforcing segregation laws. So, fear of police—mistrust of police by African Americans—a lot of that is historically based."

Bratton, the innovator, the wunderkind who had completely modernized policing, seemed taken aback by how quickly a handful of well-publicized police shootings had turned public opinion against his life's work, and how easily charges of institutional racism were being accepted as obvious truths.

"We thought we had healed this issue coming out of the '60s," he told Lemon. "Quite clearly in the last year or two, the scab that we thought had healed over has been peeled back and is still open and quite raw."

By late 2015, many officials were raising the alarm about the BLM-led movement against law enforcement. FBI Director James Comey gave a speech at the University of Chicago where he argued that the sudden spike in crime that year was no coincidence: "I do have a strong sense that some part of the explanation is a chill wind blowing through American law enforcement over the past year. And that wind is surely changing behavior."[95]

Rahm Emanuel, the Democratic mayor of Chicago, warned that police officers were becoming scared to do their jobs. He said these cops "have pulled back from the ability to interdict criminal behavior and criminals who are maybe about to engage in crime. They don't want to be a news story themselves. They don't want their career ended early, and it's having an impact."[96]

---

95 Alex Altman, "Is the Ferguson Effect For Real?" *Time*, October 29, 2015

96 Mdatcher, "'The Ferguson Effect' Myth and Reality," *Chicago Defender*, November 4, 2015

Conservative writer Heather Mac Donald wrote a *Wall Street Journal* op-ed that popularized the phrase "The Ferguson Effect." Her opening line proved to be haunting and prescient: "The nation's two-decades-long crime decline may be over."[97]

"Tough policing saves lives. It's sad but it's true," says Chris Anderson, who is one of the most thoughtful law enforcement officials I know. Born and raised in a rough section of Birmingham, Alabama, he joined a gang as a kid. His life could have gone down a predictable dead-end path. But his mom, a tough but loving local police sergeant, was not going to let her son slide into a life of crime. Between his mom's discipline and his passion for football, he straightened himself out. He worked hard and went to college, where he was both a good student and the starting tight end on the football team.

In 2016, our paths crossed serendipitously. He was retiring after more than twenty years as a homicide investigator, and I was looking for someone to host my new series, *Reasonable Doubt*, which had just been greenlit by Investigation Discovery.

Anderson is a natural. A gentle giant of a man who oozes charisma, with a warm smile and an easy, engaging laugh.

He is also a truth-teller who does not hesitate to call out anyone who is trying to bullshit him—whether it's an inmate, a witness, or another cop.

"If you want to see a decline in crime," he says, "you have to get officers out of their cars to interact with people. It's not being done now."

Anderson says officers have become reactive instead of proactive: "Here's the mindset: I'm not about to lose my job and my

---

97 Heather Mac Donald, "The New Nationwide Crime Wave," *Wall Street Journal*, May 29, 2015

benefits and my retirement because I'm out here trying to save the world. It's easier to ride around in the car, with my windows up, and just answer calls. It's very easy to do that in law enforcement. You can do that for twenty-plus years."

Anderson says it was very different in his day: "If you patrolled an area, you knew who was who, and what they were up to. You knew what guys were up to. You knew their parents and grandparents."

Chris believes broken windows policing works, but only if these quality-of-life infractions are being enforced by people with ties to the neighborhood. And he gives me a thought-provoking example.

"Let's say I'm patrolling the projects at one or two in the morning. I might see a three-year-old with a dirty diaper running around unsupervised. If it's me, I'll pick up the baby, bring it to the mom, and have a hard talk with her. But some cops who aren't from the neighborhood will pick up the baby and call CPS and have the kid taken away. What they don't realize is the mom may be working three to four jobs, trying to make ends meet. Maybe she fell asleep, exhausted, and the kid got out the door."

Chris's comment brought me back to Eric Holder's DOJ report, which concluded that the Ferguson Police Department's systemic issues with racial bias and excessive force were largely due to the fact that so many officers had no ties to the city.

Crime rates are influenced by several factors. The issue is complex, and there are many moving parts. But it is very difficult to argue that the anti-law enforcement movement, and the media's aggressive amplification of it, didn't play a significant role in the country's sudden spike in crime. The US murder rate hit a multi-generational low in 2014—the same year BLM hit the mainstream. Then, starting in 2015, it began to shoot straight back up. By 2020 and 2021, the peak years of BLM influence, the US murder rate had regressed to its bloody mid-1990s levels.[98]

The numbers are staggering. In Philadelphia, there were 248 murders in 2014. By 2021, that number more than doubled to 521.

Chicago went from 432 homicides to 695.

Cleveland, Ohio, from 64 to 170.

The list goes on and on.

Even safe and sleepy blue-city enclaves, like Portland, Oregon, and Austin, Texas, saw their murder rates nearly triple.

The one-sided media coverage of the anti-police movement had some other tangential effects on the crime rate. Residents of big blue cities elected reform-minded progressive district attorneys who stopped seeking the death penalty, ended the prosecution of juveniles as adults, reduced sentencing enhancements, eliminated cash bail, and set up diversion programs as alternatives to jail time. Even more damaging, in a direct repudiation of the broken windows philosophy, big cities implemented policies prohibiting prosecutors from filing charges for low-level crimes, including theft.

Law enforcement veterans like Chris Anderson say these ideas simply do not work: "We need to rethink what we're doing. We need more people going to jail."

The sin of legacy media was not seriously engaging with, or at the very least, platforming, some of the many law enforcement experts who were trying to warn us that the movement was leading us into dangerous territory. Whenever a police commissioner

---

98 Bryan Driscoll, "U.S. Murder Rate By Year Trend Chart," Consumer Shield, December 4, 2024

or prominent politician sounded the alarm about The Ferguson Effect, journalists would either ignore them entirely or deflect the argument by saying that the issue was "too complex," or that there wasn't enough data to support the hypothesis, or that crime wasn't up in *all* cities.

Journalists had lost sight of their north star: The Truth.

"They just jumped on the bandwagon. It was the 'in' thing," LaBarbera tells me. "The movement and the media coverage of it set back police departments by years. I wonder if they realize that now."

"Cops like myself gave blood, sweat, and tears to fix the city and bring it back from the hell it was during the crack wars," Angel Maysonet says.

It broke Angel's heart to watch the progress his generation of cops made evaporate. Now he questions whether all the sacrifices he made—all those long nights, all those times he laid his life on the line—were actually worth it.

"It's like saving your friend from almost drowning," he says, not trying to hide the bitterness and frustration. "You jump in the water and you give him CPR and save him. Four years later, he gets stage four cancer. That's what this feels like."

Chapter 7
The Death of Freddie Gray

The story of Freddie Gray begins in the historic West Baltimore neighborhood of Sandtown. In the 1950s and 1960s, it was home to a thriving Black community. Billie Holiday and Diana Ross performed at the famous Royal Theater on bustling Pennsylvania Avenue.[99] Supreme Court Justice Thurgood Marshall lived in the neighborhood, as did jazz legend Cab Calloway.[100]

Sandtown's fortunes changed after the 1968 riots, when many residents loaded up moving vans and fled to the relative safety of the suburbs. By 2015, Sandtown, once referred to as "Baltimore's Harlem," was now Baltimore's eyesore and shame. It had become a dystopian, neglected, and hopeless nightmare.

99 Jeremy Ashkenas, Larry Buchanan, Alicia DeSantis, Haeyoun Park, and Derek Watkins, "A Portrait of the Sandtown Neighborhood in Baltimore," *New York Times*, May 3, 2015

100 Michael Deibert, "Restoring Glory to a Baltimore Neighborhood," *New Lines Magazine*, March 29, 2022

One-third of the homes were boarded up and abandoned, the neighborhood's median household income was $24,000—lower than the federal poverty rate—and unemployment stood at a staggering 52 percent.[101]

Twenty-five-year-old Freddie Gray was a product of this miserable environment.

His mother, Gloria Darden, never went to high school, was illiterate, and battled a nasty heroin addiction.[102] All three of her children—Freddie, his twin sister, and his older sister—were born prematurely.

The house they lived in was so squalid, Gray's mother won a settlement from the landlord for lead-paint exposure. She firmly believed this was the cause of Freddie's learning difficulties, which caused him to have a short and disastrous stint in the public school system. Freddie was put in special ed classes and had to repeat several grades. He never could get the hang of schoolwork and dropped out after the ninth grade.

Like a lot of young men in Sandtown, his only realistic career option was street hustling and crime.

Over the next decade, Gray was arrested at least eighteen times, mostly for drug offenses, but also for assault and burglary.

His brother-in-law, Juan Grant, told CNN that Gray did what he had to do to survive: "When people come to buy narcotics or gamble or anything, and they put their money in your hand, what makes you so bad? He had responsibilities. Responsibilities don't stop because you don't have a job."[103]

---

101 William A. Galston, "Pittsburgh's Revival Lesson for Baltimore," *Wall Street Journal*, May 5, 2015

102 Nadra Nittle, "What the Alleged Suicide Attempt of Freddie Gray's Mother Says About Racism and Depression," Atlanta Black Star, October 26, 2015

103 Faith Karimi, Kim Berryman, and Dana Ford, "Who Was Freddie Gray, Whose Death Has Reignited Protests Against the Police?" CNN, July 27, 2016

At the time of his death, Gray lived with his girlfriend and her daughter in the Gilmor Homes neighborhood, a series of grim, brick, barrack-like structures that look like the tenements from The Wire.

Standing just 5'8" and weighing 145 pounds, the scrawny Gray used humor to get respect in his neighborhood.

"He was so funny," a neighbor named Raheem Gaither said. "He could have been a comedian for real, but nah. Now look at him."[104]

Freddie Gray's complicated case began on a lazy Sunday morning: April 12, 2015. The sun was out, and temperatures were already in the mid-fifties.

The streets were starting to fill up. Some residents were making their way to church. Others, like Freddie Gray, were just hanging out on street corners.

At 8:39 a.m., Brian Rice, a White, seventeen-year vet of the Baltimore Police Department, was patrolling the streets on bicycle duty when he spotted Gray. He didn't think much of him at first. The two locked eyes for a brief moment, and then, for reasons Freddie Gray would take to his grave, he suddenly started running.

Rice got on his radio and asked for help chasing down a suspect. Two other White police officers on bicycle duty—Garrett Miller and Edward Nero—heard the call and joined the pursuit.

About a minute later, Gray realized the futility of trying to outrun three cops on bicycles and surrendered. The officers handcuffed and frisked Gray. That's when they found a spring-assisted folding knife in his pocket. The weapon is illegal in the city of

[104] Faith Karimi, Kim Berryman, and Dana Ford, "Who Was Freddie Gray, Whose Death Has Reignited Protests Against the Police?" CNN, July 27, 2016

Baltimore, and the officers now believed they had probable cause to make an arrest.

Since the three arresting officers were all on bikes, they called for a police wagon to come pick Gray up.

Minutes later, Caesar Goodson, a Black sixteen-year department vet, arrived on the scene, pulling up in a large, old-fashioned paddy wagon.

By this point, an angry crowd had gathered. They were shouting at the cops, telling them to leave Gray alone. Some were recording the arrest on their phones.

The footage, which would be replayed endlessly in news reports, shows Gray thrashing about, screaming, and crying as officers stood him up and dragged him—*Weekend at Bernie's* style—to the wagon. Once there, the officers opened the rear doors, revealing a cargo area partitioned in two by a solid metal barrier. They dragged Gray into one side of the partitioned space and placed him on a bench built into the rear of the cabin. They did not fasten his seat belt like they had been trained to do. One of the officers would later claim they had to get out of there quickly because the crowd was getting hostile. Other officers would testify that even though it was official policy, police rarely, if ever, put seat belts on suspects.[105]

As the wagon left the scene, witnesses could hear Gray screaming and banging against the doors.

The officers drove down the street to get away from the mob.

When they thought they had reached a safe distance, the cops pulled over so that they could put Gray in leg shackles.

---

105 AP News, "Officers: Nobody Buckles Prisoners Into Seatbelts," CBS News, December 11, 2015

He was no more cooperative this time around, still kicking and screaming and resisting the officers.

The commotion drew another crowd and, suddenly, the cops found themselves surrounded by a second angry mob.

Frustrated, they placed Gray on his stomach and cuffed his hands to the rear of the wagon.

Once again, they left him there without fastening his seatbelt.

Witnesses at the scene said Gray was freaking out, banging the wagon so hard, it was visibly shaking.

At 8:54 a.m., the bicycle officers left the scene, and it was left to Caesar Goodson to take Gray to Central Booking. Medical experts agree that it was at some point in the ensuing twenty-five minutes, while in the back of the police wagon, that Freddie Gray suffered a fatal neck and spinal injury.

The question was: How did it happen and who was to blame?

At 8:56 a.m., Officer Goodson stopped the wagon for a third time and went around back to check on Gray. Whatever he saw must have unnerved him, because after he resumed driving, he got on the radio and asked for an officer to meet him and check on the condition of the suspect.

The unfortunate cop who answered that call was twenty-five-year-old William Porter, an African American Baltimore native. Porter's childhood dream had been to join the military, but he was turned down because he is legally colorblind. So, he went with his plan B and became a police officer.

Porter had no idea what he was walking into at 8:59 a.m., when he opened the rear wagon doors and found Freddie Gray on his stomach, his head pointing towards the door.

"Help," Gray stammered.

"What's wrong with you?"

Gray hesitated a moment and then pleaded, "Help. Help me up."

Porter went into the wagon, pulled Gray up, and sat him on the bench.

"Do you want to go to the hospital?" Porter asked.

"Yes."

Porter was skeptical. Gray was speaking normally, seemed to be breathing fine, and didn't have any visible signs of injury.

Porter hopped out of the wagon without fastening Gray's seatbelt and went to talk to Goodson.

"Take him to the hospital. He said the magic words," Porter told Goodson.

Porter would later testify, "If someone says they want to go to the hospital, they automatically reject them from Central Booking."[106]

At 9:07 a.m., Lieutenant Rice, the man who originally locked eyes with Gray, was back on the police radio. He had just arrested a new suspect and wanted the wagon to swing by and pick him up. So instead of heading straight to the hospital as he had planned, Goodson took a detour and drove over to Rice's new location.

Four minutes later, Goodson pulled up and found the original three bicycle cops who had arrested Gray with a new suspect—a man named Donta Allen. With them was Sergeant Alicia White, the sixth and final police officer who would come into contact with Freddie Gray that morning. White, who is African American, took her job very seriously and was starting to get noticed for it by the higher-ups. She was only thirty but

---

[106] Jess Bidgood, "Officer Testifies About Van Ride Leading to Freddie Gray's Death," *New York Times*, June 13, 2016

had already been promoted to sergeant. A devout Christian, her church was just blocks away from where Gray was initially arrested.

As her minister and friend, Dana Neal, told reporters, "She wanted to be a police officer because she is a Christian and wants to be a good role model for young Black women. And she wanted to be that good cop in the community and bridge the gap between the police and the neighborhoods."[107]

As the rear doors to the paddy wagon swung open yet again, White spotted Gray facing away from her, leaning over the bench, with his head down. It looked like he was praying.

White thought Gray might know something about the crime the new arrestee, Donta Allen, had just been collared for, so she asked him about it.

Gray didn't respond with words, just some audible grunts.

White assumed that meant he didn't want to cooperate and closed the doors.

That was the extent of her interaction with Freddie Gray.

At 9:16 a.m., the paddy wagon took off for the final time, with Gray on one side of the partition and Donta Allen on the other. The ride was short—just two minutes to the Western District station. Allen would later tell police that during that time, he heard a lot of banging and assumed that Gray was slamming his head against the partition. He would also tell CNN's Don Lemon, in an interview that aired a few weeks later, that the short ride was a smooth one.

---

[107] Richard Fausset, Serge F. Kovaleski, and Richard Oppel Jr., "Officers Facing Charges Find Themselves on an Unfamiliar Side of the Law," *New York Times*, May 1, 2015

At 9:18 a.m., Goodson finally pulled into the police station. When he swung the doors open, Gray's eyes were shut, his body was limp, and he didn't appear to be breathing.

Paramedics rushed him to the hospital. Over the next week, Gray remained in a coma. Doctors performed a series of surgeries, desperately trying to save his life. But he was too far gone.

On April 19, 2015, exactly one week from the day of his arrest, Freddie Gray was declared dead.

CT scans and MRIs showed that Gray had a fractured neck and a pinched spinal cord. Medical experts said his injuries were similar to what could happen if someone dove into a shallow swimming pool and hit their head.

The following night, Freddie Gray's death led most legacy newscasts.

ABC's David Muir opened his newscast with, "Good night, and we begin this Monday in Baltimore where there is an intense focus on several videos captured of the same arrest. The suspect, being put into the back of a police van. That suspect, Freddie Gray, would end up with a severed spine. He would later die. It is unclear how it happened. Late today, Baltimore police saying none of the officers described any use of force."

The news coverage over the next few days followed a now familiar pattern. The narrative was mostly driven by activists and the family's attorney. In this case, Gray's mom and stepdad had hired Billy Murphy, a prominent local Black lawyer.

Murphy was seventy-two years old, with the energy of a man half his age. He cut a memorable figure on television: a long, signature ponytail in back and a donut-shaped bald head on top. Just like Benjamin Crump, he knew how to manipulate the media and help shape their stories.

He also knew how to give attention-grabbing soundbites, like when he made the following explosive statement about Freddie Gray to CBS News: "Running while Black is not a crime. In fact, he didn't run fast enough."

It quickly became apparent that journalists had done little to no self-reflection following the fiasco in Ferguson. One of the most damning errors in the coverage of that story had been the platforming of unreliable witnesses without any cross-examination or contextualization. That's how the fictitious "Hands up! Don't shoot!" narrative became burned into the public consciousness. It's also why so many people believed that Brown had been shot in the back, even though that was empirically false.

Days after Freddie Gray's death, CNN's Anderson Cooper conducted a long phone interview with a neighborhood "witness" who insisted on staying anonymous.

"One of my relatives came in the house screaming, 'They're tasing him! They're tasing him! They're tasing one of your friends!'" He told Cooper, "I run out the door to see what's going on, but by the time I got to the actual site, I don't see the taser. He was putting it back in the holster rather than tasing him."

It is worth noting that the Department of Justice report would conclude that there was absolutely no evidence police ever tased or hit Gray. It was a point Baltimore's Black police chief was fruitlessly trying to get through to the media.

"Now police have said they didn't actually use a taser. Did you see any indication that they actually had used a taser?" Cooper asked his "witness."

"I heard the electricity. The noise from the taser," responded the anonymous man.

And with that, another false narrative was born. Since the news media was now taking everything coming from police departments with a huge grain of salt, anonymous interviews with people claiming to be local residents were given more weight than those of officers who were putting their lives on the line to protect their communities.

Based on the knowable facts at the time, reporters should have approached the Freddie Gray story with an open mind: It was, after all, a complicated story, and his death remained a mystery. All we knew for sure was that Gray had suffered his fatal injuries in the wagon. The key unanswered question was this: Did he do it to himself, by slamming his head against the partition—as Donta Allen suggested—or did Caesar Goodson deliberately drive recklessly, making sharp turns and hard stops knowing that Gray was back there without a seatbelt on? This particular act of police brutality had happened in Baltimore before, and locals even had a name for it: a "rough ride."

One of the dangerous tangential effects of these high-profile police brutality cases was that city officials were now ignoring due process and making snap decisions, trying in vain to appease the mob and avoid rioting.

On the day after Gray's death, the Baltimore PD suspended all six officers who had interacted with the suspect from the time of his arrest to his arrival at the police station. Even Alicia White, who had just briefly spoken to Gray during the wagon's final stop, was now lumped in with the "bad cops."

Of course, none of this did anything to appease the mob. For sixteen straight days, daytime protests turned into nighttime rioting.

CNN went back to its Ferguson playbook, providing wall-to-wall coverage of a poor city destroying itself in the name of "justice."

The scenes were nightmarish: fires, looting, citizens hurling weapons at police officers.

When the smoke cleared, over 350 businesses were damaged, 15 buildings were burned to the ground, 27 pharmacies were looted, 150 cars were incinerated, 20 cops were injured, two people were shot, and 486 were arrested.[108]

The rioting was so extensive that the Baltimore Orioles postponed two games and played a third in front of an empty stadium, due to security concerns.

Legacy media seemed to believe that by presenting themselves as sympathetic allies to a "long-overdue reckoning with racism," they could shield themselves from any criticism that they were exploiting violence for ratings.

But several protesters saw straight through the charade. As one told an MSNBC reporter, "My question to you is, when we were out here protesting all last week, for six straight days peacefully, there were no news cameras, there were no helicopters, there was no riot gear, and nobody heard us. So, now that we've burned down buildings and set businesses on fire and looted buildings, now all of a sudden everyone wants to hear us."[109]

The most destructive night of violence came on April 27, right after Freddie Gray's funeral. The following evening, ABC News's Byron Pitts did his best to minimize the lawlessness.

---

108 Marshall Greenlaw, "Baltimore Protests and Riots, 2015," BlackPast, December 17, 2017

109 "Criticism of Baltimore Media Coverage," Media Diversity Institute, May 5, 2015

"After ten days of peaceful protests," he reported incorrectly—there had been a lot of looting and rioting over that time period—"a small group of agitators became violent, targeting police with bricks and burning abandoned squad cars."

Pitts's report was Orwellian. As his voice-over spoke of "a small group of agitators," the video showed dozens of young people, at least fifty, hurling objects at the police. As Dan Rather used to say, "the camera never blinks."

Later in his piece, Pitts interviewed Kweisi Mfume, the former head of the NAACP, who left the organization after allegations of sexual harassment.

You might think that in the midst of high tensions and civil unrest, Pitts would look to Mfume to calm tensions. But instead, he seemed to be trying to inflame them.

"Is it Black vs. White or Black vs. blue?" Pitts asked.

"It's a little bit of both," Mfume answered.

"That legacy of race still exists?"

"It does. It does."

It was a lazy and needlessly incendiary line of questioning in the middle of a riot. For one thing, the mayor of Baltimore was Black. So were the police chief and three of the six suspended officers. So, when Pitts asked if it was "Black vs. White," it was unclear who the "White people" he was referring to actually were.

On May 1, Fox News's James Rosen filed a provocative story, in which he tried to deliver some hard truths about the rioting in Baltimore.

Rosen's piece stood out in that it dared to cross the third rail and question the mainstream narrative that the violence was simply an outpouring of understandable anger at a corrupt and racist system.

He ran a soundbite from Baltimore City Councilman Nick Mosby, who said, "The youth is showing anger for a system that's failed them."

Rosen then posed the difficult question: "But who actually ran the system that so demonstrably failed Baltimore's young Black men?"

He then pointed out that the city hadn't had a Republican mayor since 1966. The city council was all Democratic. As were all the school and union leaders. In fact, instead of being neglected, Baltimore ranked third in the nation in per-student education spending. So why was the system failing children so badly?

It was the kind of story that regular consumers of legacy media needed to see but never would.

Of course, Fox viewers weren't getting the whole story either. They needed to know that the Baltimore Police Department had recently settled a multi-million-dollar lawsuit because of a rough ride that left a suspect paralyzed. They needed to see that the poverty in Sandtown was crushing and that young people there had almost zero chance of success.

But no, everyone stayed on their side of the glass house.

President Obama, usually careful with his words, came close to prejudging the case on April 28, when he said, "This has been going on for a long time. This is not new, and we shouldn't pretend that it's new. The good news is that perhaps there's some newfound awareness, because of social media and video cameras and so forth, that there are problems and challenges when it comes to how policing and our laws are applied in certain communities, and we have to pay attention to it."[110] The quote aged poorly in light of the fact that his own Department of Justice's investigation would later exonerate all six police officers.

Al Sharpton, never known for being circumspect, said, "Freddie's death was a homicide, and those responsible must be held accountable through the most severe charges available under the law."

Beyoncé posted an image of Freddie Gray on her Instagram account with the message, "Stop killing us."

Prince quickly wrote a protest song called "Baltimore," in which he asked whether the country was hearing all the prayers for Michael Brown and Freddie Gray.

Thirty-five-year-old Marilyn Mosby, the new state's attorney for Baltimore City, was watching the developments of this case very closely.

She was brand new to the spotlight. Just a year earlier, she had been working as a lawyer for Liberty Mutual when she took a huge leap of faith and decided to run for office against a well-known and well-funded incumbent. Mosby ran as a progressive and promised to aggressively prosecute police misconduct.

The message resonated with voters, and Mosby became the youngest top prosecutor in the country. Her husband, Nick, was a member of the city council, making the two Baltimore's "it" power couple.

On May 1, 2015, Maryland's medical examiner ruled that Freddie Gray's death was a homicide. It was a controversial decision since

[110] Tanya Somanader, "President Obama on Freddie Gray's Death: "This Is Not New, and We Shouldn't Pretend That It's New," Obama White House archives, April 28, 2015

she could not pinpoint how he died or where he died but instead argued that his death resulted from "acts of omission" by officers. She argued that her conclusion was justified because police failed to secure him in a seatbelt and ignored his pleas to go to the hospital.

Later that day, Mosby gathered reporters at the steps of the downtown War Memorial and made a stunning announcement. She was throwing the book at all six of the officers who interacted with Freddie Gray on the day of his arrest.

"To the people of Baltimore and the demonstrators across America," she soberly declared, "I heard your call for 'no justice, no peace.'"

The news caught everyone off guard. Usually, in a case this complicated, a DA might take months before pressing charges.

Former Baltimore prosecutor Ivan Bates had this prescient warning: "It's easy to charge. It's hard to convict."[111]

Other legal experts were worried that she was over-charging the officers, which would make it very difficult to get jurors to vote guilty. And there was no denying—her charges were severe.

Lieutenant Rice, the man who first locked eyes with Gray, was charged with second-degree assault and involuntary manslaughter. He faced up to twenty years in prison.

Officers Nero and Miller, the two other bicycle cops, were each charged with second-degree assault and faced ten-year sentences.

William Porter, who checked in on Gray during one of the early stops, was charged with involuntary manslaughter and second-degree assault. He faced twenty years behind bars.

---

[111] Sheryl Gay Stolberg and Alan Blinder, "Marilyn Mosby, Prosecutor in Freddie Gray Case, Takes a Stand and Calms a Troubled City," *New York Times*, May 1, 2015

Alicia White, who had that brief interaction with Gray right before he was brought in for booking, was also charged with involuntary manslaughter and second-degree assault. She, too, was facing twenty years in prison.

"I didn't see that coming at all," she told a local TV station. "I was devastated. I broke down and started crying. It was hard. It was a hard pill to swallow."[112]

The most serious charges were leveled at Caesar Goodson, the driver of the wagon. He faced seven charges. Five of them felonies: involuntary manslaughter, second-degree assault, two separate manslaughter by vehicle charges, and a charge called "second-degree depraved-heart murder."

If Mosby got her way and a jury found him guilty on all counts, Goodson would likely spend the rest of his life in prison.

During her news conference, Mosby praised the protesters, telling them, "You're at the forefront of this cause, and as young people, our time is now."

Network newscasts were dominated by ecstatic reactions to Mosby's tough, "courageous" stance. Protesters partied in the streets, Freddie Gray's parents expressed gratitude, and, of course, their ponytailed lawyer, Billy Murphy, took a victory lap. "If Freddie Gray did not die in vain, we must seize this opportunity to reform police departments throughout this country," he declared.[113]

On *CBS This Morning*, the three-minute lead package was almost entirely from the prosecution's point of view.

---

112 Mariam Khan, "Baltimore Cops Charged in Freddie Gray Case Eager to Return to the Streets," ABC News, November 18, 2016

113 "Freddie Gray's Family Satisfied with Charges, Calls for Peace," WUSA, May 1, 2015

Buried in the coverage was a quick cautionary soundbite from the attorney for the Baltimore police union: "I have never seen such a hurried rush to file criminal charges, which I believe are driven by forces which are separate and apart from the application of law and the facts of these cases as we know them."

It was around this time that the first signs of public discontent with the way legacy media was covering police violence surfaced. A YouGov poll revealed that viewers believed the media was biased against the police officers, by a wide margin of 45–18.[114]

On September 9, 2015, there was another major development: Billy Murphy announced that he had reached a $6.4 million settlement between Gray's family and the city of Baltimore. He sounded conciliatory, telling reporters he hoped this would start the process of healing.

CNN's Miguel Marquez began his report on the settlement by pushing a different narrative. Over bleak shots of Sandtown, he intoned, "The neighborhood where Freddie Gray was arrested—reaction to the $6.4 million settlement—swift and angry." What followed were two "man on the street" interviews. Neither local seemed particularly upset; they just calmly and reasonably pointed out that no amount of money can ever compensate for the loss of life.

Marquez was using a cheap reporter's trick.

You go knocking on doors, sticking cameras in people's faces until you get a couple of usable bites that conform to your pre-conceived premise. It seemed like CNN was intent on keeping its racial storyline alive, even though it was unclear whether that story was *Black vs. White* or *Black vs. blue*.

[114] Peter Moore, "Poll Results: Freddie Gray," YouGov, May 7, 2015

The first officer to stand trial was Officer William Porter, the man who had checked in on Gray and asked if he wanted to go to the hospital.

The jury deliberated for three days but ended up hopelessly deadlocked on all charges. The judge declared a mistrial.

Next up was Officer Edward Nero, one of the original bicycle cops. He was acquitted of all charges.

The most critical case started in June 2016, when Caesar Goodson, the driver of the wagon, stood trial on five felony charges. Prosecutors tried to convince the jury that Goodson had killed Gray by giving him a "rough ride." However, they had very little evidence to prove it. The only solid proof the prosecution presented was surveillance footage showing Goodson making a wide right turn and briefly crossing the yellow lines on a roadway. It was not persuasive. Goodson was also found not guilty of all charges.

Fourth up was Brian Rice, the original bicycle cop. He, too, was acquitted of all charges.

On July 27, 2016, reporting from the Democratic National Convention in Philadelphia, Lester Holt cut in with some breaking news: "There were dramatic developments today involving the Baltimore police officers accused of causing a fatal injury to Freddie Gray, a man who died in their custody last year. After failing to secure a guilty verdict against four officers already brought to trial, prosecutors today dropped the charges against the remaining officers as the prosecutor suggested the legal system worked against her."

It was another stunning setback for the anti-police movement and an even bigger blow to the credibility of broadcast news. Once again, distorted coverage convinced viewers that an innocent Black man had been murdered by police, only to leave them disillusioned and confused when juries reviewed the evidence and reached the opposite conclusion.

If there was any doubt that activists and the media had gotten this case completely wrong, it was laid to rest on September 12, 2017, when the Department of Justice announced that it would not be filing civil rights charges against the "Baltimore Six."

Just like in the Michael Brown case, the DOJ punctured many of the myths that had taken root surrounding the death of Freddie Gray.

On claims that officers beat or tased him, the DOJ made the following statement: "The evidence in the matter overwhelmingly contradicted reports from some civilian witnesses that Gray was either tased or beaten by the officers. The doctor who performed Gray's autopsy and testified for the state concluded that there was no medical evidence indicating that Gray's injuries were caused by excessive force during the arrest, and no medical evidence showing that Gray had been tased."[115]

On the "rough ride" theory, the DOJ reported, "An expert on retaliatory prisoner transport practices who testified at trial for the state concluded that he had seen no evidence that Goodson made abrupt starts, stops, or turns, and that he was not sure whether Goodson had given Gray a 'rough ride.'"

The DOJ concluded by stating, "The investigation into this incident has been closed without prosecution."

"The whole case was a travesty," said former prosecutor Andrew McCarthy on Newsmax, a network for viewers who find Fox

---

[115] "Federal Officials Decline Prosecution in the Death of Freddie Gray," Department of Justice, September 12, 2017

insufficiently conservative. "It's a tragedy not just for the police officers who've been wrongly charged in this case, but also at a time when homicides hit a record number last year in Baltimore.... What [Mosby] has done is create a climate where cops have to worry about whether they're going to be prosecuted for doing their jobs."

But Mosby was completely unapologetic, blaming the *system* for her failures: "Without real substantive reforms to the current criminal justice system, we could try this case 100 times and cases just like it, and we would still end up with the same result."[116]

There is an ironic twist—maybe even a karmic one—to this story.

Marilyn Mosby is now a convicted felon herself. In 2024, she was found guilty of perjury and mortgage fraud for lying on an application to buy a home in Longboat Key, Florida.

Meantime, Alicia White, the woman Mosby tried to lock up for twenty years, was promoted by the Baltimore Police Department to captain in 2022. Then, in 2024, she was promoted again: This time, she was put in charge of running the department's Public Integrity Bureau.

---

116 Sheryl Gay Stolberg and Jess Bidgood, "All Charges Dropped Against Baltimore Officers in Freddie Gray Case," *New York Times*, July 27, 2017

Chapter 8
Back to School

I am breathing hard, speedwalking, trying to keep up with Brian McGrory, the longtime editor of *The Boston Globe*, who now runs the journalism department at my alma mater, Boston University (BU). A seemingly endless stream of students is walking towards us on Commonwealth Avenue, the campus's main street. Brian doesn't break his long, efficient strides, as he masterfully weaves his way between the crowd, never looking back to check on my progress, which is not going well. I bump into students, apologize, break into a series of awkward half jogs, all in a futile effort to catch up to Brian. It's blustery and freezing. My lungs are burning.

Ten minutes earlier, I had been sitting in Brian's warm office.

"I have to go to the other side of campus to teach a class."

"Can I sit in?" I ask.

"Sure, you up for a brisk walk?"

A brisk walk? I live in California. I hike. I play tennis. I own a Peloton. "Of course. No problem."

The speedwalk takes us across the BU campus, which mostly consists of an incongruous mix of Victorian brick townhomes and brutalist architecture, with a few post-modern buildings sprinkled in. The walk reminds me of just how depressing my hometown is in the winter. Everything is gray and drab: The sky, the buildings, even the leafless trees look sad and forlorn.

But the students walking towards us are full of life, and I am determined not to bump into any more of them. As I do a Kramer-esque move to avoid tripping over a fire hydrant, I manage to breathlessly call out to Brian, "How are you finding the students here?"

"I was expecting very fragile kids," Brian calls out over his shoulder, not breaking his relentless pace. "Participation trophies and their parents would call me complaining about their B+. That's not what happened. I rip their papers to shreds, put lots of comments on it. And no exaggeration, to a kid, they thank me. They want that feedback, and it doesn't have to be positive."

My mission, this week, is to figure out how my profession went so far off the rails. I'm thinking it has to be the schools. After all, aren't they the ones who produced all these entitled snowflakes who infiltrated newsrooms with their radical ideas? I am going to audit a lot of journalism classes at BU and am fully expecting to come face to face with the kind of kids who dominate my social media algorithms: pronoun-obsessed, mask-loving students, with tats, brightly colored hair, and declared sexual orientations so obscure I have to ask ChatGPT what they mean. I'm expecting to see kids who hate capitalism, love the Houthis, and have the disposition of Greta Thunberg whenever she speaks to world leaders. I'm expecting to find an easy scapegoat for the crisis facing broadcast journalism.

And then I walk into Brian's classroom and get hit with a big dose of reality.

Seventeen students—thirteen of them women—sit around a very large conference room table.

They are all dressed professionally, like they are at a job interview. In fact, they're much better dressed than most staff members of my LA-based shows. I keep looking for mohawks, green hair, or neck tattoos: Nothing.

I discreetly sit down in the back of the room and watch Brian lead his newswriting class.

"OK, I'm going to go around the room, and I want you to share what stories you're working on," Brian says, in his crisp, no-nonsense New England manner. "And remember, the best way not to get stuck with a bad story assignment is to come up with your own ideas."

The students are all sitting up. They are engaged and enthusiastic. They eagerly share what they're working on: solid, community-based stories about everything from the fate of small businesses to sports.

"Remember, you need to cultivate sources," Brian tells the class. "Sources become your eyes and ears. They will become very useful to you. And we never want a story with just one source."

I took a similar class back in the late 1980s, but the only people who ever read the articles I wrote were the professor and his TA. That's changed now. Brian has set up a network of small community newspapers around New England, which publish some of the students' best work. Instead of just turning in assignments for grades, these students are writing for actual readers and getting resume-building professional bylines.

I know I'm like the old man shaking his fist at the clouds, but I keep waiting for some evidence of fragility—maybe a trigger warning, or a student storming out of class in tears, heading to the comfort of a safe room filled with dolls and Silly Putty.

"Deadlines have to be met," Brian sternly warns the class. "It's the baseline. It's what we do here."

Seventeen eager heads nod.

"You cannot make mistakes," he cautions. "If you make a mistake on a little thing, people won't believe the big ones. All we have is our credibility."

Seventeen eager heads nod.

Brian even makes a salty joke: "When I was on the beat covering Plymouth, Mass, if I went to the police station and found out there was a quadruple murder, it would be the best day of my life."

I look around, expecting faux outrage. But there is none. Just laughter. The students seem to understand they'll need to develop a twisted sense of gallows humor in order to survive their chosen profession.

McGrory generously turns the last half hour of the class over to me.

"Thanks for letting me sit in on your class," I say, surveying the seventeen attentive, unlined faces: friendly, open, betraying no signs of cynicism. "So, you guys are writing stories now. You're getting bylines. When you turn in a story, how do you know whether or not it's balanced?"

A senior named Danielle raises her hand. "Ninety-nine percent of the time, the truth lies in the middle. You have to be fair."

Vanessa, a senior, chimes in: "I worked on a story about comprehensive sex education in schools. One side was against it. That was hard for me. But I had to get their side too."

Charlie, a junior, tells me, "You can't be objective. It's impossible. So, you try to be fair."

Not all the students are committed to objective reporting. One senior tells me she doesn't believe reporters should ever question someone's "lived experience." Another student, a junior, tells me, "When it comes to issues where there are two sides that have opinions, my approach is to ground myself in what is true and what is factual. You don't have to platform people who are telling lies. You have an obligation to not platform hateful opinions."

These kinds of arguments, which are also made on the network news level, are the beginning of that hellish slippery slope that turns journalists from objective reporters into activists. I wonder if the proponents of this type of thinking have ever considered who exactly is supposed to be the arbiter of what is "factual" and what qualifies as "hateful." And if someone, let's say a politician or prominent businessperson, does make a hateful comment, isn't that newsworthy?

Overall, though, these kids are all right, and most of them seem more committed to traditional journalism than many of the news managers who will soon be hiring them. They also seem unfazed by the less-than-lucrative job prospects facing them after graduation.

"It takes a special kid," McGrory says, "this far into the disruption, which is a polite word for the collapse of the business model around journalism, to still want to devote their college career to studying this."

"I'm surprised so many of these kids want to go into print. I thought they'd all want to be influencers, cutting videos on their phones," I reply, still amazed at what I saw in his classroom.

McGrory shakes his head and says, "They're warned here early on this is not going to be an easy career to make it in. You have to really be committed to it."

"So why do you think they want in?"

"It's a rare career where you can literally change the world by your work," McGrory tells me. "But you have to be prepared to do the work. All the work. The pick-and-shovel work that will lead you to where you want to go. They really, really want it and it shows."

I have always felt that I learned more in my first six months working professionally in TV news than I did in my entire four years as a student at BU. I still believe this, but now I realize that, in large part, it was due to the fact that I was an indifferent student. I had big dreams of making it in news, but school just felt like a long time-out—an obstacle preventing me from getting on with the "glamorous" life that was undoubtedly awaiting me in the real world. I did spark to some classes, like one on sports journalism, where I got to meet, interview, and write profiles on childhood sports heroes like former Red Sox "dirt dog" Butch Hobson and boxing champ Vinny Pazienza. I co-majored in film and got to make a few student movies. Also fun. But most of my time at BU was spent sitting in classes, listening to academic types who hadn't worked in the business in many years, if ever at all, drone on about theoretical abstractions.

BU still has those courses.

I sit in on one class, taught by a leftist named Joan Donovan, who left Harvard under murky circumstances, but somehow found a home in BU's journalism department.

Her class is supposed to be about "disinformation," but without any trace of irony or shame, she casually tosses out her own nuggets of misinformation as though they were obvious, empirical facts.

"When Elon Musk gave us a Sieg Heil," she tells the class, "we were told this was a chance to better understand autism."

On Musk's efforts to lead DOGE, she declares, "The 2025 tax cuts are set to expire so rich people need to find money to justify renewing their tax cuts."

In another class, purportedly teaching students how to cover government and politics, a kindly old liberal named Jerry Berger indulges himself in hysteria and conspiracy theories about Trump's nascent second term. Here is just a small sample of his takes:

"The purges we're seeing in various US agencies—you know who else committed purges? Stalin. I'm going to start comparing him to Stalin."

"Does Trump have an idea to turn the FBI into his own secret police? Time will tell."

"Trump doesn't want to be president. He wants to be king."

"Elon Musk destroyed Twitter much the same way he's trying to destroy the US government. That's the story."

After Berger's partisan rants, I worry that these kids are being fed a warped view of journalism. After class, about ten of the students agree to stay and talk to me, and I quickly realize they are taking their professor's opinions in stride.

"OK, basic question," I say. "What do you think the role of a journalist is?"

Talia, a junior, replies, "To be a fly on the wall and to hold people accountable."

"Anyone else?"

A grad student named Andrea tells me, "Information is very hard to understand. I think our job is to take that complicated information and make it more accessible to regular people."

"OK, this has become a controversial subject," I say, and notice the students tensing up a bit. "Biases. Should you keep it out of your reporting, or is it okay if it's part of your 'lived experience'?"

"In my reporting, no one knows where I stand," volunteers Myra, a senior. "Things are so polarized now. If people know where you stand, people may not trust what you report."

A senior named Mitch then tells me, "I had someone at *The Free Press* [the BU newspaper] who told me he wouldn't even vote because it might compromise his credibility."

"That is an old soul," I say, laughing. "That's the kind of thing I would hear from the generation that was retiring when I first started working in newsrooms. Okay, you guys are all saying the right things. It's like music to my ears. But are you saying everything I've read about campus radicalism is made up? Don't some people get mad at you for reporting stories right down the middle of the plate?"

The students smile and exchange knowing looks.

"I worked at a newspaper where we always tried to give both sides of the story—for and against," says a grad student named Gabriel. "And you know what we were called—fascists."

Talia pipes in again: "I had to do a story about the encampments and I'm a Jewish student, so that was tough."

"How did you handle it?" I ask, genuinely curious. "I think I would have a hard time covering that story objectively."

"I think I set [my personal feelings] aside. Looking back, it's one of my favorite stories I've ever covered."

Another student who's been quiet up until now, an undergrad named Shinanu, chimes in: "I always have to remind myself. The story is not for me. It's not about me. It was never about me."

The kids are all right.

Many people blame leftist professors for the radicalization of American newsrooms, but I think their influence is vastly overstated.

I had my share of radical professors too.

One of my favorites, Murray Levin, was a former member of the Communist Party, who would go on rants about how we shouldn't be allowed to own our own clothes, since most of our shirts and jeans were just sitting, unworn, in our closets, while there were needy homeless people who were walking around the streets barefoot. It was the late 1980s, the heart of the Reagan and Alex P. Keaton era, and his radical lectures were met with nothing more than giggles and eye rolls. Give up our Members Only jackets? God forbid.

I also took a class with the infamous leftist Howard Zinn, the author of the influential revisionist book *A People's History of the United States*. In one memorable class, guest speaker Ron Kovic whipped himself up into a Sam Kinison–style frenzy, screaming at the top of his lungs, "Pat Buchanan can suck my cock!"

Ultimately, these professors make up a loud minority. And, as I found out, most of today's students take their extremism about as seriously as we did—which is hardly at all.

For a week, I walk the halls of BU's COM building (short for "communications"—it was originally called the College of Communications, until the school administration finally figured out why people giggled every time they used the school's acronym). I marvel at how little has changed. Certainly not the architecture. Whoever designed it clearly loved beige; everything from the floors and the walls to the ceilings has the drab color palette of a grade school in desperate need of renovations. The classrooms look like something you'd see in one of those movies about poorly funded inner-city high schools. I spend the week cramming my frame into tiny school desks, sitting under foam ceilings, half expecting to see Morgan Freeman patrolling the hallways with a baseball bat. The only major change I can see from my days as a student are the free tampon dispensers in the men's rooms.

I sit in on Michael Holley's class. His twelve students may not realize it, but their teacher is a celebrity in some circles—the author of numerous Boston-centric sports books and a frequent talking head on sports-talk debate shows. He cuts a striking figure in class. Fashionable Nike sneakers, a brown blazer over a white T-shirt, designer glasses, and a smoothly shaved head.

"Journalism is everything people don't want you to know," he tells the class. "Everything else is PR."

One student tells Holley she didn't end up going to a big hockey game the night before, even though she was supposed to write a story about it.

"Why not?" Holley demands, friendly but firm.

"I had to get up for class. You want us here at eight, right?"

"OK, now hold up. What time did the game end last night? Maybe ten? You couldn't make that work?"

"I need my sleep," the student replies.

Holley arches his eyebrows, and the student lowers her head. Message received.

I go to a video journalism class taught by Tina McDuffie, a PBS TV news reporter.

"The assignments are due at 2 p.m. sharp," she tells the class in a tone that makes it clear she means business, adding, "That means at 2:01, you are late, and the work will be docked. This business is all about deadlines. They are non-negotiable."

I sit in on another class. This one's about law and ethics in journalism, taught by another celebrated author, Richard Lehr.

This is the kind of class my generation used to blow off or sleep through. But I'm sitting in a large classroom filled with dozens of students hanging onto his every word.

I wasn't finding much evidence of it at BU, but the radicalization of students in the late aughts and early to mid-2010s was real. And it was happening in the most respected journalism schools in the country.

At Stanford, Communications Professor Emeritus Ted Glasser told the school newspaper, "Journalists need to be overt and candid advocates for social justice, and it's hard to do that under the constraints of objectivity."[117]

Hakeem Jefferson, a Stanford colleague, upped the ante, equating objectivity with racism: "There's this assumption that if you really want objective journalism, just give me a staid, White person."

Not to be outdone, Andrew Heyward, a faculty member of ASU's Walter Cronkite School of Journalism and Mass Comm-

[117] Zadie Winthrop, "Should Journalists Rethink Objectivity? Stanford Professors Weigh In," *Stanford Daily*, August 20, 2020

unication, put out a report called "Beyond Objectivity." In it, he argues that objectivity has "lost its relevance."[118]

It's hard to believe that the author of a report like this has a faculty position. Even harder to believe that he once ran CBS News.

"Our conclusion?" he writes in the report. "While a few still use the word objectivity, the strong consensus is that the term is a relic of the last century's top-down, one-size-fits-all newsroom culture, usually dominated by a White male editor."

Heyward's solution is to embrace the core values of DEI: "There's a focus on diversity. We're recommending a greater, sharper, more intense focus, which actually treats diversity not just as a statistical or moral imperative, even though it's both of those things, but as a way to unlock new riches from your team."[119]

Walter Williams, author of The Journalist's Creed, started the very first journalism school at the University of Missouri in 1908. Undoubtedly, he would have been horrified to see what happened on his campus in November 2015.

During a protest about racial issues, Assistant Professor of Communications Melissa Click not only tried to block student reporters from covering the event but also grabbed the camera out of one student's hands and threateningly called out, "I need some muscle over here!"

She would later apologetically tell *The New York Times*, "I see a moment where I feel like I'm not representing my best self, and

---

[118] Andrew Heyward, "Opinion: Journalistic 'Objectivity' Has Lost Its Relevance. Maybe That's a Good Thing," Local Media Association, January 31, 2023

[119] Michelle Stermole, "Can a Journalist Be Trustworthy Without Being 'Objective'?" ASU News, January 30, 2023

I see somebody who's trying to do her best to help marginalized students."[120]

Her excuse didn't fly, and she was fired.

So where were all the Melissa Clicks at BU? Where were the radicalized students intent on destroying the foundational principles of journalism?

At some point, it hit me. The social justice warriors started infiltrating newsrooms in the early 2010s. And here I was, in 2025, roaming the dreary halls of BU looking for them. I was about a decade too late. It would be like someone going to a university in 1981 trying to find all the hippies and flower children.

Based on what I saw at my alma mater, one of the more prestigious journalism schools in the country, there is hope for the future. The students seem serious, ambitious, and have a very clear-headed sense of what their mission is.

If only the same could have been said for broadcast news in the mid-2010s.

On a summer day in 2016, there was another high-profile police shooting. This time, it was livestreamed for the whole world to see. Yet again, news reporters would betray the public's trust, making another mad rush to judgment.

[120] Daniel Victor, "Melissa Click, Missouri Professor, Defends Her Actions Against Student Journalist," *New York Times*, February 19, 2016

Chapter 9
Trigger Finger

The good-natured thirty-two-year-old who ran the cafeteria at the J.J. Hill Montessori Magnet School in St. Paul, Minnesota, was simply known as "Mr. Phil."

The school's five hundred-plus students could always count on him to greet them with a smile, a high-five, and some extra snacks he'd surreptitiously slip into their hands.

Mr. Phil had worked at the school for more than a decade, and few could remember what life was like before he got there. He was an integral part of the campus, a part of its spirit.

As one parent described him, he was like "Mr. Rogers with dreadlocks."[121]

There was something the school community could never have imagined about Mr. Phil: Once he left the school grounds

[121] Douglas Belkin, "Philando Castile Remembered as 'Mr. Rogers with Dreadlocks,'" *Wall Street Journal*, July 7, 2016

and got behind the wheel of a car, he became an entirely different person—an outlaw, known by his legal name: Philando Castile.

It was an inexplicable phenomenon. Castile was ultra-conscientious about his work but behaved like an irresponsible child when it came to driving. Over the last fourteen years of his life, Castile was stopped forty-nine separate times by the police and was convicted of thirty-five different driving-related charges.[122]

Those convictions were for things like speeding, rolling through red lights, and driving without insurance. He was so reckless that for one six-year stretch, he drove without a valid license.[123]

Each time Castile got arrested, he would call his mom, Valerie, to pick him up at the police station and drive him to the impound lot so he could get his car back. Valerie may have been disappointed in her son's behavior, but she was incensed with the police, convinced that Philando, who was African American, was being racially profiled. She would beg him to file an official complaint with the police department, but he never would.

July 6, 2016, was a hot and lazy Wednesday in St. Paul. School was out for the summer, so Castile had the full day in front of him. He went to his hairstylist to touch up his locks, got some takeout from Taco Bell, and brought it over to his sister's house for dinner. He then headed back to his apartment to pick up his girlfriend, Diamond Reynolds, and her four-year-old daughter, Dae'Anna, for a trip to the grocery store.

The apartment was shabby and located in a crime-ridden part of St. Paul. But Diamond didn't mind one bit. To her, it was paradise.

---

[122] Robin Washington, "Is Philando Castile the Ultimate Casualty of Driving While Black?" The Marshall project, July 11, 2016

[123] Sharon LaFraniere and Mitch Smith, "Philando Castile Was Pulled Over 49 Times in 13 Years, Often for Minor Infractions," *New York Times*, July 16, 2016

Reynolds had lived a hard twenty-six years. She was pretty and outgoing but had the unfortunate habit of being attracted to trouble.

Diamond was a high school dropout who spent the ensuing years going through a series of bad jobs and boyfriends. When she was twenty-two, she had her daughter, Dae'Anna, out of wedlock. It was around this time that she first started dating Philando. The two had a rocky, on-again, off-again relationship. Diamond craved excitement, and Philando was not that kind of guy. A big night for him was playing video games and going to bed before midnight. One of Diamond's friends once asked her, "Isn't it boring dating a mute button?"[124]

Diamond would break up with Philando, date jerky guys, get her heart broken, and then come back to him.

After their last break-up, Diamond hit rock bottom. She was flat-out broke, living in a homeless shelter and had so few earthly possessions, they fit into just two suitcases.

Philando—with his steady salary, 401(k), and a big-screen TV in his bedroom—offered her a lifeline. He was willing to get back together, but only if she and her daughter moved into his apartment.

It finally dawned on Diamond that boring wasn't so bad after all, and she agreed.

Philando was a steadying influence on Reynolds. She was finally starting to play the role of a responsible adult and mother. She got herself two jobs: one at a dollar store, and another cleaning rooms in a motel.

---

124 Eli Saslow, "'For Diamond Reynolds, Trying to Move Past 10 Tragic Minutes of Video,'" *Washington Post*, September 10, 2016

Even though Diamond had a checkered past, Philando never seemed to hold it against her. He showered her with gifts and doted on Dae'Anna like she was his own.

The two were starting to talk about getting married.

As Diamond would later say of the man she once found so painfully boring, "Every mother would want to have someone like my babe. Every woman would want a hard-working man with no kids like my babe. Every woman would want a man to accept their child out of wedlock that was not his, everyone would want that man to be their son, their brother, their husband."[125]

On that same hot July night, Jeronimo Yanez and his partner, Joseph Kauser, were riding in their patrol car near the Minnesota State Fairgrounds in the small suburb of Falcon Heights.

The two were longtime friends. They had met in college at Minnesota State University, Mankato, and both graduated the same year.

Between the two, Yanez was the better student, finishing near the very top of the class. It was an amazing achievement for someone who was not born into privilege.

Raised in the working-class neighborhood of South St. Paul, Minnesota, Yanez had always dreamed of a career in law enforcement, but he had few role models. No one in his large Latino family had even graduated college. His relatives had jobs, but he didn't know anyone who had an actual career.

Now, here he was, with his college buddy turned professional partner, working for the St. Anthony Police Department, and by all accounts, excelling.

---

[125] Greg Hanlon, "Philando Castile's Girlfriend Diamond Reynolds After Dallas Police Ambush, 'I Want Justice for Everyone,'" *People*, July 8, 2016

They'd been on the job for five years, and neither had received a single complaint.

Yanez's boss called his twenty-eight-year-old officer "energetic" and "intelligent" and noted that he had "a real sound ability when it comes to communicating and relating with people."[126]

At around 9:04 p.m., the officers spotted Philando, Diamond, and Dae'Anna as they were returning home from their trip to the grocery store. Philando was driving his big boat of a car: a white 1997 Oldsmobile Eighty Eight LS. Yanez would later claim that he noticed one of the car's brake lights was out, even though some witnesses disputed this.

But Yanez had another reason to be suspicious of Philando. Four days earlier, two Black men with dreadlocks had robbed a Super USA convenience store, about four miles away. The men had been caught on surveillance video, and Yanez had studied the footage.

He radioed into police dispatch and said Philando looked like one of the suspects because of his "wide-set nose."[127]

Yanez followed the Olds for about thirty seconds, before activating his police lights. Philando knew this drill all too well and immediately pulled over.

Yanez did not run Castile's plates, so he didn't know about his lengthy arrest record as he approached the car.

At 9:05 p.m., Yanez stepped up to the driver's side window and calmly greeted Castile, "Hello, sir."

126 Associated Press, "Philando Castile Case: Who Are the Key Figures in Trial of Officer Jeronimo Yanez?" NBC News, May 30, 2017

127 "Cops May Have Thought Philando Castile Was a Robbery Suspect, Noting 'Wide-set Nose,' Dispatch Audio Indicates," ABC News, July 11, 2016

"How are you?" Philando responded, also sounding calm and collected.

"Good. The reason I pulled you over is your brake lights are out, so you have only one active brake light. That's your passenger-side one. Your third brake light which is up here on top, and then this one back here, that's going to be out."

As Yanez was saying this, Kauser slowly crept up to the passenger side of the car.

"You have your license and insurance?" Yanez asked.

Philando fumbled around in his car for a moment, before handing over his proof of insurance.

He then informed Officer Yanez, "Sir, I have to tell you I do have a firearm on me."

Officer Yanez calmly said "*OK, OK,*" and then warned, "Don't reach for it then."

As he was saying this, Officer Yanez began to slowly move his hand towards his own firearm.

And then, all of a sudden, Yanez's tone changed, and he urgently called out, "Don't pull it out!"

"I'm not pulling it out!"

"Don't pull it out!!"

This was the critical moment in the encounter. Both sides agreed that Philando was reaching for something in that life-or-death moment. Diamond Reynolds would claim he was reaching for his wallet so he could show the officer his driver's license. Yanez would say he was reaching for the gun. But either way, Philando was taking an enormous chance—reaching for anything just moments after telling the officer he had a weapon in the car.

The legal question, of course, would become whether it had been reasonable for Jeronimo Yanez to fear for his life in that moment. He would testify that the image of his wife and baby flashed before his eyes. He thought he was in danger: It was fight or flight.

Yanez then did something he had never done before in his five years of law enforcement: He fired his weapon at a suspect. Not just once, but seven times. Five of the bullets hit Castile; two of them went straight into his heart.

Diamond cried out, "You just killed my boyfriend!"

Philando, slowly bleeding out, used his last words to profess his innocence: "I wasn't reaching."

"He wasn't reaching," echoed Diamond.

"Don't pull it out!" screamed Yanez. He now seemed completely unhinged, screaming at the top of his lungs.

"He wasn't," insisted Diamond calmly.

"Don't move!" Yanez shouted hysterically.

Maybe it was because Diamond Reynolds had already seen so much in her life, but somehow, in that terrifying moment, she found the strength to remain preternaturally calm. "Oh man," she said, "I can't believe you just did that."

Diamond opened the passenger door but didn't dare to get out as Officer Yanez screamed, "Don't move! Don't move!"

"Oh my God, I'm shaking," Diamond cried out, allowing some emotion to creep into her voice.

Yanez was like a record player, skipping over the same part of the song again and again. "Don't move!" he screamed, his weapon pointed straight at Diamond.

"Don't move, baby!" Diamond implored her boyfriend, even though that seemed more like a wish than an actual request. The life was quickly draining out of Philando Castile.

"Code three!" Yanez shouted into his radio. "Get the baby girl out of here!" At this point, Kauser, who was standing by the passenger side of Castile's car, gathered Dae'Anna and got her out of harm's way.

Right around this time, just forty seconds after her boyfriend had been fatally shot, Reynolds had the presence of mind to begin livestreaming what was happening on Facebook. Her account of the shooting would be watched by tens of millions of people worldwide.

"We got pulled over for a busted taillight in the back," Diamond announced to the world, as she showed Castile dying in the driver's seat, his once white T-shirt drenched in crimson. "And the police…he killed my boyfriend. He's licensed to carry."

As Diamond spoke, Castile could be heard moaning.

"He was trying to get out his ID. His wallet out of his pocket. He let the officer know he has a firearm and he was reaching for his wallet and the officer just shot him in his arm. We're waiting…"

At this point, Diamond's calm play-by-play was interrupted by Yanez, who remained visibly agitated. "Ma'am, just keep your hands where they are!" he ordered, his voice raised and quivering.

"I will, sir. No worries," Diamond replied nonchalantly. "He just shot his arm off. We got pulled over…"

Officer Yanez was coming unglued. He began to argue with Diamond on the livestream, "I told him not to reach for it. I told him to get his hands off it!"

"You told him to get his ID, sir," replied Diamond, cool as the other side of the pillow. "His driver's license. Oh my God, please don't tell me he's dead."

Diamond panned the camera over to Castile who was now slumped over, motionless.

The following night, ABC's David Muir kicked off his coverage with, "We begin tonight with that chilling piece of video livestreamed on Facebook in the moments after a man is shot by police."

At this point, the only hard piece of evidence journalists had in the case was Diamond Reynolds's livestream, which she had started *after* the shooting. If the old, foundational rules of journalism still applied, her version of what happened would have been treated with a healthy amount of skepticism. After all, it was her boyfriend who had been shot and killed by the police: She wasn't exactly an objective witness. The police account deserved, at the very least, equal weight.

But, just like in the previous high-profile cases of police violence, that's not how it played out.

Within forty-eight hours, Diamond Reynolds had lawyered up and was making the rounds of national newscasts.

On MSNBC, Tamron Hall interviewed Reynolds, her lawyer by her side, and asked a series of softball questions. Admittedly, Diamond had just suffered an immense loss, and was a very sympathetic person, but Hall had an obligation to gently challenge the narrative, to see if there might have been more to the story than a rogue cop gunning down an innocent man. Instead, she asked puffballs like, "When you see the video that you uploaded for the world to see, does it even seem real at this point?"

On *Good Morning America*, George Stephanopoulos also gave Diamond the kid-glove treatment. He offered her gushing compliments masquerading as questions: "I think all of America has been so struck by the kind of composure and strength you showed during that horrifying few minutes with the police officer. Can you explain how you remained so calm and how you decided to shoot that video?"

It is important to note that there had never been any complaints accusing Jeronimo Yanez of treating suspects of color poorly. No one ever stepped forward and said they'd heard him making racist comments or jokes. In fact, other than his statement about the suspect's "wide-set nose," which some might argue was stereotyping, there wasn't a single shred of evidence to suggest that Yanez pulled Philando over because of his skin color.

Yet, the media allowed Diamond and her lawyer to casually accuse the officer of doing just that. "If we were Caucasian, we would have not been stopped," Diamond claimed unchallenged on MSNBC.

Her attorney, Larry Rogers, chimed in: "Racism had something to do with it, unfortunately."

These statements, unsubstantiated and incendiary, were never contextualized.

The fact that Yanez was Latino, and not White, was glossed over as just an inconvenient detail.

What happened next followed a familiar pattern.

First came the rush to judgment.

Celebrities, once again, seemed determined to prove that they had no concept of due process.

John Legend tweeted, "So many people work so hard to find a reason why executing a human being during a routine traffic stop is ok. IT'S NOT OK."[128]

Josh Groban posted, "There are so many broken, backwards issues at play here it's numbing to digest. #PhilandoCastile #AltonSterling #blacklivesmatter."

---

128 John Lynch, "Celebrities Are Outraged and Heartbroken Over the Deadly Police Shootings of Alton Sterling and Philando Castile," Business Insider, July 7, 2016

Chance the Rapper apparently felt like one livestream video was sufficient evidence to convict, because he told his millions of followers, "These guys murdered this man with his 4-year-old daughter in the backseat? Is there any situation where police get arrested? Or convicted?"

Over the next forty-eight hours, broadcast coverage casually accepted the premise that Jeronimo Yanez murdered Castile and that his primary motivation was the victim's race.

Philando's sister, Allysza, told a TV reporter, "It's just like we're animals. It's basically modern-day lynching that we're seeing going on, except we're not getting hung by a tree anymore—we're getting killed on camera."[129]

Even the "Gray Lady" of journalism, *The New York Times*, ran an editorial the next day entitled "When Will the Killing Stop?" In it, Castile's mom is quoted, without context, saying, "I think he was just Black in the wrong place."[130]

In the past, elected leaders would be extremely careful about commenting on a case as sensitive as this one. The atmosphere was tense, and the threat of violence hung in the air. But when Minnesota's progressive Governor Mark Dayton was asked about Philando Castile's shooting, he didn't call for calm or ask people to wait until all the facts came in—instead, he threw oil right on the fire: "Would this have happened if the passengers in the van were White? I don't think it would have, so I'm forced to confront, and I think all of us in Minnesota are forced to confront, that this kind of racism exists."

---

[129] WCCO News, "Timeline of Key Events in Philando Castile Shooting," June 14, 2017

[130] Editorial Board, "When Will the Killing Stop?" *New York Times*, July 7, 2016

The mask of prudence and judiciousness had been ripped off, and now it seemed like everyone—from journalists to celebrities to elected officials—was going from zero to KKK in no time flat.

Broadcast news did run some obligatory sound bites from Yanez's lawyer, Thomas Kelly, who insisted, "The shooting had nothing to do with race and everything to do with the presence of that gun."[131]

But the police perspective on this shooting was just a perfunctory part of most news packages, which were dominated by overwrought family members, angry community leaders, and protesters who, once again, were flooding the streets of cities throughout America.

On July 9, 2016, NBC News's Kristen Welker led off her package with, "Thousands of demonstrators have continued to take to the streets marching against violence of all kinds. Most have been peaceful, aimed at creating a dialogue between police and communities, but a small number of protests have boiled over, putting police on constant guard."

By this point, watching legacy news had become an exercise in being able to read between the lines.

When Kristen Welker said "a small number of protests have boiled over," what she really meant was that the protests had turned violent throughout the country.

In Minneapolis, protesters chanting "We're peaceful. Y'all violent" shut down Interstate 94 and then decided they actually did have an appetite for destruction, throwing rocks, bottles, and firecrackers at the police. Twenty-one officers were hurt, and more than one hundred people were arrested.

---

131 Mitch Smith, "Minnesota Officer Was 'Reacting to the Presence of a Gun,' Lawyer Says," *New York Times*, July 9, 2016

St. Paul Police Chief Todd Axtell was furious, telling reporters, "It's really a disgrace. Protesters last night turned into criminals, and I am absolutely disgusted by the acts of some. Not all, but some."[132]

In Baton Rouge, another one hundred protesters were arrested after blocking streets and throwing rocks at police.

In Atlanta, New York, and Oakland, protesters blocked roads, threw dangerous projectiles at cops, and committed isolated cases of looting and vandalism.

Broadcast news was certainly not going to pass up the chance to run footage of the violence—it was, after all, "great TV"—but they had now gotten into the exhausting and credibility-killing habit of verbally minimizing the destruction at the exact same time they were showing it. So, even though viewers were being fed wall-to-wall coverage of fires and lawlessness, they were being told to not believe their lying eyes.

Protests—mostly peaceful, of course—continued throughout the summer of 2016. To its credit, the Ramsey County DA's office did not pull a Marilyn Mosby and rush to press charges against Yanez.

Instead, the lawyers took four months to carefully review the evidence before finally reaching a decision on November 16.

County Attorney John Choi made the announcement at a news conference carried live by many of the legacy news outlets: "I have come to the conclusion that there simply was no justification for the use of deadly force by Officer Yanez in this case."

---

132 "102 Arrested, 21 Officers Injured After I-94 Protest," CBS News, July 10, 2016

Choi was going to charge Yanez with second-degree manslaughter and two counts of dangerous discharge of a firearm. If convicted on all counts, Yanez faced twenty years in prison.

Choi's judiciousness seemed to please no one. Police advocates believed the progressive DA had it out for law enforcement.

Community activists and protesters believed the charges were too lenient.

Either way, it was going to be a very difficult case for prosecutors to win. To get the manslaughter charge to stick, they would have to prove that Yanez acted with "negligence" and "recklessness"—legal terms open to a lot of interpretation.

To get convictions on the two counts of "dangerous discharge of a firearm," prosecutors would have to prove that Yanez put Diamond and Dae'Anna's lives at risk by discharging his weapon.

Ultimately, most experts agreed that the trial would come down to one thing: Who would the jury believe—Diamond or Yanez?

As prosecutors were preparing their case, they got some devastating news. Their star witness had gotten herself in a credibility-compromising jam.

On March 3, 2017, Diamond Reynolds was arrested and accused of hitting a woman in the head with a hammer with so much force, the victim blacked out and had to be rushed to the hospital. Reynolds was charged with felony assault and, if convicted, faced up to twelve years in prison.

This should have been the lead story on every newscast.

But the same reporters who had conducted fawning interviews with Diamond after Philando's shooting now chose to gaslight their audiences. CBS and Fox, to their credit, covered the story, but the other legacy news divisions either gave it a quick mention or ignored it altogether.

It is inconceivable to think that if the roles were reversed, if Yanez had been the one arrested for a felony assault, it wouldn't have been a huge story.

On May 30, 2017, Jeronimo Yanez's trial got underway.

Fifteen jurors were selected: thirteen White and two Black. Six of the jurors were women; nine, men.

On June 6, the prosecution called Diamond Reynolds to the stand. Wearing a black top, accessorized by a large cross, she wasn't as poised as she had been on the Facebook livestream, but that vulnerability probably helped her connect with the jury.

"I felt broken, hurt, confused, lost," she testified,[133] as at least two jury members dabbed their eyes.

Reynolds was on the stand for two days and largely stuck to her original story.

On cross-examination, she did get tripped up a few times.

First, Diamond admitted that she and Philando were daily pot smokers and that there was marijuana in the car when they'd been pulled over. But she insisted she wasn't high at the time of the traffic stop. This was a major point of contention in the trial. Toxicology reports showed high levels of THC in Castile's body, even though the prosecution argued that just because he had the drug in his system didn't necessarily mean he was stoned during his fatal encounter with Officer Yanez.

Yanez's defense attorneys also got Diamond to admit that she hadn't been entirely truthful during her Facebook livestream. For example, she had said that Castile had his hands up during the traffic stop, but now she conceded that it wasn't true—his hands were never up during the encounter with Yanez.

---

133 Mitch Smith, "In Court, Diamond Reynolds Recounts Moments Before a Police Shooting," *New York Times*, June 6, 2017

She had also claimed that Philando was reaching for his wallet when Yanez opened fire, but now she said that wasn't quite accurate either—he had actually been trying to unbuckle his seat belt.

On June 9, Officer Yanez took the stand. On the livestream, he had seemed completely unglued and hysterical. In court, he tried to appear calm and stoic, but he wasn't able to maintain his composure and ended up crying on the witness stand a couple of times.

"I was scared to death. I thought I was going to die. I had no choice," he told the jurors, his voice thick with emotion.[134]

Yanez told jurors he saw Philando's gun before opening fire: "I was able to see the top of the slide and the back of the tab of the firearm and that's when I engaged with Mr. Castile and shot him."

During closing arguments, prosecutor Jeffrey Paulsen summed up the state's argument: "He [Yanez] was making assumptions and jumping to conclusions without engaging in the dialogue he was trained to have in citizen encounters like this. And that's his fault, not the fault of Philando Castile."

Defense attorney Earl Gray argued that Yanez had every reason to be on high alert as he approached the car. "We have [Castile] ignoring commands. He's got a gun. He might be the robber. He's got marijuana in his car. Those are the things in Officer Yanez's head."

On June 12, 2017, the jury began deliberating.

---

134 Matt Furber and Mitch Smith, "'I Had No Choice,' Minnesota Officer Testifies on Shooting," *New York Times*, June 9, 2017

It didn't take long for them to acquit Yanez on the two counts of dangerous discharge of a firearm. They had studied photos of the crime scene, and everyone agreed that Yanez was pointing the gun away from Diamond and her four-year-old girl when he fired at Castile.

The manslaughter charge was going to be a lot more challenging.

The first vote was 10–2 for an acquittal. Jurors would later take pains to point out that the two Black members of the jury were *not* among the holdouts.

For the next four days, the jury argued, cried, and debated.

As one anonymous juror later told Minnesota Public Radio, "What happened to Philando is not OK to any of us. Nobody felt good about any part of this. We were just asked to do a job and we did it."[135]

Ultimately, unlike the media, the jurors, who described themselves as average working folk, were able to put their emotions aside and answer the question before them. And that question was not "Did Jeronimo Yanez do the right thing when he shot Castile?" The question was, "Did the prosecution prove that he had committed manslaughter beyond a reasonable doubt?"

"It just came down to us not being able to see what was going on in the car," the same anonymous juror told Public Radio. "Some of us were saying that there was some recklessness there, but that doesn't stick because we didn't know what escalated the situation. Was he really seeing a gun? We felt [Yanez] was an honest guy…and in the end, we had to go on his word, and that's what it came down to."

---

135 Tom Weber and MPR Staff, "Yanez Juror: 'Nobody Was OK With It,'" MPR News, June 23, 2017

On June 16, 2017, Scott Pelley led off the CBS Evening News with the jury's decision: "Today, in Minnesota, a police officer was found not guilty in the shooting death of a Black driver."

Veteran reporter Dean Reynolds filed the lead package. It was long on outrage, starting off with Castile's mom screaming, "This city killed my son and the murderer gets away!" It featured soundbites from angry protesters and disappointed prosecutors but only one quick bite from the victorious defense attorneys.

ABC's Eva Pilgrim's story featured an even higher toxic imbalance. She focused on anger at the jury's decision but didn't bother to include a single soundbite from the defense.

Philando Castile's case was another Groundhog Day of terrible reporting. A suspect dead at the hands of an officer, followed by an immediate presumption of guilt, a credulous acceptance of all witness accounts, the minimization of the violence caused by "protesters," the platforming of baseless accusations of racism, and finally the assumption that yet another diverse jury would "do the right thing" and convict.

To be clear, unlike Darren Wilson, George Zimmerman, or the officers charged in the Freddie Gray fiasco, Jeronimo Yanez's actions were far more difficult to defend.

During his encounter with Castile, Yanez was completely unhinged. It is reasonable to believe that he panicked and started firing indiscriminately. It's also possible that Castile was reaching for his gun, just like Yanez claimed. Maybe in Philando's stoned mind, he wanted to show the officer the weapon—*See, this is the gun. It's registered.*

We'll never know. It was the officer's word against Diamond's, and her story had some troubling inconsistencies.

This is our system. When in doubt, a tie goes to the defendant.

Officer Yanez didn't get to celebrate his acquittal for long. The night of the jury's decision, the city of St. Anthony fired him. He never went back to law enforcement, which was probably a good thing for all concerned. He is now a teacher at a Catholic school.

The Castile family eventually settled with the city for $3 million, and Diamond Reynolds settled for $800,000.

Reynolds stood trial for the alleged hammer attack and was acquitted of the most serious charges but found guilty of a misdemeanor assault. She ended up getting one year of probation.

On June 21, five days after Yanez's trial ended, the state released the dashcam video of the shooting, which was the same footage the jury saw at trial.

The video is definitely disturbing: It shows a man getting gunned down in front of his girlfriend and a small child. But it doesn't tell us anything about whether the shooting was justified. The video comes from a camera positioned inside the squad car, so nothing inside Castile's car is visible.

Yet, for some reason, to CNN's Don Lemon, it was the most important video since the Zapruder film: "I would sit down and watch this because it's shocking. It's shocking dashcam video. It's been released of the fatal police shooting of Philando Castile last year. Few people had seen the video. It was shown in court during the trial of Jeronimo Yanez who was acquitted of the killing of Castile.... I have to warn you: This is very graphic and it's difficult to watch. Here it is."

As an illustration of how sick the culture had gotten, Trevor Noah, winner of multiple Emmys and NAACP Image Awards, went on the air that night and had this to say about the footage: "What they [the jury] are saying is that in America it is reasonable to be afraid of a person just because they are Black."

By casually tossing around evidence-free accusations of racism, the media was carelessly ripping open America's deepest wound.

Days after Philando's death, a former army reservist, inflamed by what he had come to believe was law enforcement's war on Black people, gave us a preview of how volatile the situation had become.

He decided it was time for Black people to get their revenge. And he crowned himself their avenger.

Chapter 10

Ambush!

On July 7, 2016, Private First Class Micah Xavier Johnson loaded up his vehicle for combat. It was a hot and sticky night. Even though the sun had just gone down, temperatures were still in the mid to upper eighties. But Johnson didn't have time to worry about comfort. He was on a life-or-death mission.

Johnson took stock of his black Chevrolet Tahoe.

It was packed with his tactical gear: a bulletproof vest, two semi-automatic pistols, and an AK-74 assault-style rifle—a combat weapon long used by the Russian army.

Satisfied, Johnson got behind the wheel of his SUV and began the roughly twenty-five-minute drive from the middle-class suburb of Mesquite, Texas, where he lived, to downtown Dallas, where he planned to kill.

It was a Thursday night, one day after the shooting of Philando Castile, and two days after the fatal police shooting of another Black man, Alton Sterling, in Baton Rouge, Louisiana.

In a now familiar pattern, that case garnered widespread sympathetic media coverage, but ultimately, the state concluded that the White officers acted in a "reasonable and justifiable manner." The DOJ would also look into the shooting and decline to press charges.

But Micah Johnson, who had just turned twenty-five, wouldn't live long enough to find any of that out.

There was a large BLM protest going on in Dallas that night, and he knew that lots of police officers would be there, keeping an eye on things.

His goal was to take out as many of those officers as possible. And if everything went according to plan, he would only kill the White ones.

As with most mass killers, the people who knew Johnson best insisted they didn't see it coming. He was described as "quiet" and a "loner." His mother told The Blaze, "He got upset when we ran over a squirrel."

One neighbor, a woman named Courtney Williams, remembered him as a church-going teenager: "He was just a quiet kid. No attitude, no trouble with school. Just a normal kid."[136]

Another neighbor, Angela Harris, said, "This is a nice place. I don't know why he would've been so angry."[137]

Johnson's parents split up when he was four years old, and his dad gained custody. At some point during high school, Micah moved in with his mom, Delphine, who had a stable job at

[136] Richard Fausset, Manny Fernandez, and Alan Blinder, "Micah Johnson, Gunman in Dallas, Honed Military Skills to a Deadly Conclusion," *New York Times*, July 9, 2016

[137] Jay-Newton Small, "Alleged Dallas Shooter Micah Johnson Was 'Norman Kid' from Middle-Class Neighborhood," *Time*, July 9, 2016

Citibank and owned a Leave It to Beaver-style two-story brick home in Mesquite. Everything about the house screamed "American Dream": the perfectly manicured front lawn that Micah often mowed, the tree-lined street, the American flags planted on people's lawns; even the name of the subdivision screamed comfort—Camelot.

But if moving in with his mom was supposed to help Johnson focus on his future, it didn't work. He barely graduated high school in 2009, with a 1.98 GPA. Out of 453 students in his graduating class, he ranked number 430.[138]

Johnson always dreamed of a career in law enforcement, but because of his terrible grades, that door was closed to him. So he decided to join the Army Reserve instead.

"[He] loved this country, he wanted to protect his country," Delphine said of her son's ambitions.[139]

Part of his mandatory training involved taking a rifle test. He did very poorly in that exam too, ranking near the bottom of his class.

His high school classmate, Justin Garner, who ended up in the same reserve unit, would later say, "I loved him to death, but that guy was not really a good soldier. There were certain technical skills you need as a soldier that he was lacking, like shooting, if you can believe it."[140]

Serving in the Army Reserve only takes up about one month of the year, so Micah had to find a full-time job to support himself. For a couple of years, he was a shift manager at Jimmy

---

138 Associated Press, "When Army Career Ended in Disgrace, Dallas Gunman Was Ostracized," *Chicago Tribune*, August 22, 2019

139 Rachel Herron, "Watch: Parents of Micah Xavier Johnson Speak Out," BET, July 11, 2016.

140 Associated Press, "When Army Career Ended in Disgrace, Dallas Gunman Was Ostracized," *Chicago Tribune*, August 22, 2019

John's. He then became something called a "quality assurance specialist" at a nearby truck plant. That might seem like quite a leap for someone working in fast food, but Johnson was training to become a carpentry and masonry specialist in the Reserve. Apparently, that experience was needed for his new position, and he was able to make the jump.

Johnson's squad leader was a man named Gilbert Fischbach. He remembers Johnson well and was also unimpressed with his prospects as a soldier. He says one of the reasons Johnson performed so poorly was that he was distracted, after developing a huge crush on one of his female squad mates.

"They were good friend," Fischbach recalls. "Pretty much inseparable. We had to break them up a few times."

There was one major problem with the relationship: It was mostly one-sided. Micah was in love with her, and she just saw him as a close friend—even though that seemed to come with the occasional benefits.

According to Micah's mom, the woman slept over at the house a few times. Delphine claims the girl was trying to win her over, sometimes showing up at the house with gifts.

This unidentified young woman would play a huge role in Johnson's descent into madness.

In November 2013, Johnson's unit was deployed to Afghanistan as part of the 420th Engineer Brigade. He and his crush would be going overseas together.

Everything seemed to be going well for the first six months of the deployment, but in May 2014, the woman Micah was obsessed with made a disturbing discovery: Four pairs of underwear were missing from her laundry bag. She reported it to her superiors, who took the complaint very seriously.

Officers went from bunk to bunk, making surprise inspections, in an effort to identify the thief.

When they got to Micah's quarters, they found the stolen undergarments.

This is part of what the officer wrote in the official military report:

"I ended up finding underwear under the mattress.... Once I see the underwear, I asked PFC Johnson, 'What was that?' He said it was nothing. Johnson grabbed the underwear as soon as I asked what it was."[141]

Johnson made the absurd claim that the female underwear was actually his and then tried to toss the stolen items into a dumpster.

The military immediately took away all of his weapons and placed him under twenty-four-hour escort, which meant he couldn't even take a shower or go to the bathroom without someone watching him. It was a humiliating turn of events. Word got out about what happened, and Johnson became a pariah on the base.

The woman who once considered Johnson a close friend was devastated when she found out he was the underwear thief.

"She was just torn apart," Fischbach would later say. "Not only had her best friend betrayed her trust but [he] had done something that was extraordinarily out of character."[142]

---

141 Associated Press, "Dallas Shooter Was Accused of Sexual Misconduct, Military Says," CBS News, July 29, 2016

142 Associated Press, "When Army Career Ended in Disgrace, Dallas Gunman Was Ostracized," *Chicago Tribune*, August 22, 2019

Micah's former crush filed an official sexual harassment claim, asked for a protective order, and suggested he get "mental help."

Johnson was sent back home to Texas. His military lawyer had drawn up papers, hoping the army would go easy on Micah and give him an "other-than-honorable" discharge. Somehow, he was given an honorable discharge, leading Johnson's own lawyer to shake his head and say, "Someone really screwed up."[143]

Johnson came back to Mesquite a broken man. His father, James, said he "became a loner" and "didn't like people." His mom described him as a "hermit."[144]

Johnson was adrift.

He tried to get work in construction but didn't have much luck.

He managed to get a job with a company called Touch of Kindness, which paid him to care for his autistic younger brother, who lived with him and his mom. It was a strange arrangement that involved government funds, but by all accounts, Johnson was conscientious about caring for his sibling.

The CFO of the company described Johnson as a "good employee" and a "family man."[145]

That was the side Micah Johnson was showing to outsiders. Privately, he was devolving into a spiral of rage and resentment.

His Facebook page showed his support for the New Black Panther party, which is considered a hate group by the Anti-Defamation League and the Southern Poverty Law Center.

---

143 Rachel Herron, "Here's Why Micah Xavier Johnson's Honorable Discharge From the Army Left Many Confused," BET, July 14, 2016

144 Jason Howerton, "New Details Emerge as Parents of Dallas Cop Killer Micah Johnson Break Silence," The Blaze, July 11, 2016

145 "Dallas Shooting Suspect Micah Xavier Johnson Had Rifles, Bombmaking Materials in His Home, Police Say," ABC News, July 9, 2016

Its leaders have said things like, "Every White man and every Jew is a devil by nature,"[146] and many members have expressed deeply homophobic sentiments.

Micah's profile featured the red, black, and green flag of the Black Liberation Army, an anti-capitalist extremist group that has engaged in domestic terrorism.

Perhaps these hate groups were providing him with an outlet for all the feelings of shame and pain he was experiencing after his humiliation in Afghanistan.

Johnson's social media interactions give us insights into his state of mind during this time. When a friend posted a video of a whale killing, Micah left this comment: "Why do so many Whites (not all) enjoy killing and participating in the deaths of innocent beings."[147] He then added, "Then they stand around and smile while their picture is taken with a hung, burned and brutalized black person."

He liked another social media post that read, "Kill everything blue that moves."

Johnson, who had been lackadaisical about almost everything he'd ever set out to accomplish, was suddenly highly motivated to carry out a massacre of police officers. He signed up for self-defense classes and began doing tactical drills in his backyard.

He started keeping a journal in which he outlined and diagrammed his plan of attack. He decided to use wartime "shoot and move" tactics, which he was convinced would confuse his adversaries.

---

146 "New Black Panther Party for Self Defense," Southern Poverty Law Center

147 Gina Cherelus and Erwin Seba, "Dallas Shooting Suspect's Online Posts Reflect Anger, Frustration," Reuters, July 9, 2016

He also began to stockpile weapons in his mom's home: bomb-making materials, five handguns, an assault rifle, and bulletproof vests.

On July 6, he got enraged as he watched the coverage of the Philando Castile shooting. Now, just twenty-four hours later, on this hot summer night, he would strike back. He would show the world that he wasn't someone to mess with, to humiliate, to shame. Micah Johnson would get his revenge.

At 8:57 p.m., Johnson parked his SUV in front of the El Centro Community College in Downtown Dallas. He left his hazard lights flashing and put on his body suit.

He strode purposefully towards Main Street, where officers were blocking traffic for the BLM protest. He didn't waste a second. Micah immediately raised his rifle and opened fire. *Pop! Pop! Pop! Pop!*

Within moments, three officers were dead.

The victims were forty-year-old Michael Krol, who'd been on the job for nine years; Lorne Ahrens, a forty-eight-year-old father of three; and thirty-two-year-old Patrick Zamarripa, a Latino Navy vet, who'd served three tours in Iraq and was the father of two young children.

Johnson injured three other officers in that first flurry and also managed to badly wound one of the protesters, Shetamia Taylor, a Black woman, who instinctively shielded her children when she heard the shots. That move may have saved their lives, because one of Johnson's bullets ended up shattering her tibia. She would undergo extensive surgery and ultimately make a full recovery.

In that exchange of gunfire, Johnson was hit in the leg. He was bleeding but still managed to briskly limp back to the front of the school, near the spot where he'd parked his SUV. Johnson raised his rifle and began firing rounds into the school's glass front door. Two armed school officers were inside, and they fired back, leading to a *Heat*-style shootout. Ultimately, Johnson moved on, but not before wounding both the school cops.

Johnson then spotted forty-three-year-old Brent Thompson, an officer with the Dallas transit system. Johnson stealthily snuck up behind him and gunned the officer down from behind. It was his fourth kill in as many minutes.

At this point, it was about 9:01 p.m. and the Dallas Police were in a state of confusion. Johnson's "shoot and move" tactic was so effective that officers believed there were multiple snipers firing at them in a coordinated attack.

His squad leader, Gilbert Fischbach, would later express surprise that Johnson was able to pull it off: "He didn't seem to be motivated or enthused to learn those types of tactics. These are things he was trained in but never seemed to really care about."[148]

Johnson was no longer the unmotivated soldier, who consistently finished at the bottom of his class. He was now a mass killer, staying one step ahead of an entire police force, which was determined to take him out by any means necessary.

After his fourth kill, Johnson limped around the corner and shot his way into the community college through a separate glass door. He made his way up the stairs to the second floor, staggered through the library, right past a 1,500-piece jigsaw puzzle of The Beatles, and then into a hallway.

Inexplicably, he used his own blood to write the letters "RB" twice on the walls. The meaning of those letters remains a mystery

---

[148] Associated Press, "When Army Career Ended in Disgrace, Dallas Gunman Was Ostracized," *Chicago Tribune*, August 22, 2019

to this day. Some have theorized it might have stood for "righteous blood," a biblical reference from Matthew 23:35.

Johnson then found a window in the hallway and began to shoot down at the police officers stationed below. It was during this flurry that he killed his fifth victim, Officer Michael Smith, a fifty-five-year-old former Army Ranger and father of two, who'd been a Dallas cop for three decades.

At 9:15 p.m., Johnson was finally cornered by SWAT officers in a hallway of the school. He was trapped, with nowhere to run.

For the next four hours, negotiators tried to convince Johnson to surrender, but by this point he was completely unhinged, ranting and raving—not making a lot of sense.

"He basically just lied to us," Dallas Police Chief David Brown told reporters. "Playing games, laughing at us, singing, asking how many officers did he get and that he wanted to kill some more."[149]

Johnson told the negotiators he had planted bombs throughout the city and that they would soon go off, killing more innocent civilians. This was a lie, but in the heat of the moment, no one was taking any chances.

Johnson also told negotiators why he was on this mass killing spree: "He was upset about Black Lives Matter," Brown told reporters. "He was upset about the recent police shootings. The suspect said he was upset at White people. The suspect stated that he wanted to kill White people, especially White officers."[150]

By 1 a.m., negotiations broke down, and Johnson and the SWAT team exchanged about two hundred rounds of fire.

---

[149] Ed Lavandera, "How the Dallas Massacre Unfolded," CNN, July 20, 2016

[150] Manny Fernandez, Richard Pérez-Peña, and Jonah Engel Bromwich, "Five Dallas Officers Were Killed as Payback, Police Chief Says," *New York Times*, July 8, 2016

That's when Police Chief David Brown made a historic decision. Johnson had already killed five of his officers, wounded seven others, and injured two bystanders.

The chief decided he wasn't going to risk any more lives.

So, for the first time in US law enforcement history, Brown ordered officers to strap a robot with a pound of explosives and send it down the hallway to take the suspect out.

At 1:28 a.m., the robot, which resembled Johnny 5 from the 1980s movie *Short Circuit*, was sent down the long hallway where Johnson had been trapped for the previous four hours. Johnson saw the robot coming towards him and immediately put two and two together. He panicked and started firing rounds at it, desperately trying to slow its progress. It didn't work. Seconds later, the bomb exploded.

Micah Johnson's short, tortured life was over.

On *Good Morning America*, Dan Harris opened the broadcast with, "Let's get right to the new developments in the massacre of those five police officers in Dallas. An act of madness that has injected a whole new level of anger and fear in America's already fraught debate over race and law enforcement."

He threw to old friend Matt Gutman, who was doing his best young Pat Riley impression, wearing a gray designer suit over an open white dress shirt, his hair blow-dried and poofy.

And then, the most incredible thing happened. Gutman actually filed a straight, old-school news report. No race-baiting, no wild conjectures; just a balanced, fact-driven account of what happened.

Jake Tapper of CNN conducted a live interview with Dallas Police Chief David Brown, and for the first time in years, a law enforcement official was given a mainstream platform to discuss the anti-police movements sweeping the nation.

"A majority of the African American protesters feel as though their lives don't matter as much to the police," Jake said to Brown. "What do you say to them?"

Brown, who is Black, responded with quiet passion: "We're sworn to protect you and your right to protest, and we'll give our lives for it. It's sort of like being in a relationship where you love that person, but that person can't express or show you love back. I don't know if you've been in a relationship like that before, Jake. But that's a tough relationship to be in. We show our love—because there's no greater love than to give your life for someone, and that's what we're continuing to be willing to do."

"Who do you specifically think needs to show more support to our men and women in blue?" Tapper asked.

It was an underhanded pitch, and Brown swung hard, aiming a line drive right back at Tapper and the rest of legacy media: "Media, public officials, and our communities. How media tells the story. How you sensationalize the video. How you edit the video. Show the whole story—and when you don't know the whole story, say there's more to be determined instead of jumping to conclusions without a full investigation."

It was a striking live television interview—a lifelong cop giving a prominent anchorman a much-needed refresher course on the basics of journalism.

CBS News inexplicably didn't even lead with Johnson's bloodbath, but Jeff Pegues filed a fair piece, making sure to mention, "Police do not believe Johnson had any ties to the Black Lives Matter movement and say he had no criminal record."

This piece of contextualization was critical and belonged in the piece. Micah Johnson had *no* ties to BLM. But, of course, when it was a law enforcement officer pulling the trigger, mainstream news casually accepted the narrative that the shooting was racially motivated, even when there wasn't any evidence to back that up.

Over the next few days, legacy news entertained a public debate about the BLM movement, which, up until Micah Johnson's shooting spree, had gotten a completely free pass from the press. It would be the one and only time critics of BLM would be platformed to challenge the radical movement's agenda.

The New York Times ran a piece entitled "Black Lives Matter Was Gaining Ground. Then a Sniper Opened Fire." In it, Texas's Lieutenant Governor Dan Patrick was quoted as saying, "I do blame former Black Lives Matter protests. This has to stop."[151]

Newspapers reached out to conservative voices for comments.

Rush Limbaugh called BLM "a terrorist group."[152]

Former Alaska Governor Sarah Palin said they were "a farce" and accused them of "trying to weaken America through disunity."

Joe Walsh, a Tea Party congressman from Illinois, tweeted, "This is now war. Watch out Obama. Watch out Black Lives Matter punks. Real America is coming after you."

Enrique Zamarripa, the father of one of the officers Micah Johnson gunned down, filed a $550 million lawsuit against BLM. The suit claimed that the group falsely presented itself as a social

---

[151] Michael Barbaro and Yamiche Alcindor, "Black Lives Matter Was Gaining Ground. Then a Sniper Opened Fire," *New York Times*, July 9, 2016

[152] Aamer Madhani, "Black Lives Matter: Don't Blame Movement for Dallas Police Ambush," *USA Today*, July 8, 2016

justice organization, when, in reality, its true intentions were to "further violence, severe bodily injuries, and death against police officers of all races and ethnicities, Jews, and Caucasians."[153]

The suit was not successful.

However, for the first time since its founding, BLM was facing a PR crisis.

The organization issued a statement, saying in part, "There are some that would use these events to stifle a movement for change and quicken the demise of a vibrant discourse on the human rights of Black Americans. We should reject all of this."

On July 18, 2016, Don Lemon invited David Clarke onto his CNN show to debate whether or not BLM had incited Micah Johnson's horrific mass shooting. The former sheriff of Milwaukee County made for good TV. He was a brash, outspoken, conservative Black man who spoke in support of Donald Trump at the 2016 GOP convention. He was also a bit of a wingnut who once tweeted that it would be justifiable for members of the public to violently attack journalists: "punch them in the nose & MAKE THEM TASTE THEIR OWN BLOOD." His rhetoric was so irresponsible that even Fox News had stopped booking him as a guest.

There were some thoughtful scholars who believed BLM was having a pernicious effect on American society (see Chapter 5), and they could have been invited on the show to have a meaningful exchange of ideas.

Instead, Lemon very consciously chose Clarke.

---

153 J. Weston Phippen, "A Lawsuit Accuses Black Lives Matter of Inciting a 'War on Police,'" *The Atlantic*, November 8, 2016

This tactic is called the "straw man fallacy." Get someone weak or unhinged to advocate for a position, and you immediately discredit it.

David Clarke did not disappoint, telling the CNN audience, "This anti-cop sentiment from this hateful ideology called Black Lives Matter has fueled this rage against American police officers."

Clarke's voice was thick with emotion. Lemon seemed amused, like he was sharing an inside joke with his audience: *See, this is what those "deplorables" are really like.*

"I want to know," Clarke challenged Lemon, "with all the Black-on-Black crime within the United States of America, was there any reporting on that?"

Lemon mugged for the camera and took faux offense to the question: "Please, can we keep it civil."

"I wish you had that message of civility..."

"I'd like to have a conversation..." Lemon tried to interject.

Clarke, like most zealots who are on a roll, just plowed on, talking over Lemon, "...towards this hateful ideology—those purveyors of hate—that's what we do."

Lemon pretended to look disappointed, as if he had been expecting anything more from Clarke when he booked him on his show. Lemon then threw to a commercial break, shaking his head, as if he simply couldn't tolerate Clarke's behavior for a single moment longer.

After a few minutes of selling insurance policies and soft drinks, CNN cut back to Lemon. Clarke was still in the split screen, so apparently he hadn't been asked to leave.

Lemon tried to guilt him: "Sounds like you're accusing me of inciting violence and supporting a narrative I'm not necessarily supporting, and if that's what you're accusing me of, you can leave. I don't support violence of any type."

"This whole anti-police rhetoric is based on a lie. There is no data—and you know this—there is no data, there is no research that proves any of that nonsense. None."

Clarke wasn't the first person to make this argument, even though he was one of the few allowed to voice it on a news broadcast. Despite all the unrest, rage, and anti-police sentiment, where was the smoking gun? Where were the statistics proving that American law enforcement was actually systemically racist?

A thirty-nine-year-old Black Harvard professor decided he was going to be the one to get that data. He was going to make BLM's case for them. But after a year of research, he got a shock—the facts did not back the movement's case. In fact, it was quite the opposite. Yet, when he tried to share this hard truth with the world, he was met with a cancel-culture mob, determined to silence and destroy him.

Chapter 11
The Cancellation of Roland Fryer

If your primary source of information comes from legacy news, chances are you don't know who Roland Fryer is or why his groundbreaking study on police violence caused such a firestorm.

His story was too hot for broadcast news, so the mainstream media simply looked the other way and ignored it entirely: the ultimate crime of omission.

But Fryer's story is revealing, because it shows how the anti-law enforcement movement was taking on the fervor of a religious revival. There was no tolerance for dissent, and anyone who had the audacity to question BLM's rigid dogma risked facing the wrath of an angry and vengeful mob.

By the summer of 2016, American cancel culture, which hadn't even been named yet, was making its presence felt. Online bullies were on the hunt for heretics, and when they found their prey, they showed no mercy. The punishment for thought crimes was severe: Offenders were shamed, fired, doxed, and expelled from polite society. No one got a free pass. Not even a brilliant young rock-star economist who had set out to help activists, only for them to turn on him and make him public enemy number one.

There was a glorious period when Roland Fryer was the darling of the academic elite.

In 2007, at the age of thirty, he was the youngest Black man to become a tenured professor at Harvard.

"As a pure technical economic theorist, he's of the first rate," gushed Lawrence Katz, a Harvard colleague. "But what's really incredible is that he's much more of a broad social theorist."[154]

The following year, *The Economist* named him one of the top eight young economists in the world.

"[Fryer is] destined to be a star. I mean, he's a star already, just a baby star," said legendary Harvard scholar Henry Louis Gates Jr.[155]

In 2011, the MacArthur Foundation gave him a "Genius" award.

Steven Levitt, of *Freakonomics* fame, thought the award was long overdue: "I first met Roland Fryer a decade ago. It didn't take me long to figure out he was a genius."[156]

And in 2015, he won the highly prestigious John Bates Clark Medal. Previous winners include legends like Milton Friedman, Paul Krugman, and Joseph Stiglitz.

---

154 Stephen J. Dubner, "Towards a Unified Theory of Black America," *New York Times Magazine*, March 20, 2005.

155 Stephen J. Dubner, "Towards a Unified Theory of Black America," *New York Times Magazine*, March 20, 2005.

156 Steven D. Levitt, "Roland Fryer: It's Official, He's a 'Genius,'" Freakanomics.com, September 26, 2011

If it's possible for an economist to become a pop-culture star, Fryer was on the fast track to becoming one. Good-looking, opinionated, and comfortable in front of the camera, he made otherwise boring academic symposiums interesting with his blunt and oftentimes provocative proclamations. He had the energy and cadence of a stand-up comedian—something he actually dabbled in on the occasional open mic night.

Fryer was so entertaining, he was invited to be a guest on *The Colbert Report*, making him one of the few Ivy League professors to appear on late-night comedy shows, which usually feature vapid conversations with singers, actors, comedians, and athletes.

While Fryer definitely had a flair for showmanship, his true passion was education. Specifically, he was determined to use data-driven analysis to find ways to improve the performances of African American students.

His work caught the attention of New York Mayor Michael Bloomberg, who appointed him Chief Equality Officer of the city's Department of Education. For the 2008–09 school year, Fryer taught two classes a week at Harvard and then took the train to New York to work his second job.

"I basically want to figure out where Blacks went wrong," Fryer told a magazine writer, in his typical blunt style. "One could rattle off all the statistics about Blacks not doing so well. You can look at the Black-White differential in out-of-wedlock births or infant mortality or life expectancy. Blacks are the worst-performing ethnic group on SAT's. Blacks earn less than Whites. They are still just not doing well, period."[157]

[157] Stephen J. Dubner, "Towards a Unified Theory of Black America," *New York Times Magazine*, March 20, 2005.

Fryer was iconoclastic and intellectually insatiable. To him, there were no third-rail issues. He published a study that showed there was a social stigma toward Black kids who excelled in school. He also looked into the possibility of incentivizing African American students with cash to get them to improve their grades.

"We became friends. He was almost like an adopted son,"[158] said Glenn Loury, a Brown professor, who saw a lot of himself in Fryer. Both were Black economists pushing the boundaries of academic inquiry. "He did not make the White people feel comfortable in their soft racism, their soft liberal racism. He didn't dance for them."

Nothing was off the table for Fryer. The only thing that mattered to him was a fearless pursuit of truth.

He once saw a drawing of a slave trader licking the cheek of a Black man about to be shipped to North America. It was a bizarre and disturbing image, and Fryer couldn't get it out of his mind. Then he came up with a wild theory. Since Blacks have higher salt sensitivity and higher rates of hypertension, could the slave trader have been tasting the sweat of the man for salt to see if he could survive the overseas trip? He shared this theory with a colleague who initially found it "absolutely crazy," but later admitted the idea was plausible.

"I want to have an honest discussion about race in a time and place where I don't think we can," Fryer once told a reporter. "As soon as you say something like, 'Well, could the Black-White score gap be genetics?' everyone gets tensed up. But why shouldn't that be on the table?"[159]

---

158 Rob Montz, "Harvard Canceled Its Best Black Professor. Why?" documentary, posted March 9, 2022, Good Kid Productions

159 Stephen J. Dubner, "Towards a Unified Theory of Black America," *New York Times Magazine*, March 20, 2005

The study that got Roland Fryer cancelled was not supposed to be controversial. "It started back in 2014. We were all mesmerized by what happened to Michael Brown," Fryer told the hosts of the *TRIGGERnometry* podcast.[160] "I wanted to do something. I thought it would help."

Like the rest of the nation, Fryer and his students were riveted by the wall-to-wall coverage of the demonstrations and rioting in Ferguson. "You know, protesting is not my thing, but data is my thing. So, I decided I was going to collect a bunch of data and try to understand what really is going on when it comes to racial differences in police use of force."[161]

In 2015, Fryer assembled a diverse team of student volunteers to do the hard work. Over the course of a year, they would spend three thousand hours poring over police reports, trying to find concrete evidence that cops were more likely to kill Black suspects than White ones.

Fryer always kept an open mind and always let the facts lead him, but he had to admit, he was pretty sure he knew how this study was going to turn out. "I thought I would be able to show that the police are biased very easily," he said. "I grew up not liking the police."

There is absolutely nothing about Roland Fryer's background that would have indicated he was destined for great things. In fact, statistically, he was much more likely to have ended up like Michael Brown or Eric Garner than a celebrated member of the intelligentsia.

---

160 Konstantin Kisin and Francis Foster, hosts, *Triggernometry*, June 16, 2024

161 Quoctrung Bui and Amanda Cox, "Surprising New Evidence Shows Bias in Police Use of Force but Not in Shootings," *New York Times*, July 11, 2016

Born in Daytona Beach, Florida, in 1977, he was immediately abandoned by his mother. Four years later, his father got a job selling Xerox copy machines in Lewisville, Texas, so they packed up the moving vans and relocated. Roland describes his father as a degenerate gambler and an abusive alcoholic. He lives with the painful memory of his father, blinded by anger, lashing him with a garden hose. When he was in the third grade, Roland watched in horror as his father, in the throes of another violent rage, beat his girlfriend up so badly, she ended up hospitalized.

Roland's only respite came during summers, when he would fly back to Florida to stay with his grandmother, who was known to everyone as "Fats." She was a strict, no-nonsense schoolteacher, who believed in Roland and affectionately called him "Juju."

Fats's sister, Ernestine, lived nearby, and Roland would spend a lot of time at her house as well. It was like going from *Little House on the Prairie* to *Breaking Bad.* Ernestine ran a large crack ring. She would take him on her "business trips" to Miami—a euphemistic way of saying he stayed in the car while she went into seedy places to buy cocaine. Roland remembers sitting in his aunt's kitchen, watching her cooking up crack in the same frying pan she used to make him pancakes. The business was a family affair. Fryer says his cousins, many with gold chains and gold teeth, always hung out at Ernestine's house, waiting for their next assignment. The family ultimately got busted and several of them ended up doing significant prison time.

Back in Texas, Roland became a troubled teen. "I didn't care if I lived or died," he recalls.[162]

---

[162] Stephen J. Dubner, "Towards a Unified Theory of Black America," *New York Times Magazine*, March 20, 2005.

At thirteen, he got a fake birth certificate, which enabled him to get a job at McDonald's. This deceit was not so he could flip burgers for minimum wage, but so he'd have access to the register from which he could steal cash. By the time he was fourteen, he owned a gun, was dealing marijuana, and regularly shoplifted from department stores.

When Roland was fifteen, his father was convicted of rape and went to prison. The teenager was left to fend for himself.

That year, Fryer had a frightening run-in with police. It was this incident that he would later credit for completely turning his life around.

One afternoon, a couple of White cops thought he matched the description of a crack dealer. They pulled him over, drew their guns, and made him lie face-first on the pavement.

"Who the hell wants to have a police officer put their hands on them or yell and scream at them?" Roland would later say. "Every Black man I know has had this experience. Every one of them. It's hard to believe the world is your oyster if the police can rough you up without punishment. And when I talk to minority youth, almost every single one of them mentions lower-level use of force as the reason why they believe the world is corrupt."[163]

As fate would have it, the same night Roland got roughed up by the police, he was supposed to take part in a burglary. The incident with the cops shook him up so badly, he told his friends his nerves were shot and he was going to have to bail out. That turned out to be fortuitous. His friends went ahead with the attempted burglary, got busted, and ended up doing time.

---

163 Quoctrung Bui and Amanda Cox, "Surprising New Evidence Shows Bias in Police Use of Force but Not in Shootings," *New York Times*, July 11, 2016

Roland Fryer says the events of that day were a complete game changer. When he found out his friends got arrested, something clicked and he resolved to end his life of crime and apply himself to sports and schoolwork.

Fast-forward six years: Roland was proudly holding up a diploma, after graduating magna cum laude from UT Arlington. Four years later, he got a PhD from Penn State.

Even now, all these years later, Fryer can't believe how the trajectory of his life changed so radically: "I always think I'm supposed to be dead, not alive, much less at Harvard."

Years later, as data from his research project began to pour in, Fryer's long-held antipathy towards the police was put to the test. Tanaya Devi, one of Roland's research assistants, recalls the moment it became clear that the study on law enforcement violence was not turning out as he'd expected: "I remember Roland walking in and saying, 'What do the numbers look like?' And I said, 'I just don't want to say it out loud.' And he said, 'What do you mean you don't want to say it out loud?' We couldn't find bias in the lethal use of force."[164]

"It was the most surprising result of my career," Fryer says.[165]

Essentially, what Fryer's team found was that there was a clear difference in the way police used non-lethal force against suspects. For example, cops were 21 percent more likely to draw

164 Rob Montz, "Harvard Canceled Its Best Black Professor. Why?" documentary, posted March 9, 2022, Good Kid Productions, YouTube

165 Quoctrung Bui and Amanda Cox, "Surprising New Evidence Shows Bias in Police Use of Force but Not in Shootings," *New York Times*, July 11, 2016

their guns or pull out a baton against a Black suspect compared to a White one.[166]

But the explosive part of his study, the part that challenged the orthodoxy of the BLM-inspired anti-law enforcement movement, was that the data showed police were 27.4 percent *less* likely to fire at a Black suspect than at a White one.

Fryer didn't try to fight the evidence, even though it ran contrary to what he had been expecting. Instead, he got to work, writing a 105-page report. In it, he didn't minimize the fact that there was racial bias in non-lethal police encounters with Black suspects. But he did believe the finding that Whites were more likely to get shot was extremely significant, and he called into question the claims being made by protesters around the country:

> The importance of our results for racial inequality in America is unclear. It is plausible that racial differences in lower level uses of force are simply a distraction and movements such as Black Lives Matter should seek solutions within their own communities rather than changing the behaviors of police and other external forces.[167]

Before releasing the study, Fryer showed his report to a few of his colleagues, who cautioned him, "Don't publish this. You'll ruin your career."[168]

---

[166] Roland G. Fryer Jr., "An Empirical Analysis of Racial Differences in Police Use of Force," Working Paper No. 22399 (National Bureau of Economic Research, 2016

[167] Ibid.

[168] Patrick McDonald, "Prof Says, 'All Hell Broke Loose' at Harvard After His Study Found No Racial Bias in Police Shootings," Campus Reform, February 27, 2024

Fryer says their reactions only made him more determined to share his report: "They said, 'It's so different, Roland. It's so different. You don't want to publish this. Put it away for now.' I said, 'Well, you just guaranteed I'm going to put it out no matter what.'"

Fryer released the paper in July 2016, just a few days after the Philando Castile shooting and Micah Johnson's assassination of five Dallas police officers.

He expected to get some pushback, but he was sure he could handle whatever heat came his way. He was an iconoclast, and it's not like he hadn't ruffled feathers in the past.

For the first couple of days, there was radio silence. Broadcast news didn't touch the story, and Fryer thought maybe the report wasn't that big a deal after all. As he put it, "There was something there for everyone not to like."

But that all changed on July 11, when *The New York Times* ran a story called "Surprising New Evidence Shows Bias in Police Use of Force but Not in Shootings."

And that's when, as Roland remembers, "all hell broke loose."

First came the condemnations. Wesley Lowery, a young Black journalist who was making a name for himself at The Washington Post, called Fryer's work "a nonsensical Harvard study."[169] He also asked, "Since when are economists authorities on police shootings?"

Snopes, the website which claims to be the arbiter of truth and misinformation, gave the study a "false" rating, calling it "an unvetted working paper" and a "work in progress."

Fryer has always maintained that these critiques, which questioned his methodology, were transparently false and politically

---

[169] Daniel Engber, "Was This Study Even Peer-Reviewed?" *Slate*, July 25, 2016

motivated. He used the same standards and practices that he always had—the same ones his colleagues used in their work.

But now, the same elite intelligentsia that had been celebrating him seemed intent on destroying him…and for what, exactly? Being the bearer of bad news?

The impulse to punish truth-tellers is deeply ingrained in human psychology. In 1632, Galileo published a book positing that the earth revolves around the sun. This was so upsetting to the Roman Church that it arrested him, put him on trial, and convicted him of heresy. Galileo lived out the rest of his years under house arrest.

And now, Fryer, who was simply trying to move the national debate on policing towards data-driven evidence, found himself the target of anger and abuse.

X (formerly Twitter) even reportedly suspended users who posted links to Fryer's study, under the guise of "misinformation": a modern euphemism for censorship.

For a couple of years, I co-hosted a modestly successful podcast called *Cancelled*. My co-host and I recorded about fifty episodes featuring in-depth conversations with people who had just been expelled from society by the online mob.

It was one show you definitely never wanted to be invited on as a guest.

Some of the people we spoke to, like former televangelist Ted Haggard, had brought the trouble on themselves. If you're going to preach about the evils of homosexuality, it's probably not a good idea to get caught buying meth and paying for "massages" from a male prostitute.

But many of our other guests were guilty of nothing more than thought crimes. Soap star Antonio Sabàto Jr. was banished from Hollywood after openly supporting President Trump in 2016. We spoke to him from Florida, where he was trying to scrape together a living working construction jobs.

The drummer of the heavy metal group System of a Down was targeted for his conservative beliefs.

Alan Dershowitz, once a beloved and frequent guest on legacy cable news shows, became persona non grata after representing President Trump in one of his impeachment trials. This, *despite* his public insistence that he was not a Republican and planned to vote against the president.

Dr. Drew, the beloved avuncular addiction specialist, had to go into hiding after he dared to question the wisdom of universal lockdowns during COVID.

As I found out firsthand, all these cases had one thing in common: An intolerant and ascendant far-left movement was making very public examples of anyone who dared challenge its dogmas.

The results were chilling.

A Cato Institute poll revealed that 77 percent of conservatives and 59 percent of independents said they were afraid to reveal their true political opinions.[170] Even more shocking, one-third of the respondents said they feared that if they were honest about their true political beliefs, they could get fired. It might sound like people were getting paranoid, but as the old saying goes, just because you think everyone is out to get you, doesn't mean they aren't. Case in point: That same poll showed that 50 percent of liberals thought that anyone who supported President Trump should be fired from their jobs.

170 Ed Dean, "Most Americans Afraid to Share Their Political Views, New Poll Shows," *Florida Daily*, August 7, 2020

The public shaming and excommunication of anyone who transgressed from a rigid set of progressive doctrines was not just a spontaneous phenomenon of the social media age. It was calculated and highly effective. It allowed a relatively small percentage of radicals to hijack the nation's political discourse. These activists shut the Overton Window so tightly that Americans, who usually pride themselves on free speech, knew that to research, question, or express differing opinions on a wide range of subjects—such as climate change, transgenderism, COVID, and the BLM agenda—would do nothing more than get them an invitation on my podcast.

Roland Fryer was now facing the fury of these radicals.

The man who had overcome an abusive childhood, rogue cops, and a self-destructive life of crime was now being taken down by keyboard warriors and Ivy League professors who wore blazers with patches on their elbows.

After *The New York Times* published its article, he started getting credible death threats and needed twenty-four-hour police protection for forty days. "It was crazy," he recalls.

And then, a former personal assistant accused him of sexual harassment. Fryer has always denied the charges, and many of the students who worked for him rushed to his defense, but this accusation was all Harvard needed to silence him. Since Fryer had tenure, he couldn't be fired outright. But he could be marginalized.

The school permanently shut down his lab. All of his research work was abruptly stopped, and he was given a two-year suspension.

As one of his assistants said, "This is the most cold-blooded murder I have ever seen."

Years later, Roland Fryer remained defiant. “I think the truth helps us, right? False narratives do not,” he said on *The Invisible Men* podcast. “I find it insulting that people would change the truth because they think they’re trying to help us. The truth is enough. I’m just following the data wherever it leads.”

Truth as a north star. Letting facts lead instead of leading facts to a predetermined destination. Roland Fryer thought the way reporters are supposed to.

But journalists, who had lost sight of their core mission, ignored his story. Out of the dozens of news people I interviewed for this book, only a handful even knew who Fryer was, and not a single one could remember hearing someone pitch his study, or the story of his cancellation, in a morning meeting.

So, instead of an elevated and thoughtful discussion about police violence with actual data points, broadcast news chose to present the debate about the American justice system using two proxies: on the side of law and order, a once-in-a-lifetime, shoot-from-the-hip president; on the side of the social justice movement, a professional athlete who seemed to be cosplaying the role of revolutionary as his physical abilities were deteriorating.

This made-for-TV fight lacked nuance, thoughtfulness, and hard facts, but it provided broadcast news with all the ingredients it craved: race, rage, conflict, emotion, and a battle between “good” and “evil.”

Chapter 12
The President vs. The Quarterback

In some ways, the two men were strikingly similar. Donald Trump and Colin Kaepernick both grew up in religious households; they were both more instinctive than analytical by nature; and most critically, they were both masters of reinvention who beat staggering odds to become two of the most famous and polarizing people on the planet.

Of course, when you examined their immutable characteristics, they were worlds apart. The two were born into completely different generations, different socio-economic classes, and most obviously, different races.

Nineteen-year-old Heidi Russo became pregnant with Colin in 1987. When she broke the news to her boyfriend, it did not go well. On Heidi's YouTube channel, she claims he told her, "My parents are going to kill me. It's going to ruin my life. You need to get rid of it."

She refused, and he immediately broke up with her, leaving Heidi on her own. In November of that year, she gave birth to Colin and, for six agonizing weeks, weighed the pros and cons of keeping her son. Deep down, she knew she couldn't give him a good home. She was still a teenager, she was single, and she didn't know the first thing about raising a child, let alone a biracial one. Heidi was Italian American. The baby's father was Black.

When Colin was six weeks old, Heidi was introduced to Rick and Teresa Kaepernick, a White couple looking to adopt. After a lot of tears and prayer, she reluctantly concluded they could give Colin the stable home life he deserved.

"It is the toughest decision I ever made," Heidi told the Denver Fox affiliate in 2013, after Colin had become a breakout star in the NFL. "For me personally, I was in a situation that wasn't planned. Certainly, I wasn't able to give Colin the life I wanted him to have."

Rick and Teresa embodied rock-solid stability. They'd been sweethearts since they were fourteen. They already had two children but had lost two others due to congenital heart defects. Devout Christians, they prayed for guidance and came to the realization that adoption was the best way for them to grow their family.

The fact that Colin was biracial didn't bother them in the least.

"Colin knew from the very beginning that he was different," Rick said. "I mean, it was pretty obvious. Either my wife or I had an affair, or something else was going on, right? So, when he was asked about the color of his skin, we'd just say, 'You've got such beautiful brown skin. We're jealous!'"[171]

---

171 Andrew Corsello, "CK1: Colin Kaepernick," *GQ*, August 14, 2013

The Kaepernicks were solidly middle-class. Teresa was a nurse and Rick worked in the cheese and dairy business.

When Colin was four, Rick got a great job offer out west and moved his family from Wisconsin to Turlock, California.

Smack in the heart of the state's agricultural Central Valley, Turlock has the feel of a Midwestern city, without the harsh winters. When the Kaepernicks arrived in the early '90s, it had a population of around forty-two thousand people, roughly 2 percent of whom were Black.

Colin would never forget the lingering stares he got walking around the small city, or the classmates who said Rick and Teresa couldn't possibly be his parents because they were both White. Those slights stung, and he never let go of them.

Colin would later say that even though his parents did their best, they struggled to see the world through his eyes. "I know my parents loved me, but there were still very problematic things that I went through."[172]

As an example, he said there was a time when he wanted to get cornrows, but his mom refused, saying he would look like "a little thug."

"I think it's important to show, 'No, this can happen in your own home,'" Colin would later say. "And how do we move forward collectively while addressing the racism that is being perpetuated."

Colin was struggling with his identity, but he found a refuge in sports. He was such a natural, his family nicknamed him "Bo," as in Bo Jackson.

---

172 Skyler Caruso, "All About Colin Kaepernick's Adoptive Parents, Rick and Teresa Kaepernick," *People*, March 10, 2023

He was a three-sport star in high school, playing basketball, football, and baseball. As a starting pitcher, he threw two no-hitters, blowing away overmatched hitters with his fierce 95-mph fastball. He was so impressive that the Cubs would eventually draft him. But Kaepernick's true love was football.

Amazingly, the man who would be known in the NFL for his scrambling ability and speed didn't gain a single positive rushing yard in high school. "Yes, I was fast," he told *GQ*. "Yes, my coaches knew I was fast. But we had no backup QB. So, they told me not to run."

Major college programs had no interest in Kaepernick, even though he was clearly athletic and had a 4.1 GPA. He was considered too scrawny, with only 170 pounds on his 6'4" frame. Scouts were also unimpressed with his throwing motion, which was considered awkward and not up to Division I standards.

The best Kaepernick could do was accept a scholarship at the University of Nevada, which planned to play him at safety.

In the fifth game of his freshman year, the starting quarterback got hurt and Kaepernick was rushed in as an emergency replacement. He made the most of the opportunity, throwing for 384 yards, four touchdown passes, and scrambling for another 60 yards. A star was born that day, albeit in a losing cause.

The coaching staff then made him the starter, and he held onto the job for the next four years.

During his college career, Kaepernick went 32–16 and became the first college quarterback with at least ten thousand passing yards and four thousand rushing yards.[173]

[173] Chris Murray, "Colin Kaepernick Makes ESPN's List of Top 75 College QBs. But He Still Seems Underrated," Nevada Sportsnet, May 23, 2023

In 2011, Kaepernick entered the NFL draft, and even though scouts still had major reservations about his throwing motion, he was scooped up by the San Francisco 49ers in the second round.

Colin spent his rookie season riding the bench, watching veteran quarterback Alex Smith lead the Niners to a 13–3 record and the NFC title game.

Just like in his college career, it would take an injury for Kaepernick to get a chance to play.

That opportunity came on November 11, 2012, when Alex Smith got knocked out of a game against the Rams with a concussion. Kaepernick came in and played a dynamic half of football. The following week, on Monday Night Football, he carved up the Bears, which had a top-notch defense.

A few days later, Alex Smith was medically cleared to return to the field, but the 49ers head coach, the iconoclastic Jim Harbaugh, decided that Kaepernick would keep the job.

Kaepernick was in a tough spot. Smith was less than gracious about the demotion, and the sports-talk pundits were divided, but Colin kept his head down and had a magical season.

In his very first playoff game, a rout of the Packers, he set an NFL playoff record by rushing for 181 yards as a quarterback.

In the NFC championship game against Atlanta, the Niners were down by 17, and their Cinderella season seemed to be coming to a close, but Colin, playing like a veteran, cooly led his team to a huge comeback win and a trip to the Super Bowl against the Ravens.

It was the ultimate middle finger to the football intelligentsia. Just five years earlier, he couldn't get a single decent college football program to give him a scholarship—and now, here he was, about to lead his team in the biggest game in all of sports.

Kaepernick came up just short in the Super Bowl but he had made his mark. He was poised to become the league's next big star.

As Ron Jaworski, a retired NFL star turned ESPN analyst said, "I truly believe Colin Kaepernick could be one of the greatest quarterbacks ever. I love his skill set. I think the sky's the limit."

People who first learned about Colin Kaepernick through his activism might be surprised to know that he was a completely different guy when he first came into the league. His hair was short, and reporters often used words like "shy" and "polite" to describe him.

In fact, the only culture-war controversy he found himself in involved his tattoos. Kaepernick got addicted to ink in his sophomore year of college. By the time he hit the pros, he had dozens of visible tattoos, many of them bible passages. This might seem like no big deal by modern standards, but NFL quarterbacks at the time tended to be clean-cut. Peyton Manning and Tom Brady, by far the biggest stars at the position, were the types of guys who played golf, loved Will Ferrell movies, and popped in Hootie & the Blowfish CDs to unwind.

A Sporting News writer named David Whitley took exception to Kaepernick's sleeve tattoos and wrote, "NFL quarterback is the ultimate position of influence and responsibility. He is the CEO of a high-profile organization, and you don't want your CEO to look like he just got paroled."[174]

The writer was accused of being a racist, but he quickly pointed out that he had two adopted Black daughters, and the

---

174 James Nye, "Race Row Erupts Over Columnist Who Said African American NFL Star Colin Kaepernick Shouldn't Be a Quarterback Because He Has Tattoos and 'Looks Like He Just Got Paroled,'" *Daily Mail*, November 30, 2012

controversy quickly faded away. (He might not have gotten off so easily if he had written his column a few years later when cancel culture was in full swing.)

Kaepernick downplayed the controversy, simply saying, "I want to try to break that perfect football mold. I don't want to be someone who can be put in that category. I want to be my own person. I want my own style. I want to be someone who can't really be compared to anybody."[175]

Kaepernick's sophomore season proved he was no fluke, as he led the 49ers to the NFC championship game. He seemed well on his way to being an elite NFL quarterback, which meant fame, generational wealth, and huge commercial endorsements.

What no one suspected was that Kaepernick's best days were already behind him.

In the second week of the following season, Kaepernick was fined for allegedly calling Bears defensive lineman Lamarr Houston the "N" word during a game. Kaepernick has always maintained that he didn't use the slur, but Houston told reporters he most definitely did.

That incident set the tone for a dreary season in which the 49ers didn't even make the playoffs and Kaepernick's play regressed. Many scouts believed he had lost focus and that his mechanics were getting sloppy again.

In 2015, the wheels completely came off as Kaepernick continued to regress. After going 2–6, and playing fundamentally poor football, he was benched for the forgettable Blaine Gabbert. In the span of two years, Kaepernick had inexplicably gone from the future face of the league to a benchwarmer.

---

[175] Peter King, "Colin Kaepernick Does Not Care What You Think About His Tattoos," *Sports Illustrated*, July 23, 2013

In the offseason, Kaepernick demanded to be traded.

The team refused.

But they might have accommodated him, had they known that a new Colin Kaepernick would be showing up to training camp later that summer. His days as a starting quarterback were mostly behind him, but Kaepernick was about to pivot and make his mark on the world in a whole new way: as a polarizing figure in the culture wars. A hero to some, a villain to others. He would become such a flashpoint in the fight over American law enforcement that he would find himself in a feud with no less than the leader of the free world.

***

Donald Trump could have happily skated through life, anonymously enjoying the best the world has to offer. But something—some drive for attention, some drive for beating the odds, some need for adrenaline—never allowed Donald John Trump to sit back and enjoy all the privileges he had been born into. Instead, his life was filled with spectacular triumphs, public failures, bitter feuds, and an almost compulsive need to be in a constant state of crisis.

By the time Trump was born in 1946, his father, Fred, was already a rich, successful land developer. The family, which would grow to five kids, lived in Jamaica Estates, a wealthy neighborhood in Queens.

Fred was a tough guy—a ruthless businessman and an uncompromising disciplinarian at home. Trump would later refer to his dad as his "inspiration."

His mother, Mary Anne, was born in Scotland and didn't emigrate to the US until she was eighteen. She wanted her children to have God in their lives and regularly took them to a Presbyterian church, which is where Trump was baptized.

"People are shocked when they find…out I am Protestant," Trump said on the campaign trail in 2015. "And I go to church and I love God and I love my church."[176]

Despite his exposure to religion, Trump was a difficult child. As he wrote in his bestselling 1987 book *The Art of the Deal*, "Even in elementary school, I was a very assertive, aggressive kid, a bit of a troublemaker."

When Trump was thirteen, his parents, fed up with his bad behavior, sent him off to a military academy. It seemed to do the trick. Trump straightened out his act and ended up going to U Penn, graduating with a degree in economics in 1968.

Unlike other students who had to send out dozens of resumes in the hopes of getting a low-paying entry-level job, Trump went right to work for Fred. In 1971, when he was just twenty-five, his father handed over the keys to the kingdom, making his fourth child the CEO of the family's real estate business.

Trump made the front page of *The New York Times* for the first time in 1973, but in a way that even the publicity-hungry future president couldn't have wanted. In the October 16 edition of the paper, there's a photo of young Trump, in a three-piece suit, standing in front of his car with the vanity plate "DJT." The headlines over his picture read, "Major Landlord Accused of Anti-Black Bias in City." In his first quote in *The New York Times*, Trump responded to the charges with a blanket denial. "They are absolutely ridiculous," he told the paper. "We have never discriminated, and we never would."[177]

---

[176] Kelsey Dallas, "What Has Donald Trump Said About Religion?" *Deseret News*, July 18, 2024

[177] David W. Dunlap, "1973, Meet Donald Trump," *New York Times*, July 30, 2015

The case was settled two years later, with Trump agreeing to some concessions to the Urban League. But as he would later repeatedly point out, he never admitted to any wrongdoing.

In 1976, he made it back into the paper of record. This time, as the subject of a glowing profile which began with these lines: "He is tall, lean and blond, with dazzling white teeth, and he looks ever so much like Robert Redford. He arrives around town in a chauffeured silver Cadillac with his initials, DJT, on the plates. He dates slinky fashion models, belongs to the most elegant clubs and at only 30 years of age, estimates that he's worth 'more than $200 million.'"[178]

Trump was designing a carefully crafted image, but few people outside the five boroughs knew who he was. The 1980s changed all that. The decade when Americans once again embraced capitalism and conspicuous consumption was the perfect fit for Donald J. Trump. He was a walking, talking Gordon Gekko and, through force of will, turned himself into a national celebrity.

During those halcyon days, Captain Capitalism was everywhere: opening Trump Tower on Fifth Avenue, casinos in Atlantic City, and golf courses; buying the New Jersey Generals of the USFL; sitting courtside at NBA games; and going to championship fights.

Reporters, who could always count on him for a memorable, hyperbolic quote, kept him on speed dial and he happily returned their calls.

Trump had successfully branded himself as the embodiment of "the good life." After a hard day of dealmaking and self-promotion, he would hit New York's vibrant nightlife, usually with

---

178 Judy Klemesrud, "Donald Trump, Real Estate Promoter, Builds Image as He Buys Buildings," *New York Times*, November 1, 1976

a beautiful woman by his side. As he walked through clubs filled with Manhattan's fabulous crowd, few knew that the drink in his hand was either a Diet Coke or a club soda. He had sworn off booze after watching his alcoholic brother, Fred Jr., drink himself into an early grave.

The carefully constructed image of Trump as "The Alpha Male" resonated in the world of hip-hop. Rappers like Jay-Z, Nas, and the Beastie Boys made positive references to him in their songs.

In their song "Skypager," the conscious group A Tribe Called Quest rapped that their beepers went off as often as Trump received checks.[179]

And Yung Joc bragged that people in his neighborhood had given him a Trump-inspired nickname.

The unlikely future president also made guest-starring appearances on prime-time sitcoms like *The Fresh Prince of Bel-Air*, *Suddenly Susan*, and *The Nanny*. He even hosted *Saturday Night Live* twice. For someone who wasn't a trained actor, he was a natural in front of the camera and seemed willing to poke fun at himself.

The 1990s were not as kind to Trump. Six of his businesses declared bankruptcy, and he ended up going through two divorces.

But Trump is the king of reinvention.

In 2004, he jumped on an emerging phenomenon called reality TV, agreeing to host a new show called *The Apprentice*. This turned out to be a lifeline for the fallen tycoon, who, according to his tax returns, lost $90 million that year. Not only was the show a critical success and a ratings winner but it also restored Trump's public image as an American titan of business. It also

179 Ja'han Jones, "Hip-Hop's Most Memorable Lines About Donald Trump," MSNBC, August 8, 2023

improved his bottom line. A *New York Times* investigation estimates that through his direct salary and licensing deals, Trump made $427 million from the show.[180]

By 2011, Trump was starting to dip his toe into the world of conservative politics, and it was clear from the start that he was going to follow a scorched-earth policy. In early 2011, he made the media rounds, questioning whether President Barack Obama had really been born in America.

"Right now, I have some real doubts," Trump told the *Today* show.[181]

"He doesn't have a birth certificate or he hasn't provided it," Trump told ABC News.

Trump would later have to concede that Obama was born in the US, but his public birther campaign endeared him to the right flank of the GOP.

Despite that, no one imagined that a real estate developer turned reality TV star could be much more than a political gadfly. Certainly, no one imagined he could make a serious run for the White House. But Donald Trump, the master of hype, media manipulation, and reinvention, was about to shock the world.

On June 16, 2015, he came down the escalators of Trump Tower to announce his candidacy for the highest office in the Western world. Always the showman, he unveiled a new marketing slogan for the campaign: "Make America Great Again." Most Republican insiders and Beltway pundits considered his candidacy nothing more than a "joke," or a "publicity stunt."

In 2016, Donald Trump would prove them all wrong.

---

180 Mike McIntire, Russ Buettner, and Susanne Craig, "How Reality-TV Fame Handed Trump a $427-Million Lifeline," *New York Times*, September 28, 2020

181 Allison Kite, "Five Years of Donald Trump's 'Birther' Statements," *Wall Street Journal*, September 16, 2016

***

A brand-new Colin Kaepernick showed up to the 49ers' training camp in the summer of 2016. The "shy" and "polite" kid from small-town California had started growing out his hair and suddenly seemed more interested in the social justice movements rocking the country than in regaining his starting job.

His social media posts took on a militant tone. After Alton Sterling was shot, he tweeted, "This is what lynchings look like in 2016! Another murder in the streets because [of] the color of a man's skin."[182]

After the shooting of Philando Castile, he posted, "We are under attack! It's clear as day! Less than 24hrs later another body in the street!"

During one summer practice, Kaepernick caused a stir when he wore socks depicting cartoon pigs in police hats.

"If I had had the chance to interview him," says Michael Holley, a prominent sports columnist and author, "I would start at the beginning. What led to this? There's nothing from previous interviews to suggest this would happen. What happened?"

His teammates were also confused, not sure what to make of Colin 2.0. It was like he'd shown up that summer with a whole new personality. Some speculated he was being influenced by his new girlfriend, Nessa Diab, a TV and radio personality, who was an outspoken supporter of BLM.

Outside of San Francisco, there weren't a lot of people talking about Kaepernick's new SJW persona. He didn't play in the

---

182 John Branch, "The Awakening of Colin Kaepernick," *New York Times*, September 17, 2017

team's first two preseason games and it seemed likely he would start the season riding the bench.

On August 26, during the team's third preseason game, NFL Network reporter Steve Wyche noticed that Kaepernick was not standing for the national anthem. He immediately knew he had a huge story on his hands.

"History has shown us," Wyche reflected, "that when people have tread on the flag or the national anthem, the emotional reaction is very, very explosive."[183]

Wyche approached Kaepernick after the game and asked why he didn't stand for the anthem. The answer he got was fiery and blunt—the type of answer Donald Trump was becoming known for on the campaign trail.

"I am not going to stand up and show pride in a flag for a country that oppresses Black people and people of color," the quarterback declared. "To me, this is bigger than football and it would be selfish on my part to look the other way. There are bodies in the street and people getting paid leave and getting away with murder."

Kaepernick also said he wasn't going to stop his protest until he saw "significant change" for minorities.

The story became an instant sensation. Kaepernick was venerated as a courageous athlete who was risking everything to fight for social change. Mainstream news reporters portrayed him as a selfless hero, following in the footsteps of legendary athletes like Tommie Smith, John Carlos, Muhammad Ali, and Billie Jean King, who risked alienating mainstream America to fight for progressive causes.

---

[183] Rhiannon Walker, "One Year Later, Steve Wyche Reflects on Breaking the Colin Kaepernick Story," Andscape, August 28, 2017

It is worth noting that there is also a long tradition of conservative athletes taking the same risks to further their beliefs. But it would be difficult to argue that Herschel Walker, Riley Gaines, or Harrison Butker—to name just a few—have been treated with the same reverence.

On September 1, 2016, the 49ers played their final preseason game in San Diego. The Chargers marketed the game as Military Appreciation Night, and the fans did not take kindly to Kaepernick's refusal to honor the flag. He was booed every time he touched the ball. This may have contributed to Kaepernick's terrible on-field performance, which led new coach Chip Kelly to announce that the former star would start the season on the bench.

Legacy news was operating under an alternate reality; one in which Kaepernick was still one of the best quarterbacks in the league and his protest was an act of selfless sacrifice.

ABC's Kayna Whitworth, reporting from San Diego, tossed to her package by saying, "One of Colin Kaepernick's teammates joined him in taking a knee, and a Seattle Seahawks player also didn't stand for the national anthem. But this morning, Kaepernick says he's willing to make real change and plans on donating a million dollars to charities that he's been working with to help end racial inequality."

That last seemingly anodyne line was an error repeated over and over by reporters covering the story. If Whitworth had been following sound journalistic practices, she would have said, "But this morning, Kaepernick says he's willing to make real changes and plans on donating a million dollars to charities that he's been working with to help end what *he sees as a crisis of racial inequality*." This small change in wording is the difference between reporting and advocacy. In the report that aired, Whitworth accepted Kaepernick's charges as empirical truths. The second version attributes the claim to Kaepernick's point of view, therefore not accepting the veracity of his claims.

Over the next couple of years, reporters would dutifully report that the quarterback was fighting against "police brutality," "the murder of young Black men by law enforcement," or "systemic racism," leaving no room to doubt whether or not Kaepernick's allegations were actually correct.

While mainstream outlets were treating Kaepernick as the next coming of Gandhi, the Fox universe was doing the exact opposite.

On August 31, Fox Business Channel put together a panel to "debate" his protest. In reality, they had assembled a group of like-minded conservatives trying to one-up each other with the best zingers.

Mark Simone, a New York City radio talk show host, said, "Everyone has the right to be an idiot, but I think he's abusing the privilege."

Kelly Riddell from *The Washington Times* chimed in with, "He gets paid—what? $200,000 a week to sit on the bench. I think the US has been pretty good to Colin and he should be grateful."

The polarization was intensifying. Viewers of mainstream news broadcasts would never learn that Supreme Court Justice Ruth Bader Ginsburg, a liberal icon, called Kaepernick's protest "dumb and disrespectful."[184] People in the conservative news eco-system would never hear that some elite White athletes, like Travis Kelce, were supporting Kaepernick's protest.

---

[184] Christine Hauser, "Ruth Bader Ginsburg Calls Colin Kaepernick's National Anthem Protest 'Dumb,'" *New York Times*, October 11, 2016

***

The establishment and chattering class never saw it coming.

Using a potent mix of bombast, humor, preternatural confidence, name-calling, and exaggerations, the former reality TV star emerged as the winner of the GOP primary season, besting a field of seventeen.

Trump's appeal to voters was due, in part, to his incessant calls for law and order. During his acceptance speech at the 2016 GOP convention, he thundered, "The attacks on our police and the terrorism in our cities threaten our very way of life."

This stance made him the perfect foil for the growing anti-police movement. As far as journalists were concerned, Trump was Bull Connor and Kaepernick was Martin Luther King.

Trump, the politician, didn't always have an adversarial relationship with the press.

During the primary season, he had dominated the airwaves. Always the showman, Trump knew just how to get loads of free airtime through a mixture of charm, provocative soundbites, and an eagerness to court controversies and outrage.

According to a Media Research Center (MRC) study, Trump got 60 percent of the prime-time coverage during the primary season, more than his sixteen Republican opponents *combined.* A study by *The New York Times* estimated that Trump was able to generate roughly $1.9 billion in free airtime during the 2016 primary season, six times more than his closest rival, Ted Cruz.[185]

185 Nicholas Confessore and Karen Yourish, "$2 Billion Worth of Free Media for Donald Trump," *New York Times*, March 15, 2016

"What I know," the Texas senator said at the time, "is that the media was involved in a lovefest, giving Donald Trump two billion dollars in free media."[186]

Well-placed sources within CNN report that the Rubio campaign would often call the network's top brass, complaining bitterly about its "All-Trump" 24/7 coverage.

There were also internal divisions within the network. Jeff Zucker, CNN's legendary boss, believed in identifying two to three huge stories and owning them. He saw Donald Trump as one of those huge stories: a larger-than-life figure making an improbable run for the White House.

But many journalists at the network thought Zucker was creating a monster and blamed him for the candidate's stunning rise.

"Trump should be kissing Zucker's feet," says one high-ranking source.

But others, like veteran anchor and reporter Ashleigh Banfield, think the CNN boss was simply following his strong news instincts and has little to apologize for: "Jeff Zucker is one of the best producers TV news has ever seen. He knows how to make great, compelling stories. Did he lose his way with Trump? I think we all did."

Once the dust settled and it became clear that the 2016 election would be a matchup between Donald Trump and Hillary Clinton, the tone and tenor of the coverage drastically changed. Broadcast news turned openly hostile to Trump. It wasn't a case of bias. It was straight-up activism. Journalists who had treated

---

186 "Pre-Primary News Coverage of the 2016 Presidential Race," Shorenstein Center, June 13, 2016

Trump as a novelty now saw him as an existential threat and believed it was their duty to stop him.

"Trump changed everything. We've never seen anyone like him in American politics. We've never seen someone have such open disdain for the press before," says former CNN reporter Dan Simon.

"I watched Trump break norms every day," says Banfield. "You can't blame journalists for having whiplash covering him. But over time, a lot of seasoned journalists lost their way."

Donald Trump put the media on tilt.

Instead of simply reporting on a candidate prone to demagoguery, news reporters began engaging in it themselves. Instead of simply covering Trump, they became active participants in the story, seeing themselves as the last line of defense between American democracy and someone they dubiously labelled as a wannabe dictator.

One of the most deleterious decisions came from *The New York Times*, when Dean Baquet, the venerable paper's editor, changed the rules of campaign coverage by allowing reporters to take their gloves off and go after Trump.

"Dean Baquet changed things when he let loose the hounds on Trump," said Bill Applegate, the late great legendary TV newsman and station manager. "He removed the obligation of reporters to be objective because he felt Trump posed such a threat to democracy. *The New York Times* is still the north star for newsrooms around the country. And he provided the permission structure for them to set objectivity aside and attack."

The result of this shift was jaw-dropping. A study found that a stunning 91 percent of the TV news coverage of Trump in the fall of 2016 was not just negative, but "hostile."[187]

To be fair, the president was openly antagonistic towards journalists, calling news he didn't like "fake" and labeling reporters "enemies of the people."

Even some of the biggest names at Fox News Channel became the targets of Trump's fury.

Take Shepard Smith.

He was one of Roger Ailes's first hires when he launched Fox News in 1996.

Shepard, then thirty-two, had worked his way up through the minor leagues of broadcast news, starting in Panama City, Florida, before jumping to Fort Myers, Orlando, and then Miami.

When he arrived, he felt like Tom Cruise in *The Firm*: a new hire in a too-good-to-be-true environment.

"Fox did a lot of things better in many ways," he says of the early days of the network. "We teased well. People stayed with us longer. I think our average viewer stayed with us for something like 21 minutes at a time and the competition only got 7 minutes. The length of tune in was killing the competition."

Smith says there was no written handbook, no explicit orders that came down from management demanding a conservative spin on stories. "There was no directive," he says. "But you knew what to do. It was all subtle. For example, we were all conditioned to believe that *The New York Times* had become far left and evil. I didn't realize it at the time, but this was part of our conditioning."

---

[187] Hadas Gold, "Study: 91 Percent of Coverage on Evening Newscasts Was Negative to Donald Trump," Politico, October 25, 2016

Smith is a grinder who takes pride in his work ethic. His coverage of huge stories like Princess Diana's funeral, President Clinton's impeachment, and the Columbine massacre got the attention of the FNC brass.

In 1999, he was given his own show. Unlike some of the partisan hosts on FNC, Smith was determined to maintain the highest journalistic standards: "I wanted to tell the truth as simply as possible," he says, looking back on his days anchoring the desk. "I wanted everything to be as transparent as possible."

The approach worked. By 2003, Shepard had one of the top five rated shows on cable. Even frequent critics of Fox News had to begrudgingly admit that he was anchoring a solid, journalistically sound newscast.

For the next sixteen years, Smith was in TV nirvana. His show was a consistent ratings winner, and he was rewarded with an annual contract worth $15 million.[188]

But things were changing at Fox News. Shepard says the management team got addicted to scouring social media sites and would overreact whenever they saw negative comments from viewers: "If they went on Twitter and 8 percent of the comments were angry about some story, they would want you to leave those facts out. There was no appetite for *damn it—we're just going to tell the truth*!"

Shepard Smith's fall from grace within the Fox News universe was indirectly related to the Trump of it all.

"I'm the moderator of the show," he says. "Whenever someone said something on my air that was demonstrably untrue, I interrupted and set the record straight."

---

[188] Stephen Battaglio, "Shepard Smith, Respected Nonpartisan Voice at Fox News, Is Leaving the Network," *Los Angeles Times*, October 11, 2019

When Shepard was calling out Democrats, viewers and management had no problem with it, but when it was Trump—that was a completely different story.

"I would go on and say *why is it lie after lie after lie*? And the bosses would say, 'Shepard, watch your tone.' Honestly, I still don't know how to cover Trump properly."

Some of the late-night opinion hosts on Fox started taking shots at Shepard for not being sufficiently supportive of the president.

Smith was able to brush those criticisms off.

But things got a lot more personal when Trump himself tried to rally MAGA Nation against him.

The president tweeted to his sixty million followers that Shepard was "HOPELESS & CLUELESS" and repeatedly made the false claim that Shepard's show was the lowest-rated one on Fox News.

Smith eventually left Fox to start a show at CNBC but insists it had nothing to do with the president singling him out for criticism: "No, not at all. Full stop. Attacks from the president are not uncommon. In my case, the commentary was neither unique nor influential. I stepped away because it was the right time and the best decision for my family and me."

***

By late September, Colin Kaepernick's once mighty 49ers were 1–2 and would only win one more game that season. Kaepernick was riding the bench; yet, by becoming a hero to the counterculture, he had become one of the biggest names in the league. Just like Trump, reporters couldn't resist sticking a mic in his face, knowing he was always good for a shoot-from-the-hip headline-grabbing soundbite.

This is exactly what happened the day after the first debate between Trump and Hillary Clinton.

"Both are proven liars," the benchwarmer said, "and it almost seems like they're trying to debate who's less racist.... You have to pick the lesser of two evils, but in the end, it's still evil."[189]

Donald Trump, never one to take a punch without throwing a counter, was asked about Kaepernick's protest by a conservative Seattle talk-show host. "I have followed it and I think it's personally not a good thing," the candidate replied. "I think it's a terrible thing, and you know, maybe he should find a country that works better for him. Let him try. It won't happen."

TV news had exactly what they wanted: a public feud between a presidential candidate and a cultural icon.

Reporters rushed back to Kaepernick to get his response, and he was more than happy to deliver: "It's a very ignorant statement that if you don't agree with what's going on here, and that if you want justice, and liberty and freedom for all, that you should leave the country. Um, no. He always says, 'Make America great again.' Well, America has never been great for people of color, and you know, that's something that needs to be addressed. Let's make America great for the first time."

It was a calorie-free made-for-TV debate. The only way news would engage with the possibility that the BLM-led anti-law enforcement movement was flawed was to make Trump, whom they were vilifying as a unique threat to American democracy, its spokesperson.

---

[189] Yamiche Alcindor, "Colin Kaepernick Says Presidential Candidates Were Trying to 'Debate Who's Less Racist,'" *New York Times*, September 28, 2016

Kaepernick didn't have a particularly sophisticated understanding of the issues he was advocating for. At one point, he made a tortured comparison between police training and getting a cosmetology license. He also praised former Cuban dictator Fidel Castro, who murdered fifteen to eighteen thousand of his own citizens and turned the island into a large prison state. "One thing Fidel Castro did do is they have the highest literacy rate because they invest more in their education system than they do in their prison system," the quarterback falsely declared.

Kaepernick would later admit to NFL Media, "I'm still growing up.... I'm trying to educate myself more and more."

By the end of 2016, Kaepernick's PR team stopped letting him speak to the press.

"He was honored at Harvard. A big award," recalls Michael Holley. "But he didn't speak at Harvard. Is that a coincidence? Probably not."

By 2017, Kaepernick was out of a job and Trump was the leader of the free world.

In October of that year, Kaepernick sued the NFL, claiming that team owners "have colluded to deprive Mr. Kaepernick of employment rights in retaliation for Mr. Kaepernick's leadership and advocacy for equality and social justice and his bringing awareness to peculiar institutions still undermining racial equality in the United States."

The two sides would later reach a confidential settlement, reportedly for a nominal amount.

But Kaepernick's lack of even a single job offer created a new national debate: Was he being blackballed? After all, no-name quarterbacks like Trevone Boykin, Christian Hackenberg, and

Brad Kaaya were on NFL rosters. Wouldn't Kaepernick be an upgrade over those guys?

But at this point in his career, Kaepernick was strictly a backup. A reclamation project at best. And most NFL teams want their backups to fade into the background and quietly hold a clipboard until they're needed.

As Hall of Fame Cleveland Browns lineman Joe Thomas tweeted, "Teams don't currently view him as a starting QB, and NFL teams accept ZERO distractions from their backup QB's."

A mythology has built up around Kaepernick: that he was a special talent who sacrificed his promising career for a cause bigger than himself. Truth is, he was overrated. Based on advanced Quarterback Rating (QBR) metrics, he never once ranked in the top half of NFL quarterbacks in his five seasons in the league, and he finished among the very worst three times.

In 2019, I had the chance to spend an afternoon in Miami with NFL legends Ray Lewis and Lawrence Taylor, who were thinking of starting a show and wanted to feel me out as a potential producer. The conversation naturally drifted to Kaepernick, and I was surprised at the ferocity of their reactions. Lewis, in particular, not only thought his kneeling during the anthem was disrespectful but also dismissed Colin's talents as a player. I'm a Patriots fan and asked Lewis to compare facing Kaepernick versus Tom Brady. The hall of famer just laughed and dismissively waved his hands at what he clearly considered an absurd question.

Kaepernick would never play in the NFL again, but he got paid top dollar—reportedly $40 million—to become the face of a controversial Nike campaign.[190] Colin's image was plastered on

[190] Dan Cancian, "Colin Kaepernick Net Worth: How Much Will Nike Deal Pay?" *Newsweek*, September 4, 2018

billboards all over the country with the iconic Nike swoosh and the following words in bold font: "Believe in something. Even if it means sacrificing everything."

Kaepernick may have been out of professional sports, but in 2017, his protest went viral. On one September weekend, more than two hundred NFL players knelt during the anthem.

Donald Trump took them all on.

Campaigning for an Alabama Senate candidate, the president told an adoring crowd, "Wouldn't you love to see one of these NFL owners, when somebody disrespects our flag, to say, 'Get that son of a bitch off the field now! Out!'"

A couple of nights later, ABC News's *Nightline*, in full TDS mode, ran an incendiary piece, which attempted to portray Trump's comments as racist.

In the piece, the reporter intones, "Many view Trump's harsh language about the actions of athletes in a league whose players are predominantly Black in stark contrast to his comments about the demonstrations in Charlottesville."

The piece then cuts to neo-Nazis marching in Charlottesville, chanting, "Jews will not replace us!"

It then cuts to President Trump saying, "But you had people that were very fine people on both sides."

ABC was perpetuating a toxic lie that persists to this day, despite direct evidence proving that the infamous "very fine people" quote was taken out of context. Even the left-leaning fact-checking website Snopes labels the claim as "false."[191]

But ABC used that utterly false premise as the foundation of their editorial masquerading as a news piece. One of their

---

191 Taija PerryCook, "No, Trump Did Not Call Neo-Nazis and White Supremacists 'Very Fine People,'" Snopes, June 21, 2024

reporters even asked Trump's spokeswoman whether the president believed some of the kneeling players were "fine people."

The network's shameful piece ends with an inflammatory conclusion delivered by Matthew Dowd: "It's ludicrous to say that none of this has been about race. That's what the entire aspect of this whole thing has been about: discrimination, racism, and police brutality."

In truth, broadcast news was proving over and over again that it had no interest in a tough and honest discussion about police brutality. The story they wanted to exploit was race. As Roland Fryer found out the hard way, the media would ignore information that did not conform to the predetermined conclusion that law enforcement was systemically targeting Black men and that the justice system was irredeemably racist.

There were no exceptions to this rule.

If there were, Tony Timpa would be a household name.

Chapter 13
Who Is Tony Timpa?

In early 2015, *The Washington Post* established a database to keep track of police shootings in the United States. For those hoping it would help back the claims of the anti-law enforcement movement, the results were once again a disappointment.

The most striking thing revealed by the data is that, fortunately, very few unarmed people are killed by law enforcement. Between 2015 and 2019, there were roughly 275 million interactions between cops and citizens,[192] and only 340 of those resulted in an officer killing a suspect who did not have a weapon on them. When you crunch the numbers, that is a fractional .000001 percent. Death by neck restraint, the way Eric Garner

[192] Susannah N. Tapp and Elizabeth Davis, "Contacts Between Police and the Public, 2020," Bureau of Justice Statistics, November 2022

and George Floyd were killed, accounted for only 1–2 percent of all police killings.[193]

Of course, the optimum number would be zero. These cases are all tragic and it is appropriate for people to ask tough questions when law enforcement officers, who have been entrusted to protect and serve their communities, use deadly force. But the statistics from *The Washington Post*'s database do not point to any kind of a national crisis, which raises the disturbing question of why legacy media decided to make police brutality the defining story of the decade.

To put it in perspective, during that same five-year period, a study from Johns Hopkins found that medical errors killed a staggering 250,000 Americans each and every year, making it the third leading cause of death, after heart disease and cancer.[194] If journalists wanted to shine a spotlight on a systemic crisis in American society, this would have been highly impactful. But it was a complicated story to tell—there were too many numbers and stats. The visuals weren't appealing—just exteriors of hospitals and file footage of doctors making their rounds. No news director was going to pay much attention to this epic healthcare scandal when you could simply point cameras at passionate protests in the streets during the day, followed by lawlessness at night.

Just like Roland Fryer's Harvard study, *The Washington Post*'s databank did reveal some racial disparities that are worth considering.

---

[193] Brenden Beck, Joseph Antonelli, and Angela LaScala-Gruenewald, "Neck Restraint Bans, Law Enforcement Officer Unions, and Police Killings," *Criminology and Public Policy*, 23 (2024): 663–688

[194] Ray Sipherd, "The Third Leading Cause of Death in the US Most Doctors Don't Want You to Know About," CNBC, February 22, 2018

Of the 340 fatal shootings of unarmed suspects during the 2015–2019 period, 141 of the victims were White and 111 Black: a 56–44 percent split. Since African Americans make up just 13 percent of the population, that number is disproportionately high. Turning the Rubik's Cube another way, FBI stats show that Black people committed 51 percent of murders and 36 percent of all violent crimes in 2019, leading some in law enforcement to argue that this data point alone is enough to explain the disparity in the numbers.[195]

To be clear, there are compelling historical reasons for these disparities, and they should be studied and debated…just not by journalists. Legacy news was hammering home the doctrinaire claim that law enforcement was specifically targeting Black men in the 2010s, despite the fact that every attempt to substantiate that argument with hard data backfired. Journalists refused to acknowledge those hard truths and stubbornly continued to amplify the dubious claims of activists.

America was wrestling with its ghosts and sacrificing its living in the process.

As Bill Maher always admonishes his audience, "You need to live in the time you're in."

The media committed many sins in its mis-coverage of police violence in the 2010s, but its greatest crime, by far, was ignoring the two-thirds of cases in which an unarmed suspect killed by police was not African American.

Legacy news simply refused to cover those stories. Journalists seemed scared that it would open them up to accusations of engaging in "All Lives Matter" relativism.

---

[195] "2019 Crime in the United States," Federal Bureau of Investigation

After all, if the story was truly about police violence, and not race, every legacy network would have been sending teams of reporters down to Dallas in the summer of 2016.

Tony Timpa was the embodiment of what activists fashionably called "White privilege." He was thirty-two, had a $250,000-a-year job at his dad's trucking company, a fancy convertible, and an expensive downtown apartment. He also had an eight-year-old son and a beautiful fiancée. But Timpa was living proof that there are some things money just can't buy—like mental health.

Timpa, along with his two sisters, grew up in the affluent Dallas suburb of Rockwall. His biological mother, Vicki, used to read him a children's book about a little boy named Peter Pat. In the story, Peter thinks he's old enough to go out on a walk by himself but ends up getting lost. A helpful police officer ends up saving the day, bringing Peter home.

"He loved the police. He trusted the police," remembered Vicki. "They made him feel safe in this big world, even back in 1984 when he was born."[196]

Despite living in comfort and abundance, Timpa was an unhappy child, plagued by demons. Years later, those demons would be given proper names: depression, anxiety, and schizophrenia.

Timpa carried a heavy burden as a teenager. He felt like he was dying inside, but few people knew he was suffering, as he successfully masked his pain with an outwardly gregarious personality. In high school, he began to anesthetize his feelings with drugs. First pot, and then meth.

[196] Cory Smith, "Dallas Police Officers Under Investigation Following Death of Unarmed Man," NBC DFW, September 19, 2017

Despite the drugs and mental illness, Timpa was the starting center for his high school varsity football team and managed to do well enough in school to get accepted to Baylor University in Waco, Texas.

In college, things began to unravel. Timpa was no longer able to fool people with his "good-time-Tony" mask. He sank deeper into depression and drug use, and his family had to pull him out of school several times to check him into rehab facilities. Those stints helped him hold it together just long enough to graduate.

After leaving Baylor, Timpa fell back into the comfort of his family's safety net. His father owned a successful trucking logistics company and brought Tony in at a fat salary and the lofty title of director of operations. Timpa's dad would always insist that this wasn't pure nepotism—that his son was an invaluable part of the company. In some ways, Tony did seem like he was pulling his life together. He fell in love, married young, and, when he was just twenty-four, had a son named Kolton. He belonged to a church, played golf, loved skiing, and was described by his friends with the old familiar words "fun" and "outgoing."

He was fooling everyone again. But the demons would not loosen their grip on Tony Timpa.

He continued to drink and take drugs excessively and fell right back into his old pattern of checking in and out of rehab. After officially being diagnosed with depression and schizophrenia, he was prescribed medications that can lead to weight gain. That may explain why Timpa became clinically obese. The former high school athlete, who stood 5'11", ballooned to over 220 pounds. By the time he was twenty-seven, he was visiting cardiologists, complaining about arrhythmia and shortness of breath. Doctors diagnosed him with an enlarged heart. Timpa was falling apart both physically and mentally.

His first wife, unable to deal with the agonizing ups and downs of living with a mentally ill addict, left him.

Timpa quickly rebounded and hastily got engaged to a Polish immigrant.

On August 10, 2016, Tony Timpa's demons were running the show. He was off his meds, which left him in a confused and delusional state. That morning, he confessed to his family that he was spiraling again. The plan was for him to take the day off from work, rest, and wait for his stepmother to pick him up so she could check him back into a facility later that day. Timpa's illness had other ideas.

Tony spent the last day of his life on a bender. He did some lines of coke and, in the evening, took a tour of some of Dallas's seedier establishments. He visited a head shop and then went to a porn store with the ironic name "New Fine Arts." At around ten that night, something kicked in. Some small part of Tony Timpa that desperately wanted to be well, to be a father to his eight-year-old son, took charge. He pulled out his cell phone and dialed 911—he was going to call the cops on himself. Little did Tony Timpa know: The only responsible thing he did that entire day would directly lead to his death.

"911 operator."

Tony had called for help, but now he didn't seem to know how to put it into words. After a long period of silence, he finally sputtered out, "I'm schizophrenic."

Tony asked for someone to come pick him up. The 911 operator asked for his address, but this was too much for Timpa to process. There was a voice in the background. It seemed like

Tony was having two conversations at once. One with the operator and the other with some mystery person standing next to him.

"What is your name?" the 911 operator demanded. Even though she was presumably trained to talk to people in distress, this operator had the demeanor of a bored TSA employee aggravated that someone didn't remove the keys from their pocket before walking through the metal detector.

"Tony Timpa."

"Anyone have weapons?"

"I don't," Tony told the operator. "I don't know about my partner here."

He had met a guy named Frederick Johnson during his bender, but it's unclear whether that's who he was referring to as his "partner." It's possible no one was there at all, and it was just someone he had conjured up in his delusional state.

"Have you been taking your medication?"

"Gosh. I skipped today."

"So, what are you diagnosed with—schizophrenia and what?"

"There's other stuff," Tony replied. "I forgot. Depression, anxiety, bad childhood."

"Bipolar?"

"Yes."

"Feel like harming yourself or anyone else?"

"No, but this guy here's not talking anymore. It's weird. Daryl."

Real or not, Daryl was scaring Tony, and after unsuccessfully trying to tell the 911 operator where he was, Timpa abruptly hung up the phone.

Moments later, the operator called him back.

"There's a guy acting real weird and it's giving me a bad time," Tony explained.

"Who's the guy you're with?"

Silence.

"What's going on?" the operator pressed.

"He's acting like he's not going to let me go."

"How did you get there?"

"I drove here with him. I don't know who he is," Tony said. "He went around the corner. He won't give me my key. I've got a great $80,000 car, and I think I'm getting set up with a lot of people coming."

There was a long pause.

Then a very loud honk.

And then a lot of screaming.

Tony Timpa was having a full psychotic break. He had started running up and down Mockingbird Lane, a very busy Dallas street, stopping traffic. Then, to the horror of onlookers, he climbed on top of a bus. Other 911 operators were getting calls from witnesses reporting that a man who was "on something" was going crazy.

Two private security guards managed to chase him down. They handcuffed him, zip-tied his feet, and then waited for police to get to the scene.

A Crisis Intervention Team (CIT) call went out. It ordered officers to perform a five-man takedown of Timpa. This would involve four officers getting a hold of one of his limbs, and a fifth securing his head. This takedown requires special training and is intended to prevent someone who's having a mental health crisis from hurting themselves or others.

The first cop to arrive at the scene was Supervising Police Sergeant Kevin Mansell. It was 10:36 p.m. and Timpa was sitting barefoot in a grassy area, right by the sidewalk. He was in a bad state, screaming and thrashing about. At one point, Timpa rolled himself into the street and had to be lifted up and brought back to the safety of the grassy area.

Within ten minutes, two paramedics and four officers arrived at the scene. Three of the officers were wearing bodycams and recorded everything that happened.

The footage starts with Timpa crying out in agony, "Don't hurt me!"

"We're not going to hurt you, bro," responded one of the officers calmly.

Timpa was on his stomach.

Officer Dustin Dillard, a White male, and officer Danny Vasquez, Latino, each had a knee pressed on Timpa's back.

"No!" Timpa cried out, thrashing around.

"Tony! Tony! Tony!" the officers commanded.

That only made him scream louder, "Nooo!"

Timpa began to grunt and make guttural noises.

"We're not going to hurt you. You need to relax," one of the officers said soothingly. "What did you take today?"

"Coke."

After about two minutes, Vasquez removed his knee from Timpa's back. But Dillard kept the pressure on and would continue to do so for a total of fourteen minutes and seven seconds—almost five minutes longer than Derek Chauvin kept his knee pressed on George Floyd's neck.

For more than ten minutes, Timpa continued to cry, scream, and beg. He yelled out "help me!" more than thirty-five times. His screams sounded primal and deranged.

At one point, he pathetically begged, "Kill me! Kill me! I need to die!"

At around 11:30 p.m., Timpa stopped struggling and shouting. Despite this, Officer Dillard kept his knee pressed against

Timpa's back. The other officers, noticing the change, started making jokes.

"He asleep?" one asked as the others laughed.

"Shit, if I was squirming that much I'd be sleeping too."

One of the officers gave Timpa a little shake but he remained motionless on the ground.

"Tony, time for school!" taunted one officer.

Another then tried to imitate Timpa in an exaggerated slurred voice: "I don't want to go to school."

More laughter. The humor was juvenile, but the officers were having a great time, trying to one-up each other's playground punchlines.

"First day. You can't be late!"

"We bought new shoes for the first day of school. Come on."

"We made breakfast. Scrambled eggs. Your favorite. Waffles."

"Rooty-tooty-fruity waffles!"

The officers were cracking each other up as Timpa remained motionless.

Finally, the medics arrived and put him on a stretcher and loaded him into the ambulance.

Dustin Dillard, who had kept his knee on Timpa's back the entire time, stood by the EMTs, grinning.

"I hope I didn't kill him," he said to more laughter.

The medics were trying to revive Timpa, but weren't having any luck.

"He's not breathing," one of them called out to Dillard.

"Fuck," Dillard said. It seemed to suddenly dawn on him that this might not be a laughing matter.

The medic looked up and simply said, "He's dead."

Vicki Timpa was heartbroken when she found out her son died. But the call from the Dallas PD left her with more questions than answers. They weren't clear about what happened, and each time she called, officers kept changing their story. On one call, they told her he had a fatal heart attack in a bar.[197]

Vicki is a fighter, and she wasn't going to let the police off the hook until she found out exactly how her son died. She hired Geoff Henley, a former prosecutor turned private attorney. Henley is an iconoclastic figure in Texas. He once wrote a book called *Beyond Reasonable Doubt*, which tries to make the case against God's existence—not the most popular position to take in Texas.

"Not my best work," he laughs. Geoff is friendly and a bit flamboyant, and if you close your eyes while listening to him, you could swear you were talking to Saul Goodman.

Henley says he knew something was very wrong when he finally got his hands on the medical examiner's report.

In his autopsy report, the ME wrote he found cocaine in Timpa's system and concluded that he was suffering from "excited delirium syndrome" at the time of his death:

> People affected by EDS are witnessed to exhibit erratic or aggressive behavior and will often "throw off" attempts at restraint, requiring multiple people to subdue them. The person will appear to be calm and suddenly become unresponsive.[198]

---

197 Billy Binion, "Tony Timpa Wrongful Death Trial Ends With 2 Out of 3 Cops Getting Qualified Immunity," *Reason Magazine*, September 27, 2023

198 Katie Wedell and Cara Kelly, "'Excited Delirium' Cited as a Factor in Many Fatal Police Restraint Cases. Some Say It's Bogus," *USA Today*, June 13, 2020

But what really caught Henley's eye was the ME's conclusion, which did not jibe with Tony Timpa dying of a heart attack in a bar:

> Although the decedent only had superficial injuries, the manner of death will be ruled a homicide, as the stress of being restrained and extreme physical exertion contributed to his demise.

Henley kept pressing the Dallas PD to come clean and explain what really happened, but "the city stonewalled us."

Finally, six months later, he got his hands on the bodycam footage and watched the final minutes of Tony Timpa's life slip away as officers yukked it up.

The footage was compelling, and it should have been a slam-dunk story for the news media. Here were officers, caught on tape, having a good old time as a man in their care died in front of their eyes. But outside of local news, Henley couldn't get anyone to touch the story.

"I had press conferences. I wasn't getting any coverage," Henley says. "Every time we sent out a press release—nothing. I have eighty-five to one hundred contacts on my email list and I would send it out. Silence."

"Did you try to get activists involved?" I ask.

"We went to the NAACP. They weren't terribly interested."

"I have to ask the sixty-four-thousand-dollar question. If Tony Timpa was Black, do you believe there would have been a massive crush of media coverage?"

Henley pauses for a moment before answering with a sigh, "The short answer is yes. I think it would have been explosive. I really do."

In 2017, a Dallas grand jury convened and agreed to indict three of the officers involved: Sgt. Kevin Mansell, who showed up first on the scene; Danny Vasquez, who had his knee on Timpa's back for the first two minutes of the encounter; and Dustin Dillard, who had his knee pressed on Timpa the entire time.

Despite the indictment, there was no criminal trial. In 2019, the Dallas DA unilaterally decided to dismiss all charges.

Mike Mata, president of the Dallas Police Association, said, "Unfortunately, he died. I'm sorry for that. I'm sorry for the family. But those officers didn't kill him. The use of cocaine killed him."[199]

Henley, not surprisingly, disagrees: "I think that there is absolutely a compelling argument to be made that Dustin Dillard committed either criminally negligent homicide or that he recklessly caused the death of Tony Timpa."

Timpa's case may not have gotten any national media attention, but it ended in the same way almost all the other high-profile cases did—with no criminal convictions against the officers.

But there was one key difference.

In those other cases, the city almost always made quick multimillion-dollar settlements with the victims' families. Not here.

The Timpas had to file a civil suit against the officers, which didn't get heard until 2023, seven years after Tony's death.

The case was tried in front of an eight-person jury of five men and three women.

The defense argued that the officers had followed protocol that night and that Timpa died because of his drug use and

[199] "DA Drops Charges for 3 Dallas Officers Accused in Man's Death," Fox 4 Dallas, March 29, 2019

pre-existing heart condition—not because of the way he was restrained. In many ways, this argument was similar to what was presented to the Eric Garner grand jury.

Henley countered that the officers violated Timpa's Fourth Amendment rights by using excessive force when they tried to restrain him. He then made the audacious request that the jury award the family $300 million in damages. He told them that would be the only way to send a message to the Dallas PD.

The jury's verdict had something in it for everyone. It did find three of the officers liable for Timpa's death but only agreed to award $1 million in damages to his son.

Timpa's mom, Vicki, tearfully told the Dallas CBS TV station, "I don't have any closure. With no apologies, with no admitting anything other than they said they made a mistake."

One of the officers who was found liable, Raymond Dominguez, was contrite. Not so much for Timpa's death, but for the way he and the other officers joked as he lay dying: "I don't think my apology will ever be enough, but that's all I have to offer."

Dustin Dillard, the officer who kept his knee on Timpa's back the whole time, was more defiant: "I did not hurt Mr. Timpa. I did not kill Mr. Timpa. I did nothing wrong."[200]

A few months after the civil trial, the Dallas City Council finally agreed to settle with the Timpa family for $2.5 million.

In an ironic postscript to this case, Dustin Dillard was promoted to senior corporal in 2022. In this new role, part of his responsibilities would involve training rookie officers.

---

200 Ryan Mills, "Jury Finds Three Dallas Officers Liable for George Floyd-Like Death of Tony Timpa," *National Review*, September 27, 2023

The public does not know about Tony Timpa's tragic story because it did not fit a predetermined storyline. Had it gotten the media attention it deserved, people might have seen that police violence affects people of all races.

A few years later, a stoned ex-con crossed paths with a police officer who had a history of using excessive force.

Their deadly encounter had a lot of similarities with Tony Timpa's.

The major difference was that this victim was Black.

And within hours, the country was pushed to the brink of a civil war.

Part Three
Hellfire

"The party told you to reject the evidence of your eyes and ears. It was their final, most essential command."

—GEORGE ORWELL

Chapter 14
The Killing of George Floyd

George Floyd had less than an hour to live when he walked into Cup Foods, an iconic convenience store in a diverse working-class neighborhood of Minneapolis. Once inside, Floyd was fidgety, dancing to music only he could hear, laughing at jokes in his own head.

To be fair, there were lots of reasons to feel good on the evening of May 25, 2020. The previous week, Minnesota Governor Tim Walz had partially lifted the state's COVID stay-at-home orders—among the most Draconian in the country. And after a long, hard winter, the city was finally getting a taste of summer. It was almost 8 p.m., but the sun was still above the horizon, and temperatures were mild, in the low seventies.

However, Floyd's jovial mood was more likely due to the fact that he had just ingested a massive amount of fentanyl.

His autopsy would later reveal that he had 11 ng/mL of the drug in his blood. Anything over 10 is considered very dangerous and possibly fatal.

Floyd, wearing jeans and a tank top, walked up to the clerk, a Black teenager named Christopher Martin. He asked for a pack of cigarettes and handed him a twenty-dollar bill as payment.

"He seemed very friendly, approachable, talkative, but he did seem high," Martin would later testify.[201]

As Floyd left the store with his cigarettes and change, Martin watched as he walked across the street to a parked 2001 Mercedes-Benz SUV.

The teenager then held the twenty up to the light and his heart sank. "I noticed that it had a blue pigment to it," Martin recalled, "kind of how a $100 bill would have, and I found that odd, so I assumed it was fake."

Cup Foods had a strict policy: Any clerk who accepted a counterfeit bill would have that amount taken out of their paycheck.

Martin reported what happened to his boss and was told to grab a co-worker and go out to Floyd's car to see if they could convince him to come back inside and work things out.

It was a fool's errand.

Martin was nineteen. Floyd was forty-six, 6'4", and weighed over 220 pounds. To make the situation even more uncomfortable, as Martin approached the car, he saw that Floyd was not alone. Sitting next to him, in the front passenger seat, was a forty-two-year-old man named Morries Hall. Some people described him as a friend, but Floyd's girlfriend couldn't stand him. She thought he was an opportunist who sold George drugs and didn't

[201] Chris McGreal, "Chauvin Trial: Cashier Tells of Guilt Over Role in Events That Led to George Floyd's Death," *The Guardian*, March 31, 2021

care about his wellbeing. In the back seat was a woman named Shawanda Hill. She didn't know Floyd well but had bumped into him at the convenience store and he had offered to give her a ride home.

Floyd rolled down his window and spoke to the teenager. He wasn't hostile or aggressive but made it clear that he wasn't going back into the store.

Dejected, Martin walked back into Cup Foods, only to have his manager order him to go back out to Floyd's car and try again.

Martin did as he was told, but by the time he got back to the car, Floyd was asleep. Shawanda was on her cell trying to get someone to pick her up since it was clear that Floyd wasn't up to the task. She felt pity for the teenager who was standing in front of the car looking forlorn. She tried to wake Floyd up but had no luck.

When Martin told his manager that he couldn't get Floyd to come back inside, the boss ordered a different employee to call the police. The call to 911 was made at 8:01 p.m. In it, Floyd was described as "awfully drunk," and "not in control of himself."

It took police seven minutes to arrive at the scene. During that time, Floyd dozed in the car, which he had borrowed that morning from a friend. It seems likely he was crashing from the fentanyl he'd taken, which can sometimes cause a short "euphoric rush" followed by exhaustion.

Floyd was making one bad decision after another. Something he had struggled with his entire life.

George Floyd grew up in a drab and dangerous Houston housing project called Cuney Homes. Six members of the Floyd family were squeezed into their Section 8 apartment: George, his mom, his two older sisters, and two younger brothers. His father, a professional jazz and R&B guitarist, hadn't been in the picture for years.

Floyd's mom worked long hours flipping burgers, so George had to step up and help raise his two younger brothers. He hand-washed their clothes in the sink and MacGyvered banana-and-mayo sandwiches.

Floyd, who was nicknamed "Perry" by family members, took on these adult responsibilities with good cheer.

"He didn't mind doing it," said his aunt, Angela Harrelson. "He tried to be an example as much as he could. And there was a lot of pressure, too, not having a father figure around. And that was really, really hard for him."[202]

"We all grew up poor," said his childhood friend Vaughn Dickerson. "[But] Floyd's household was a bit poorer than ours."

Despite this, George had big dreams. In second grade, he turned in a school paper, in which he was asked to set some goals for himself:

When I grow up, I want to be a Supreme Court Judge.

When people say, 'Your honor, he did rob the bank,' I will say, 'Be seated.'

And if he doesn't, I will tell the guard to take him out.

Then I will beat my hammer on the desk.

Then everybody will be quiet.[203]

In high school, Floyd was a standout two-sport star, and he made sure everyone knew about it. Classmates remember him strutting around campus boasting that he was going to change the world.

---

[202] Gabrielle Banks, Julian Gill, John Tedesco, and Jordan Rubio, "George Floyd: 'I'm Gonna Change the World,'" *Houston Chronicle*, April 20, 2021

[203] Toluse Olorunnipa, "George Floyd," *Britannica*, April 14, 2025

As the starting tight end for his varsity football team, he used to ham it up, pulling stunts like kissing the chalk in the end zone after catching a touchdown pass.

But his true passion was basketball. He was the starting power forward and co-captain of his varsity team. Some people thought he had a chance to go pro.

Around this time, he became good friends with Stephen Jackson, who would go on to have a very solid fourteen-year NBA career. Even though Floyd was four years older, the two were close and called each other "twin" because everyone thought they looked so much alike.

"I tell people all the time," Jackson says, "[t]he only difference between me and my twin…is that I had more opportunities. If George would have had more opportunities, he might have been a pro athlete in two sports."[204]

One thing separating Floyd from better opportunities was his schoolwork. He graduated a year late due to poor grades and had to settle for a basketball scholarship at South Florida Community College—not exactly a hoops powerhouse. He started right away and played fairly well.

Two years later, he transferred to Texas A&M–Kingsville, after being recruited by their football coach. But his grades were so bad, he never met the academic requirements to play on the team.

In 1997, he dropped out of college and returned to the Third Ward.

Floyd's sports dreams were dead, but he still aspired to make his mark on the world. He thought he might do it through rap.

---

[204] Manny Fernandez and Audra D. S. Burch, "George Floyd, from 'I Want to Touch the World' to 'I Can't Breathe,'" *New York Times*, April 20, 2021

Going by the name "Big Floyd," George displayed some self-awareness and vulnerability in his rhymes, rapping about how, up until that point, he had never been able to live up to his potential.

His rap dreams never materialized, and Floyd began to spiral into a life of crime. In the ten years after he dropped out of college, he was arrested and convicted on nine separate charges. The most alarming incident occurred in 2007. Floyd, posing as a water department employee, rang the front doorbell of a Houston residence. Aracely Henriquez, who was home alone, naively opened the door. Floyd drew his gun, pointed it at her stomach, and ordered her to walk into the living room. Five of his accomplices then stormed the house, ransacked it, and stole everything of value.

Floyd did five years in prison for that felony. He got out in 2013, determined to turn his life around. He joined a church and committed himself to God. But his struggles with drug addiction continued.

In 2017, after another relapse, his pastor encouraged him to enroll in a rehabilitation program specifically tailored for Black men. But there was a catch: It was located in Minneapolis. By this point, Floyd had fathered five children with different moms, and they all lived in Texas. It is unclear whether he was involved in their lives, but a move would mean taking himself completely out of the picture. Floyd ultimately decided to head north.

Once in Minneapolis, Floyd moved into a townhome with a couple of roommates and got himself two security guard jobs. One was at a downtown homeless shelter. The other, at a nightclub called the Conga Latin Bistro.

"Right away, I liked his attitude," said Jovanni Thunstrom, the club owner who was also Floyd's landlord. "He would shake your hand with both hands. He would bend down to greet you."[205]

Floyd was complex. The same man who terrorized a woman by pointing a gun at her during a home invasion robbery could also show flashes of empathy.

In 2017, while on the clock at the homeless shelter, he noticed a woman who seemed distraught. He approached her and gently asked if she'd like for them to pray together. That was the start of a romantic relationship with Courtney Ross. They would stay together until the day he died.

In 2018, George's mother passed away. The loss hit him hard, and he was unable to process the pain. Instead of turning to his faith, he turned back to his old mistress: drugs.

The next two years were bleak. Ross would later admit that the two "both suffered with opioid addiction."[206]

In March 2020, Floyd lost both of his security jobs due to the COVID lockdowns. Without the routine of work, the wheels completely came off. Within weeks, he was in the hospital, fighting for his life after overdosing on heroin.

***

Police dispatch must not have taken the 911 call from Cup Foods too seriously, because the officers they sent over were both newbies.

Twenty-six-year-old Alexander Kueng was on his third day of work as a Minneapolis police officer.

---

205 Manny Fernandez and Audra D. S. Burch, "George Floyd, from 'I Want to Touch the World' to 'I Can't Breathe,'" *New York Times*, April 20, 2021

206 Bill Chappell, "Courtroom Video: Floyd's Girlfriend Testifies on Day 4 of Derek Chauvin Trial," NPR, April 1, 2021

Kueng was more cerebral than the stereotypical cop. At the University of Minnesota, he had earned a sociology of law degree. He also studied Russian and took a class on American race relations.

Kueng had a special reason to want to be in law enforcement. As a Black man, he believed there was an issue with the way cops treated people of color, and wanted to join the force to make a positive change.

As the BLM movement was getting a firm foothold in American mainstream culture, Kueng got blowback from friends and family who bought into the narrative that law enforcement perpetuated White supremacy. But he stood firm in his conviction that the way to effect change was from inside the system.

"That's part of the reason why he wanted to become a police officer," said his mother, Joni Kueng. "To bridge the gap in the community, change the narrative between the officers and the Black community."[207]

His partner, that day, took a far more circuitous route to the Minneapolis PD.

At thirty-seven, Thomas Lane was a lot older than most rookie cops. A high school dropout, he had lost fifteen years, drifting in and out of a series of dead-end jobs. During that time, he had been a construction worker, restaurant server, nightclub bouncer, and Home Depot salesperson.

When he got married in his early thirties, he decided it was time to embark on a career. Law enforcement was a natural fit—it ran in his bloodline. His great-great grandfather had been the Minneapolis police chief in 1911. If Thomas made it to the

---

[207] Kim Barker, "The Black Officer Who Detained George Floyd Had Pledged to Fix the Police," *New York Times*, June 27, 2020

force, he would become the third generation of Lanes to put on the uniform.

So, even though he was well into his thirties, Lane went back to school, buckled down, and got a degree from the University of Minnesota.

When he got hired by the Minneapolis PD, it was the start of a brand-new chapter in his life.

***

Lane was on day four of his new job when he knocked on the window of George Floyd's car.

"Let me see your hands," he commanded authoritatively.

"I'm sorry. I'm sorry. I'm sorry. I'm sorry," Floyd gushed emotionally.

"Stay in the car. Let me see your hands! Both hands!"

"I didn't do nothing."

Lane, showing his lack of seasoning, immediately drew his weapon and pointed it at Floyd.

"Get your fucking hands up right now!" he barked.

"Alright. What did I do though? What did I do?" Floyd pleaded.

"Put your hands up there," Lane directed, gesturing towards the dashboard.

Floyd was disoriented and not following orders.

"Put your fucking hands up! Jesus Christ!" Lane was clearly getting frustrated. "Keep your fucking hands on the wheel!"

Lane and Kueng were getting nowhere. George Floyd would be obsequious towards the officers one moment, and then completely ignore everything they were saying the next.

"Step away from the vehicle. Step away from me!" Lane commanded again.

Floyd began to cry, "Please don't shoot me! Please man!"

"We're not going to shoot you."

Lane and Kueng grabbed Floyd's arms and pulled him out of the car. They cuffed him and ordered him to walk with them. But Floyd refused and used his considerable weight to sit down in the middle of the street.

"Stop resisting, Floyd!" Shawanda scolded from the back seat.

Floyd finally allowed the cops to lead him away from the car and to a sidewalk directly across the street from Cup Foods. The rookie officers seated Floyd on the ground with his back against the wall of a building.

"You know why we're here?" Kueng asked Floyd kindly.

"Why?"

"We're here because it sounds like you gave a fake bill to individuals there."

"Yes."

"You understand that?"

"Yes."

"You know why we pulled you out of the car?"

Floyd was silent, like a small child being scolded.

"Because you were not listening to anything we told you," Kueng said, answering his own question.

"I didn't know what was going on."

"You listen to us, and we'll tell you what's going on, all right? When you're moving around like that, it makes us think way more is going on that we need to know."

"Right."

Floyd seemed calm sitting on the ground, but when the officers stood him up and started walking him over to the squad car, he began to panic again.

"Ouchhhhie!" he screamed.

"Are you on something right now, man?" Lane asked.

"No, nothing."

"Because you're acting real erratic."

"I'm scared man. God, man."

The officers managed to shuffle Floyd over to the squad car that was parked right in front of Cup Foods, but the second they tried to get him into the back seat, all hell broke loose.

For the next four minutes, the officers tried everything to get Floyd into the car. They reasoned with him, bargained, tried to shove him inside using force—but nothing worked; he was too big and seemed to be having a full-on panic attack. He kept telling the officers that he was claustrophobic and at one point yelled out, "I can't breathe," even though neither of the officers was restricting his airway.

Floyd's meltdown was remarkably similar to Tony Timpa's. He was having some sort of a psychotic break, but the two rookie officers were in over their heads. To make things worse, a small crowd had gathered to watch the spectacle.

At 8:17 p.m., the rookie officers breathed a sigh of relief. Another police car pulled up with two veteran officers.

The rookies knew one of the cops well. He was a nineteen-year veteran who had been their field training officer.

His name was Derek Chauvin.

He was a blank slate. A phlegmatic man who had many acquaintances but few friends.

The death of George Floyd would make him the most hated man in the Western world, but media attempts to paint him as a singularly evil and corrupt person were reductionist. Like Floyd himself, Chauvin lived in a gray area. At times, he could be cruel and heartless, but he also had moments of tenderness and compassion.

Derek grew up in a middle-class neighborhood near St. Paul. His childhood was largely unremarkable, other than his parents divorcing when he was young.

Chauvin, like rookie Officer Lane, was a poor student and a high school dropout.

After giving up on his education, he spent the next couple of years working as a cook at McDonald's and then at a cheap buffet restaurant. But Chauvin had ambition and knew exactly what he wanted: a career in law enforcement. In 1997, he left the world of low-end dining behind after enlisting in the US Army as a military policeman.

He ended up doing two stints in Hohenfels, Germany. Chauvin took the assignments very seriously. While other officers went out drinking, he abstained and offered to be their designated driver.

"He was a regular guy, didn't stand out, did his job, kept his uniform clean and kept his equipment accounted for," Jerry Obieglo, his platoon sergeant, remembered. "I had no complaints."[208]

In 2001, Chauvin came back home and got hired by the Minneapolis PD. At first, he excelled at the job. He was commended by two

[208] Stephen Montemayor and Jennifer Bjorhus, "Even to Friends, Former Officer Derek Chauvin Was an Enigma," *Minnesota Star Tribune*, August 8, 2020

women for the way he handled their domestic violence calls. In 2006, he was recommended for the Medal of Valor.

One night in 2010, Chauvin pulled his squad car up to a local hospital and brought someone in for a health check. One of the employees, a beautiful Asian woman, caught his eye and he boldly approached her and asked for her number.

That woman was Kellie May Xiong, an immigrant from Laos with two children from a previous marriage. The two fell in love and got married—and Chauvin suddenly had an instant family.

"Under all that uniform, he's just a softie," Kellie said. "He's such a gentleman. He still opens the door for me, still puts my coat on for me. After my divorce, I had a list of must-haves if I were ever to be in a relationship, and he fit all of them."[209]

To make extra money—usually about $250 a night—Chauvin worked security for local bars and restaurants. The gigs were easy, and most nights he didn't even have to get out of the squad car. But when he did, he had a reputation for overreacting.

One of the places he worked for was the El Nuevo Rodeo bar. In a curious twist, George Floyd did some security gigs there as well. No one has been able to establish whether they knew each other, but Chauvin has always maintained that they didn't.

The bar's owner, Maya Santamaria, said Derek Chauvin was usually mellow but had a hair-trigger temper. "I saw both sides of him," she said. "Pepper spraying everybody, sometimes using holds that were not apparently the most legal of holds, getting freaked out if there were a lot of Black clientele in our club and needing backup right away for no apparent reason."

---

[209] S. M. Chavey, "Refugee Once Shamed for Her Looks Vying to Be the First Hmong Mrs. Minnesota," *Twin Cities Pioneer Press*, June 4, 2018

It is worth noting that Santamaria is the only acquaintance of Chauvin who has so much as implied that he held racist views.

But his aggression was well documented.

As a member of the Minneapolis PD, he was involved in four shootings and had somewhere between fifteen and eighteen complaints filed against him.

In 2007, Melissa Borton, a White woman, was stopped for going ten miles per hour over the speed limit. Even though she had a newborn and a dog in her car, Chauvin and his partner pulled her out and put her in the back of their squad car.

She asked them why she was being detained, and they said she matched the description of a suspect.

Fifteen minutes later, she was let go without an explanation.

Shaken up by the encounter, she filed a formal complaint the next day. After a perfunctory review, Chauvin received a letter of reprimand.

Melissa Borton would later say, "I lived to complain. George Floyd didn't."[210]

****

Back in front of Cup Foods, Chauvin was trying to help the two rookie cops he'd trained to get George Floyd into the squad car. But they weren't having any luck. Floyd was in a state of delirium, screaming, crying, and resisting any attempts to put him in the back seat.

At 8:19 p.m., Chauvin decided it was time to use the Maximal Restraint Technique, which is taught to all members of the Minneapolis PD. The three officers forced George Floyd into the

---

210 Erin B. Logan, "Minneapolis Woman Recalls Run-In with Officer Charged in George Floyd Killing: 'I Lived to Complain,'" *LA Times*, June 4, 2020

prone position on the street. Lane held down Floyd's legs. Kueng restrained his back. Derek Chauvin put his knee on Floyd's neck.

For the next four minutes and forty-five seconds, Floyd continued to struggle and shout.

"I can't breathe, Mama. I love you, Reese. I love you!"

"I can't do nothing! My face is gone!"

He also cried out "I can't breathe" a total of twenty-seven times.

About ten people had gathered in front of Cup Foods, and a few of them whipped out their phones and began recording the incident.

Some members of the crowd started shouting at the cops.

"Check his pulse! He's not moving!" yelled one woman, who happened to be an off-duty firefighter.

"He's not responsive right now, bro. Bro, are you serious? Is he breathing? Check his pulse!" said Donald Williams, a professional MMA fighter who went by the bitterly ironic nickname "The Deathwish." He had stumbled onto the scene and couldn't believe what he was seeing.

Williams was fighting the impulse to tackle Chauvin, to force him off of Floyd's neck. But he took long, deep breaths and reminded himself that this would accomplish nothing other than turning his kids into orphans.

"I had so much rage," he later said. "But I had to stay in my body. I was lost."[211]

Williams became the conscience and voice of the crowd, berating the cops to show some mercy:

"You're a bum, bro. You're definitely a bum!"

---

211 Jon Wertheim, "Police Killed George Floyd. An MMA Fighter Punched Back," *Sports Illustrated*, May 25, 2021

Officer Tou Thao, Chauvin's partner, was on crowd control duty. He breezily ignored all the cries of outrage, ordering everyone to step back onto the sidewalk, and at one point joked, "This is why you don't do drugs, kids."

Thao, thirty-four, was a nine-year veteran with a checkered career of his own. A Hmong American like Chauvin's wife, he was hired by the Minneapolis PD through a diversity program.

He had been the subject of six separate citizen complaints.

The most serious one came in 2017, when a Black man sued the city, claiming Thao beat him up, leaving him with broken teeth and bruises. The case was ultimately settled for $25,000.

During the first four minutes and forty-five seconds of Chauvin's neck restraint, Floyd struggled and resisted. But then, he went into convulsions and seemed to be having a seizure.

Thomas Lane was worried and asked Chauvin if they should roll Floyd onto his side to help with his breathing.

"No, we're good like this," the veteran cop replied dismissively.

After Floyd's apparent seizure ended, he became completely motionless. His body went limp.

For the next agonizing three minutes and fifty-one seconds, Chauvin kept his knee on the back of Floyd's neck while bystanders screamed and pleaded with the officers.

"Get off his neck!"

"Bro, are you serious?"

"You're going to let him kill a man in front of you, bro!"

"They don't care."

"Look at him! He's enjoying that!"

At one point, Derek Chauvin reached for the mace in his pocket and looked up at the crowd as if to warn them not to come closer. Some swore he appeared to be smirking, but that is open to interpretation; perhaps a litmus test for one's personal view of law enforcement.

The bystanders weren't the only ones alarmed by what was happening. For the second time in the span of a few minutes, Lane, the rookie cop, asked the veteran Chauvin whether they should roll Floyd over. Again, the answer was no.

Even after the medics arrived on the scene, Derek Chauvin kept his knee pressed on Floyd's neck for almost an entire additional minute.

The medics finally lifted Floyd onto a stretcher and put him in an ambulance. Lane followed them inside and performed CPR, but it was no use. George "Perry" Floyd was dead.

Broadcast news would soon reduce this tragedy to its most simplistic and incendiary image: Derek Chauvin, a White cop, with his knee on the neck of a Black man who died in his custody.

In the alternative conservative media ecosystem, a counter-narrative was being formed. Some pundits claimed that since George Floyd had so much fentanyl in his system, he probably would have overdosed anyway. They also argued that Chauvin was guilty of nothing more than following procedure.

There was a kernel of truth to this argument—but only a kernel. Minneapolis officers were trained in the Maximum Restraint Technique. The official police guide read:

> The Maximum Restraint Technique shall only be used in situations where handcuffed subjects are combative and still pose a threat to themselves, officers or others, or could cause significant damage to property if not properly restrained.

Derek Chauvin was following proper procedure, as established by the Minneapolis PD, when he *initially* used the neck restraint on Floyd. However, that same manual also instructs officers as follows: "As soon as reasonably possible, any person restrained using the MRT who is in the prone position shall be placed in the following positions...." In other words, the method is meant to be used for a very short period of time—just long enough to subdue the suspect.

"You can't leave someone on their stomach for that long," says retired LAPD Homicide Detective Sal LaBarbera. "That's not the way to do it. Roll him over. Sit him up. If they did that, none of this would have ever happened."

Chris Anderson, a retired Birmingham detective agrees, "If Derek Chauvin did the neck restraint for a minute, that would have been OK. You could have just put him in a vehicle after that. You had more than enough officers on scene who could have physically restrained Floyd and gotten him into the squad car and then he could have been properly transferred to the jail."

Chris pauses and considers his words carefully: "What you saw was an absolute murder. There's no way around it."

For eight years, the anti-law enforcement movement had been rallying around a series of flawed, cherry-picked cases.

But with Derek Chauvin, BLM finally hit paydirt.

Unlike the other cases explored in this book, a fair-minded examination of the evidence can only lead to one conclusion: Derek Chauvin murdered George Floyd.

Even if someone wants to give Derek Chauvin the benefit of the doubt and excuse the entire first four minutes and forty-five seconds of the neck restraint while Floyd was resisting, how do you excuse him for continuing MRT for another full minute while Floyd was having an apparent seizure? And even if you can wrap your mind around that, it's almost impossible to justify maintaining the neck restraint for yet another three minutes and fifty-one seconds while Floyd lay on the ground, completely motionless and unresponsive.

If broadcast news had upheld its obligation to hold truth as its north star, if it had not committed repeated crimes of omission and had told the entire story of police violence in the 2010s, people would have been justifiably upset and disgusted by Derek Chauvin's crime.

There would have been condemnations.

Maybe even a few protests.

But because of the malpractice committed by legacy news, millions of people were under the belief that the murder of George Floyd was not a tragic outlier event committed by a rogue cop. They believed it was just the latest example of a systemically corrupt and racist American justice system.

Even though there was zero evidence that the killing of George Floyd had anything to do with race, the image of a middle-aged White cop nonchalantly pressing his knee into the neck of a Black man, seemingly smirking while the life drained out of his body, was a gut punch to the majority of Americans.

LeBron James, a billionaire athlete who lived in a $23 million Brentwood mansion, echoed this feeling when he tweeted, "We're literally hunted EVERYDAY/EVERYTIME we step foot outside the comfort of our homes!"

The media had ripped open the scab of America's original sin of racism and released a highly volatile mix of fury and resentment.

Outraged Americans were about to ignore COVID stay-at-home orders and take to the streets.

Most wanted to make their voices heard, wanted to fight for meaningful change.

But others were out for revenge.

They were determined to burn it all down.

Chapter 15
American Inferno

The following day was eerily quiet. Even though the video of Floyd's death had already gone viral, most Americans were still reluctant to step outside of their homes and protest. Understandable, considering that for two and a half straight months, elected leaders, public health officials, and the media had waged a relentless campaign to keep the public compliant, isolated, and inside.

There was a small protest in Minneapolis that night involving a few hundred people, and things did get a bit unruly—some squad cars were vandalized and a couple of police stations were tagged with graffiti—but city leaders must have breathed a huge sigh of relief; they could handle this.

Little did anyone know, this would be the country's final night of peace for the rest of the summer.

Despite the relative calm, Minnesota officials knew they had a potentially explosive situation on their hands and that the city could easily spiral into lawlessness.

About eighteen hours after Floyd was pronounced dead, Minneapolis's first Black police chief, Medaria Arradondo, tried to lower the temperature by announcing that all four officers had been fired. Outside of grumblings from the president of the Minneapolis police union and some conservative commentators on Twitter, no one seemed too concerned about the lack of due process.

While Arradondo tried to calm the public and lower the temperature, the city's uber-progressive young mayor, Jacob Frey, seemed more interested in scoring political points.

"Being Black in America should not be a death sentence,"[212] he pronounced, ignoring the fact that one of the fired officers was himself Black, and that there was no evidence that Chauvin had been motivated by anything more than a general indifference to human life. Tellingly, during Chauvin's murder trial the following year, prosecutors would never bring race up as a motive.

It was once standard practice for TV newscasts to report the race of both the suspects and victims in crime stories. For years, this rankled social justice activists. They pressured news outlets to stop doing it, arguing that it reinforced racial stereotypes and was causing the public to favor harsh sentencing laws. Besides, these critics argued, a suspect's race was completely irrelevant and broadcasting it served no public good. Gradually, news outlets began to change. By the early 2010s, not only was a suspect's

---

212 Erin Donaghue, "Four Minneapolis Police Officers Fired After Death of Unarmed Man George Floyd," CBS News, May 28, 2020

race rarely mentioned but newscasts were dedicating less airtime to crime stories in general.

Of course, these new standards were repeatedly ignored during the coverage of police violence in the 2010s. All of a sudden, the media reverted to its old playbook. The racial identity of the victims was always mentioned. And the race of the officers was mentioned too, but only if it fit the predetermined storyline.

On May 26, 2020, David Muir opened *ABC World News Tonight* wearing a funereal-black suit-and-tie combo. "The US nearing a very difficult milestone with the Corona virus," he somberly told his audience. "But we're going to begin here this evening with tension building tonight in Minneapolis after an unarmed Black man died after being arrested and pinned to the ground by an officer. He can be heard on video saying, 'I can't breathe.' Tonight, four police officers have now been fired."

Muir tossed to reporter Alex Perez, who irresponsibly opened his package by also pushing the race angle: "Tonight, the Black man in this horrifying video, on the ground and in handcuffs, is dead. The White officer, with his knee on his neck along with three other officers—all fired."

Perez had willfully declined to mention that two of the three "other officers" were men of color.

Over at CBS, anchor Norah O'Donnell, in addition to misidentifying the victim as "George Lloyd," also leaned into the racial framing of the story: "There's breaking news in the shocking case of an unarmed African American man who died after being handcuffed and then pinned to the ground by Minneapolis police."

The next afternoon, President Trump, who won his improbable bid for the White House, in large part, on a platform of law and order, expressed his outrage at Floyd's death. "I feel very, very badly," he told reporters. "That's a very shocking sight."[213]

Joe Biden, who would unseat the president five months later, took it a step further. Echoing the language of BLM, he framed Chauvin's actions as something more than just an isolated incident, calling it "part of an ingrained, systemic cycle of injustice that still exists in this country."[214]

On May 27, 2020, two days after Floyd's death, the dam broke. In a spontaneous outpouring of anger and grief, hundreds of thousands of people took to the streets from coast to coast. In many states, the protesters were defying strict stay-at-home orders.

It was the perfect storm. After eight years of relentlessly being fed a one-sided and misleading view of police brutality, and after two months of being isolated and locked down in their homes—unable to earn a living or send their children to school—the American psyche had broken. The nation was a powder keg, ready to explode.

Following a now familiar pattern, the daytime would mostly be devoted to legitimate protesting. The night, to destruction. But this time, the scale was different: The Floyd riots exploded with a ferocity that stunned the country and its leaders. For weeks, cities across America would devolve into a fiery, anarchic, dystopian nightmare.

In that first night of violence, demonstrators in Los Angeles completely blocked the normally gridlocked 101 Freeway. In Saint Louis, one man was killed after protesters blocked one of

---

213 Jill Colvin and Colleen Long, "Trump Tries a New Response After George Floyd's Death," AP, May 28, 2020

214 Quint Forgey, "'George Floyd's Life Mattered': Biden Condemns Death of Black Man in Minneapolis Custody," Politico, May 27, 2020

the city's busy freeways. In Chicago, six people were shot and one killed during a rally.

But Minneapolis got the worst of it by far. There was widespread looting. Big chain stores like Target and AutoZone were wiped clean, but the true price of the lawlessness was paid by the hundreds of small business owners who lost their stores to vandalism and arson.

A disgusted Minneapolis police spokesperson, John Elder, said, "Tonight was a different night of protesting than it was just the night before."[215]

Things would only get exponentially worse.

The following day, May 28, 2020, the Floyd family hired old friend Benjamin Crump to represent them. Over the ensuing weeks, the social justice lawyer would continue to raise the heat, calling the killing of Floyd "torture." He also publicly claimed that "we have two justice systems in America. One for Black America and one for White America."[216]

Meantime, the pandemic was largely forgotten as protesters in more than two thousand cities and towns marched by the thousands, chanting, singing, and screaming for systemic change. Some made radical proposals that, just months earlier, would have been viewed as absurd and dangerously naive: Defund the police, end capitalism, close all prisons, and release all convicts.

It didn't seem to occur to many of these nouveaux radicals that the system they were so intent on destroying seemed to be working just fine. The four officers had been fired and would

---

215 Matt Furber, John Eligon, and Audra D. S. Burch, "Minneapolis Police, Long Accused of Racism, Face Wrath of Wounded City," *New York Times*, May 27, 2020

216 Nicquel Terry Ellis, "George Floyd's Family Lawyer Ben Crump Has Often Been the Man Behind the Mourners," *USA Today*, June 3, 2020.

soon be charged with felonies. The president had spoken out against Derek Chauvin. His opponent, Joe Biden, had done the same. Even conservative stalwarts like Rush Limbaugh and Sean Hannity denounced Derek Chauvin. In fact, other than a few random voices on the fringes of alternative right-wing media, you would have been hard pressed to find anyone defending The Minneapolis Four.

In New York, CNN was having a hard time convincing its reporters to go out into the field. Between the deadly pandemic, rampant lawlessness on the streets, and an overwhelmed police department, staff members felt they were being asked to risk their lives to cover the story.

Dan Simon, a CNN reporter at the time, agreed to provide live coverage of the unrest in San Francisco and Portland. "It was an out-of-control wildfire and by this point the genie was out of the bottle," he says of the madness in the streets—fueled, in part, by nearly a decade of one-sided news coverage of police brutality. "The media overplayed its hand. There were some high-profile incidents caught on tape. It created a false narrative, and it was the media's responsibility to set the record straight. But it didn't. It was a failure of public officials and the media."

Many reporters complained that network producers were repeating the mistakes made during Ferguson. They wanted great TV—which meant visuals of angry mobs, fires, and looting. But constantly airing those images only served to encourage more people to join in, especially once it became clear that law enforcement was doing little to stop the destruction.

There were others who argued that it was the fecklessness of politicians, especially progressives who supported the BLM movement, that allowed the violence to escalate to dystopian levels. In particular, they pointed the finger at a highly controversial decision made by Minneapolis Mayor Jacob Frey.

On May 28, an angry mob, thousands strong, surrounded the city's Third Precinct. The location had significance, since that's where the four fired officers had been stationed. The crowd threw rocks, projectiles, and Molotov cocktails at the building. The outlaws were fearless, sensing correctly that they could act with impunity since city leaders had ordered police officers not to retaliate. At 10:09 p.m., after rioters jumped over the fences surrounding the precinct, Frey made a decision that was unprecedented in American history. Determined to avoid a direct confrontation between law enforcement and "protesters," he ordered the evacuation of the Third Precinct.

As law enforcement officers ran for their lives, the mob stormed in, destroying, looting, and vandalizing just about everything in sight. Still thirsty for vengeance, they set the building on fire and blocked any attempts by firefighters to put the flames out.

By the time the sun came up, the precinct was a simmering burnt shell. It immediately became a powerful flashpoint in what had quickly become a politically polarized debate.

President Trump lashed out at Frey's decision to retreat, calling him "very weak" and a "radical left mayor."

He also tweeted, "These THUGS are dishonoring the memory of George Floyd and I won't let that happen."

While the destruction of the Third Precinct packed a powerful symbolic punch, small business owners in working-class South Minneapolis were suffering heartbreaking losses.

Rory Purnell was at home, watching helplessly as TV news showed mobs indiscriminately setting fire to the buildings near his barbershop. Determined to save the business he had worked so hard to build, he raced back into town, planning to put up a sign declaring it was Black-owned.

"We're seeing people getting out of cars with bats and stuff," he said. "I just begged them—leave the barbershop alone." [217]

It didn't work. His business was set on fire, just like most of the others on his street.

By May 28, even liberal Minnesota Governor Tim Walz had seen enough and activated the National Guard. "Let's be very clear," he said. "The situation in Minneapolis is no longer, in any way, about the murder of George Floyd. It is about attacking civil society, instilling fear and disrupting our great cities."

Many politicians and community leaders realized that they now had an obligation to condemn not just the killing of George Floyd but also the deadly rioting that was intensifying by the night.

For some reason, legacy news seemed incapable of holding onto both those thoughts at the same time.

Many reporters were encouraged to minimize or flat-out gaslight their audiences about the destruction.

NPR changed its internal guidelines, encouraging reporters to avoid using the term "riot," in favor of words like "protest" or "uprising."

The Oxford dictionary defines "riot" as "a violent disturbance of the peace by a crowd." It was Orwellian to deny that this was exactly what was happening on a large scale.

It's worth noting that it wasn't all violence and mayhem—there were indeed massive peaceful demonstrations. An objective news organization would have treated the protests and the riots

[217] Jim Wu, "Protests Continue to Rage After Death of George Floyd," *New York Times*, May 28, 2020

as two distinct events. Instead, legacy news insisted on conflating the two, gaslighting the public about the true scale of the riots. This would be like a TV reporter stressing that despite a deadly 7.6 earthquake, the ground was calm for most of the day.

Liz Collin was a trusted face in Minneapolis. For twelve years, she had been an anchor and reporter for the CBS affiliate, WCCO. With her perfectly coiffed blond hair, piercing blue eyes, and just the hint of a smile on her lips, she had all the ingredients news directors look for in on-air talent: good looks, smarts, and warmth.

But as the protests raged on, viewers couldn't help but notice that Liz Collin was missing from the station's broadcasts. Turns out she had been pulled off the anchor chair by station management. The reason? She had committed the cardinal sin of being married to a cop.

"They considered it to be a conflict of interest," she explains, reflecting on those strange, disorienting days.

But Collin didn't have time to dwell on what she saw as an unfair decision by station management. Left-wing activists, who had convinced themselves that anyone affiliated with the police, in any way at all, deserved to have their lives destroyed, doxed her. "I had so many death threats. There were four separate protests at my home."

In one incident, about one hundred BLM supporters gathered in front of her house and smashed pinata effigies of Collin, demanding that she and her husband be fired.[218]

This was peak cancel culture. Radical activists, who knew their views were still on the fringe of American public opinion,

---

[218] Neal Justin, "Liz Collin, WCCO Anchor and Wife of Former Police Union Chief Bob Kroll, Leaves Station," *Minneapolis Star Tribune*, January 25, 2022

made examples out of people like Collin for thought crimes, both real and imagined. Heretics were swiftly punished by being publicly shamed, fired, or doxed. The goal was to create an atmosphere in which people feared expressing any opinions that might challenge the movement's doctrinaire positions.

"People saw what was happening in my situation," Collin says. "They were trying to send a message."

Message received. Collin helplessly watched as her station caved in to the demands of protesters.

"There was a memo that came out to all the CBS-owned-and-operated stations," she recalls. "It said not to use the word 'riot.' It also mandated that half the people interviewed on camera had to be people of color or from a protected class. That's not so easy to accomplish in Minneapolis."

News managers throughout the country did what they do best: Overreact. No one wanted to make a decision that could be labeled "racist" or held up as an example of "White supremacy."

So, in newsrooms from coast to coast, professional ethics were cast aside, and veteran journalists were forced to swallow hard and come to peace with the twisted logic of those who insisted that truth and objectivity were just code words for racism.

Throughout that deadly summer of rage, reporters were expected to contextualize, minimize, and in some cases, excuse the violence.

This led to credibility-killing on-air absurdities. For example, MSNBC's Ali Velshi did a live shot in front of a building fully engulfed in flames and described the scene as not "generally speaking unruly." [219]

---

[219] Nikolas Lanum, "Pro-Choice Protests the Latest in Liberal Media's History of Defending Violence by Left-Wing Activists," Fox News, May 10, 2022

CNN anchor Chris Cuomo minimized the rioting in New York by asking, "Please show me where it says protests are supposed to be polite and peaceful?"

But the gaslighter-in-chief was Cuomo's counterpart at CNN, Don Lemon. He described the scenes of deadly violence in Minneapolis as merely "outbursts of anger." He also claimed that the coordinated looting sprees in New York were due to "economic desperation." And over live footage of rioters pillaging stores in Los Angeles, he told his viewers, "So do not get it twisted and think that this is something that has never happened before and this is so terrible and these savages and all that. This is how the country was started."

A generation earlier, during the 1992 riots in Los Angeles, network news managed to strike a balance—objectively reporting on *both* the widespread violence and the outrage over the acquittal of the police officers involved in the Rodney King beating.

Here's how NBC's Tom Brokaw opened his newscast a few days into the riots: "As fires, looting, and street violence continue—a lawless reaction to the acquittal of four White police officers in the beating of Black motorist Rodney King. National Guardsmen are being deployed to neighborhoods not yet under assault."

Dan Rather was also in truth-telling mode, opening the *CBS Evening News* with this straightforward account: "Two thousand National Guardsmen are in Los Angeles tonight in case they're needed to keep order," he gravely told his viewers. "In violence following the Rodney King verdict, at least ten people have been killed, 200 injured and there have been 300 arrests. Property damage—100 million and expected to rise."

On ABC, Peter Jennings masterfully, and somewhat poetically, spoke to the horror many people felt from both the verdict and the senseless destruction that followed: "Good evening. This has been a day in which people all over the country have been using words and phrases such as outrage, powerlessness, wanton violence and hopelessness, anger, frustration, betrayal, and racism. Some Americans were completely shocked at the verdict in the Rodney King case and the violence which followed."

Jennings then tossed to a package that, in stark contrast to the reporting in 2020, gave voice to the true victims of riots: the working-class people who live in the neighborhoods being destroyed. As one Black police officer said, "I haven't heard anyone mention Rodney King. It's just people taking advantage of the situation right now."

Days into the 2020 riots, there still weren't many voices calling for calm and reconciliation. Former President Obama made a statement that, while characteristically mild in tone, made it clear where his sympathies lay: "It's natural to wish for life 'to just get back to normal' as a pandemic and economic crisis upend everything around us. But we have to remember that for millions of Americans, being treated differently on account of race is tragically, painfully, maddeningly 'normal'—whether it's while dealing with the healthcare system, or jogging down the street, or just watching birds in the park."[220]

President Trump made another attempt at empathy, saying, "I understand the hurt. I understand the pain." But his aggressive message to the rioters, delivered through a tweet, was not exactly soothing: "When the looting starts, the shooting starts."

---

220 Maggie Astor, "What Trump, Biden and Obama Said About the Death of George Floyd," *New York Times*, May 29, 2020

This incendiary tweet prompted the social media giant to take the unprecedented step of adding a warning label to the president's message.

Celebrities, of course, also felt the need to weigh in. While many of the messages were fairly anodyne, some major stars with massive followings raised the temperature even higher with angry and emotional social media posts.

Beyoncé, who had a staggering 156 million followers on Instagram, posted a video in which she said, "We're broken, and we're disgusted. No more seeing people of color as less than human."

Nicki Minaj tweeted to her twenty million followers, "White people have been using violence against black people since the beginning of time. We didn't invent violence & looting. Let your voice be heard. #BlackLivesMatter."

The NBA's Washington Wizards put out a statement in all caps that screamed, "WE WILL NO LONGER TOLERATE THE ASSASSINATION OF PEOPLE OF COLOR IN THIS COUNTRY. WE WILL NO LONGER ACCEPT THE ABUSE OF POWER FROM LAW ENFORCEMENT!"

Celebrities posted pictures of themselves taking part in BLM protests. Among them were mega-stars like Madonna, Ariana Grande, Pink, Stephen Curry, Jamie Foxx, and Ben Affleck.

Some, like Seth Rogen, Steve Carell, and Justin Timberlake, went one step further, donating money to organizations that were bailing out people arrested for participating in the riots.

By Friday, May 29, 2020, the US was in crisis. Seemingly everyone in power, from small-town police chiefs to the president of the United States, had underestimated the explosiveness of the civil disobedience.

"Quite candidly, right now, we do not have the numbers," admitted Minnesota Governor Tim Walz. "We cannot arrest people when we're trying to hold ground because of the sheer size, the dynamics, and the wanton violence that's coming out here. There's simply more of them than us."[221]

Seven states called in the National Guard. Many big cities imposed curfews, and California, Minnesota, and Pennsylvania all declared official states of emergency. But none of these measures stopped the violence. If anything, the protests were growing larger and more menacing by the day. Some worried that the US was actually on the brink of civil war.

Dr. David Kilcullen, a diplomat and leading expert on counter-insurgency strategy, said, "To me, current conditions feel disturbingly similar to things I have seen in Iraq, Lebanon, Libya, Somalia and Cambodia."[222]

In what seemed like a desperate attempt to calm the public before the start of the weekend, authorities arrested Derek Chauvin and charged him with third-degree murder and second-degree manslaughter.

"This is by far the fastest that we've ever charged a police officer," County Attorney Mike Freeman told reporters.[223]

If it was supposed to appease those bent on destruction, it didn't work.

The final weekend of May 2020 would go down as one of the bloodiest and most lawless in American history.

---

221 "'Absolute Chaos' in Minneapolis as Protests Grow Across U.S.," *New York Times*, May 30, 2020

222 CJ Werleman, "Is the United States on the Brink of Another Civil War?" *Byline Times*, June 1, 2020

223 "Former MPD Officer Derek Chauvin in Custody, Charged With Murder in George Floyd's Death," CBS News, May 29, 2020

Cities burned, police cars were torched, freeways were blocked, windows were smashed, stores were looted, innocent people were murdered, and thousands of family-owned businesses—some of which were barely staying afloat during the pandemic—were completely destroyed.

It was the weekend when CNN, which had been credulously amplifying the message of radical agitators for eight straight years, found *itself* the target of angry rioters. Ironically, a fast-moving SWAT team was the only thing that saved employees at the network's Atlanta headquarters from a charging mob.

The legacy networks spent the weekend showing image after image of widespread anarchy and violence. Reporters continuously contradicted their own visuals, insisting that, despite what everyone was watching on their screens, the protests were actually mostly peaceful. Confused viewers had to decide whether to trust their eyes or their ears.

Things were chaotic at *CBS Mornings*, the network's flagship show anchored by Gayle King.

"COVID happened and we all had to work from home," recalls Lisa Bacon, who was an editorial producer for the show. "Every day we would run COVID death counts, but as soon as George Floyd died, the pandemic was gone. It didn't matter."

Bacon, a Harvard graduate, is a veteran news and entertainment producer, perhaps best known for being the executive producer of Joan Rivers's snarky *Fashion Police* show on E!

At CBS, the team held meetings twice a day: first at 6 a.m. and then at noon. Bacon doesn't remember hearing any discussions about how to cover the story. "No one spoke up. Not one person said maybe we should get the other side to the Floyd story."

Bacon says emotions were running high that summer. One reporter wanted management to donate money to BLM and Floyd's family. "I have to give some credit to CBS," she says. "They said no. You can't be donating money to BLM and then claim you're staying neutral."

Bacon says that Gayle King, the face of the show, was struggling to keep her emotions in check. At one morning meeting, someone pitched a story about an elderly African American woman who'd been pulled over by the cops.

"'You know,'" Bacon recalls Gayle telling the team, "'the police are only doing that because she's Black.'"

"I want to give Gayle King a lot of credit," Bacon says. "She works very hard. She is very involved. She wants to break news. But when it came to this story, she couldn't separate herself from it. She believed in what the activists were fighting for with all her heart."

While legacy networks were conflating the protests with the riots and gaslighting the public about the latter, Fox was conflating the protests and the riots and gaslighting the public about the former.

In its coverage, the network rarely emphasized the scale and passion of the demonstrations. Whatever one personally thinks about the merits of the movement, somewhere between 6–10 percent of all Americans took part in at least one protest that summer.[224] In and of itself, that is a huge story that deserved a lot of thoughtful coverage.

But to its credit, Fox covered some important stories that legacy media was too snakebitten to touch.

---

224 Larry Buchanan, Quoctrung Bui, and Jugal K. Patel, "Black Lives Matter May Be the Largest Movement in U.S. History," *New York Times*, July 3, 2020

For example, on May 31, Fox's Mark Meredith did a live shot from Washington, DC, reporting that aggressive protesters had surrounded the White House and become criminally violent. They not only threw bricks, bottles, and fireworks at law enforcement but also punched, kicked, and tossed buckets of urine on them. Sixty Secret Service agents were injured in the clash—eleven of them so badly that they had to be hospitalized.

On just about any other day, this would have been an obvious lead story. But outside of Fox News, only CBS gave it significant airtime.

On Monday, June 1, CNN's Anderson Cooper dropped any remaining pretense of journalistic objectivity. Instead of opening his show with something resembling news, he instead delivered an angry, partisan screed.

"Good evening," he said authoritatively. "We are witnessing a failure of presidential leadership at a time when this country, when we the people need it—perhaps more than ever in our lifetime. Tonight, with flash-bang grenades going off and tear gas in the air, the President of the Unites States, a wannabe wartime president, has what he hoped was his MacArthur moment, his Patton promise, calling himself our law-and-order president. He said he'll bring active-duty military troops into our American states and cities to dominate—his words—*dominate*, in the wake of the police killing of George Floyd a week ago." Cooper ended with a flourish, "What happened in the past hour would be comical, if it wasn't so dangerous and so destructive."

Cooper probably thought he was having his "Walter Cronkite turning on the Vietnam War moment," but the truth was he had already lost his credibility on this story back in the early Trayvon Martin days. Despite his distinguished appearance and mild temperament, his bias had been glaringly obvious to anyone paying even the slightest bit of attention. Cooper's show was well produced and compelling. It would have made a great entry into the crowded field of cable opinion shows—if only he'd honestly labeled it as such.

In a panicked attempt to "meet the moment," TV news pushed out some unintentionally comedic pieces. *PBS NewsHour* ran a package on cultural biases in the workplace. One of the "experts" they interviewed claimed that strict schedules and time management were Eurocentric and therefore racist.

NBC ran an uncritical story about the push for the use of gender-neutral pronouns in the workplace. CBS ran a piece about cultural appropriation in food, arguing that it was "problematic" for White chefs to profit from making traditionally Black dishes.

CBS Mornings' Gayle King fronted a six-minute segment on White privilege. One of her guests was Ibram X. Kendi, a recently hired CBS News contributor. This was a shocking lapse in judgment since Kendi was best known for saying things like, "The only remedy to past discrimination is present discrimination"[225] and "Whiteness prevents White people from connecting to humanity."

Her second guest was Robin DiAngelo, a White professor from a small-time college, who hit the jackpot by writing the bestseller *White Fragility: Why It's So Hard for White People to Talk About Racism.*

"Good to see you both," Gayle King said, turning first to DiAngelo. "So, I would like you to explain first, what White

[225] Ibram X. Kendi, "Ibram X. Kendi Defines What It Means to Be an Antiracist," Penguin, June 9, 2020

privilege is exactly, and why White people have such a hard time seeing it because it's so clear to most Black people I know."

"White privilege is the automatic, taken-for-granted advantage bestowed upon White people living in a society based on the premise of White as the human ideal," DiAngelo said to approving murmurs. "From its founding [this country] established White advantage as a matter of law, and today as a matter of policy and practice."

These are provocative and inflammatory opinions, arguably worthy of discussion, but definitely necessitating a healthy dose of skepticism and probing follow-up questions. Gayle King would not be providing any of that.

She didn't push back when it was asserted that White children as young as three were being conditioned to be White supremacists. She didn't ask a follow-up question when Ibram X. Kendi made the counterfactual claim that "too many unarmed Black men are being shot while armed White men are just being arrested." She had nothing to say when Kendi made the Catch-22 argument that the surest sign a White person is racist is if they deny it. She didn't even challenge DiAngelo when she claimed that White people do not care about racial justice and that "the status quo of our society is racism."

If the summer of 2020 was supposed to be a seminal moment in the US—a long-overdue national reckoning with racism—it was hard to tell from the reporting. A lot of the news coverage, especially in print, was veering into outright silliness. *The Guardian* printed an article claiming that gardening was racist. *The Hill* published an article arguing that libraries reinforced White supremacy. Many outlets published a PETA blog post claiming that milk was a symbol of—you guessed it—White supremacy.

It was like those old Mad Libs books. Editors and news directors were sending out reporters to cover stories on "(add noun or verb) is racist." Just fill in the blank, and you had your story for the day.

Sound like an exaggeration?

Major newspapers and magazines actually published articles claiming that the following things were racist: ballet, dieting, lifting weights, geology, owning dogs, opera, being nice, tipping, veganism, yoga, and even zombies.[226]

Meantime, the violence continued.

The president's tough talk was cheering up his demoralized supporters but further inflaming the protesters. Blue-city politicians were trying the gentle approach: making it clear that they empathized with the cause, but not the violence. That didn't seem to help either.

On June 3, 2020, after eight straight nights of violence, Minnesota Attorney General Keith Ellison threw the protesters another bone. The state was now going to charge Derek Chauvin with second-degree murder instead of the previously announced third-degree charge. Additionally, the other three officers had all been arrested and charged with aiding and abetting the murder of George Floyd.

This hasty decision was met with praise from the Floyd family attorney Benjamin Crump, who issued the following statement: "This is a bittersweet moment. We are all deeply satisfied

[226] Michael Deacon, "Everything Is Racist Nowadays… and Here's an A-Z to Prove It," *The Telegraph*, November 19, 2024

that Attorney General Ellison took decisive action, arresting & charging ALL the officers involved."[227]

The following day, the major US networks ran wall-to-wall coverage of a reverential memorial service for George Floyd in Minneapolis. But that, too, did nothing to stop the madness.

The rage was feeding on itself.

Around this time, a poll showed that 67 percent of Americans now supported BLM.[228] It was an amazing achievement for the organization's three founding members, who had captured the public's broad support despite being openly anti-capitalist, anti-West, anti-family, and anti-Semitic.

BLM had exploited a sense of guilt in the collective American psyche, and now many of their empathetic White allies were struggling to find an outlet for their shame.

At rallies around the country, some White people started performing a ritual—washing the feet of Black protesters and community leaders. The White people performing these acts of penance seemed to be in a state of religious hysteria. Some wept, their eyes bulging wide, as they looked to the crowd for approval.

This trend of self-blame inevitably led to hostility towards America's history and its founding fathers. Statues of Christopher Columbus were destroyed or taken down in five US cities. A statue of George Washington in Portland was spray-painted with "genocidal colonist" and "BLM" before being wrapped in an American flag, set on fire, and pulled down. Statues of other

---

227 Bill Chappell, "Chauvin and 3 Former Officers Face New Charges Over George Floyd's Death," NPR, June 3, 2020

228 Juliana Menasce Horowitz, Kiana Cox, and Kiley Hurst, "Views of Race, Policing and Black Lives Matter in the 5 Years Since George Floyd's Killing," Pew Research Center, May 7, 2025

founding fathers like Benjamin Franklin, Thomas Jefferson, and Alexander Hamilton were also vandalized or destroyed.

By June 7, wide-scale protests had spread overseas. Massive demonstrations were held in far-flung locations like Australia, France, Germany, and Spain.

During his brief life, George Floyd was a complex man who never could outrun his demons for very long. In death, he had suddenly become the symbol of a movement.

On June 9, 2020, he was laid to rest in his hometown of Houston. It was a send-off worthy of a martyr and a statesman. Celebrities and dignitaries were in attendance. Minneapolis Mayor Jacob Frey knelt by his casket and sobbed into his COVID mask.

Floyd's funeral was carried live by most major legacy news outlets—an honor not even afforded to Nelson Madela. The service ran for more than four hours. A horse-drawn carriage then carried Floyd's gold-colored casket to the cemetery.

It's hard to pinpoint when and why the violence stopped. The rage just slowly burned itself out. In most American cities, things started to calm down by mid-June. But there were some notable exceptions. Portland, Oregon, which had a Black population of just 5.6 percent, was the scene of one hundred straight nights of violence.

By the time the smoke literally cleared, the George Floyd riots had caused close to $2 billion in damages—the costliest in American history.

Somewhere between nineteen and twenty-five people were killed during the rioting, making it one of the deadliest.

In August 2020, legacy news returned to live coverage of another working-class city setting itself on fire. This time it was Kenosha,

Wisconsin. The inciting incident was the non-lethal police shooting of a man named Jacob Blake, who had violated a restraining order by entering the house of his children's mother without permission, had taken one of the kids, and was trying to get away while armed with a knife. The officers would not be charged in the case.

There were also major protests in September of that year when a grand jury decided not to indict the police officers involved in the fatal shooting of Breonna Taylor, an EMT, during a no-knock drug raid.

And the country was on edge the following April, when the jury in the Derek Chauvin murder trial began deliberations. They ultimately found him guilty of all charges, and he was sentenced to twenty-two and a half years in prison.

Peace prevailed.

The other three officers involved in Floyd's killing were later convicted of every charge brought against them in both federal and state courts.

After Chauvin's trial, the media's coverage of police violence began to dissipate.

The fever was breaking.

It would be nice to think this might have been because the movement succeeded in making meaningful changes to American policing. But the data tells a different story. The number of police killings of unarmed men has not changed much since 2020. These incidents were relatively rare then and, thankfully, remain so now.

However, if you include armed suspects, police actually got more trigger-happy since the death of George Floyd. In 2024,

American law enforcement killed 1,226 suspects—an *increase* of 18 percent from 2019.[229]

But the media looked the other way. The most important story of the 2010s became nothing more than an afterthought in the 2020s.

Legacy news spent eight years race-baiting and cherry-picking cases.

It spent eight years platforming witnesses who made wild claims that too often turned out to be lies.

It spent eight years ignoring or attacking any evidence that contradicted the claims of activists.

It spent eight years refusing to investigate BLM despite the fact that, behind the catchy name, the movement had problematic beliefs and associations.

It spent eight years cutting itself off from law-enforcement contacts who could have provided much-needed balance to its coverage of the high-profile cases of alleged police brutality.

It spent eight years tirelessly contextualizing the deadly violence of the riots but never contextualized the police killings themselves.

It spent eight years boosting ratings by giving viewers a front-row seat to the captivating spectacle of working-class American cities burning to the ground.

It spent eight years feeding us a steady diet of outrage porn, leading the public to believe that Black men were being routinely hunted down by racist cops.

Broadcast news was complicit in bringing us to the brink of civil war.

---

[229] Steven Rich, Tim Arango, and Nicholas Bogel-Burroughs, "Since George Floyd's Murder, Police Killings Keep Rising, Not Falling," *New York Times*, May 24, 2025

In the end, news betrayed its values.

Journalists turned from being truth-tellers to activists.

Reporters manipulated the facts, distorted evidence, and gaslit their audiences.

It was malpractice.

But ultimately, broadcast news paid a steep price for its unethical coverage. Legacy news lost viewers; it lost influence; and, most importantly, it lost the country's trust.

Epilogue

"The truth will set you free, but
first it will piss you off."

—GLORIA STEINEM

Chapter 16

Pottery Barn Rules

Let's assess the damage.

The major legacy networks—NBC, ABC, and CBS—lost more than 60 percent of their combined nightly news audience from 1995 to 2025.[230]

In the cable universe, CNN lost about half its viewership.

If you ask the managers running these newsrooms to explain how this happened, they will likely give you a lengthy answer, blaming things like changing viewing habits, the proliferation of social media, and cord-cutting. All of those answers are legitimate, but they obfuscate the core issue: TV news lost the trust of the public. If you are in the business of truth-telling, you cannot succeed if people don't believe what you're saying.

An alarming 2024 Gallup poll asked Americans whether they trusted broadcast journalists to report the news "fully, accurately

---

[230] "Network TV: Evening News Ratings Over Time by Network," Pew Research Center, July 9, 2015

and fairly." Only 31 percent answered yes. An overwhelming 69 percent said they had little to "no trust at all."[231]

And yet, when I interviewed news executives for this project and suggested that a return to real objective journalism might be the business's only path back to relevance and profitability, they dismissed the idea. *No, that would never work. Audiences have been conditioned to expect news that conforms to their biases.*

"I'm pessimistic. Journalism as we practiced it is dead and on life support," says veteran anchor Terry Anzur.

Pat Lalama agrees with that bleak assessment: "Will the networks ever get back to true journalism? No, it's never going to happen. It's done. They are clouded by their own arrogance."

It is true that nobody doubles down on failure quite like television executives do.

In the late 1990s, when HBO ushered in the new era of premium content with critically acclaimed shows like *Oz* and *The Sopranos*, the legacy gatekeepers dug their heels in and continued to greenlight the same old stale diet of broad, formulaic shows that hadn't worked in years. As a result, the prime-time audience for network TV was cut by more than half between 2005 and 2025.

I've personally pitched shows to executives at cable networks that have lost 80 percent of their audience. These empty suits are allergic to unique ideas, and after passing on anything even slightly outside the box, will proceed to authoritatively explain what "works" and what "doesn't." I've had to bite my tongue to keep from asking them if they are so in tune with what the audience wants, why doesn't anyone watch their network anymore?

[231] Megan Brenan, "Americans' Trust in Media Remains at Trend Low," Gallup, October 14, 2024

Are arrogance and an unwillingness to change the only things keeping news executives from recommitting themselves to true journalism?

In my opinion, it runs deeper than that. For one thing, there are cultural issues.

Unlike the early days of TV news, when the business was staffed with scrappy, blue-collar reporters, broadcast journalism is now almost exclusively the domain of highly educated white-collar employees. Most of the staff are steeped in blue-bubble culture. They take boutique fitness classes, shop at the local co-op, fuss over imaginary gluten allergies, do juice cleanses, and post every meal they eat on Instagram.

TV executives and anchors move in even loftier circles. They are the 1 percent the Bernie Bros rail against. They go to swanky parties in the Hamptons, rub elbows with celebrities, send their kids to the "right" private schools, and tend to use the word "summer" as a verb. Entry into this idyllic blue-bubble world comes with a price tag. One is expected to be sympathetic to the progressive ideals laid out in those "In This House" signs people used to post on their front lawns.

"There are very few advantages to being old and retired," the late legendary newsman Bill Applegate told me. "But one advantage is you get to tell the truth. If I was still working, I would have kept quiet."

Applegate said the corporate pressure to conform and fall in line was palpable: "If I ran CBS News and tried to change things, I would have been gone. I don't think you can have anyone run a network news division today without political bias."

There's another compelling reason network executives are reluctant to recommit themselves to real journalism: It's hard work.

True journalism requires a lot of sweat equity: cultivating sources, digging, challenging, probing. It needs fearless journalists who are willing to challenge authority, question dogmas, and deliver hard truths.

Diane Dimond embodied those characteristics, and she, too, is pessimistic: "I want to hope against hope that my chosen career straightens itself out. But it will take a sea change in the colleges and in newsrooms. I'm not holding my breath."

There's also the issue of money. TV news has been slashing budgets across the board for years. Of course, these cuts rarely affect management. But it does leave many TV newsrooms severely short-staffed. This means that producers have to rely on quick, easy stories to fill their news blocks, which means more coverage of fires, crime, high-speed chases, natural disasters, and panels of bloviating talking heads filling up time. It is reactive news. Proactive news requires hiring tough investigative journalists and then giving them the time and resources to break stories. It is expensive and requires patience and a willingness to delay gratification.

A lot of people argue that objective news may sound good in theory, but when push comes to shove, nobody actually wants to watch it. I believe nothing could be further from the truth. A journalistically sound, well-paced and well-written newscast can be exhilarating.

If biased, activist news were a blockbuster movie, it would be one of those formulaic hero's journey films. The good guys would be likeable and charismatic. The bad guys would be over-the-top baddies. We would know exactly how the film would turn out from the very first frame. Those movies can make a lot of money. They have their place. But would we be happy if that was literally all the studios pushed out?

Real journalism, on the other hand, is like a great whodunnit or legal drama. There are a bunch of surprising twists and turns. Someone who seems innocent one moment suddenly appears guilty the next. New evidence is constantly being revealed, changing our perspectives on the story. It is compelling and unpredictable.

I'm not naïve enough to think that Fox News and MSNBC will suddenly embrace old-school journalism: They are successfully serving up a steady diet of comforting confirmation bias to their viewers. But it's the other news divisions—the ones dying a quick and agonizing death—that have the opportunity to save themselves and the profession.

"The old networks are atrophying. The people have been fed Cheetos. At some point they need a salad," says Ashleigh Banfield. "They're feeling sick and they want to get healthy."

Yes, Americans are hungry for real journalism.

The upstart cable network NewsNation, which has dedicated itself to straight-down-the-middle reporting, saw a 22 percent increase in viewership in 2024.[232]

Bari Weiss left *The New York Times* to form her own digital news platform. The Free Press is a lively and stimulating site that fearlessly tackles all sorts of taboo issues, including transgender extremism, anti-Semitism on campuses, social media censorship, and right-wing "wokeism." The writers are curious, smart, and unafraid to challenge the dogma of both the right and the left. In October 2025, Weiss sold The Free Press, which started as a

---

232 BMN Staff, "NewsNation Earns Highest Ratings in Network History During November," Barrett Media, November 27, 2024

Substack newsletter, to Paramount for a reported $150 million. As part of the deal, she was named editor in chief of CBS News.

Shepard Smith also proved that viewers crave truth. His unbiased newscast on FNC did extraordinarily well, despite not pandering by serving comfort food to its mostly conservative viewers.

"We have to shift the fundamental rules of journalism," Smith says about the path forward for journalism. "We have to cover the whole story. The parts we like and the parts we don't."

And that's what this all comes down to: Truth.

Many broadcast journalists have tied themselves into knots trying to justify their crimes of omission. They attempt to deflect the profession's malpractice with lazy excuses about how the anti-law enforcement movement was a generational event and the profession had to meet the moment. They warn us not to be "simplistic" and insist that these issues are "very complex."

These are all excuses.

Truth is simple and real. There is no "your truth" or "my truth": There is only The Truth. The willingness, even eagerness, of industry leaders to support ideas that ran counter to the foundational principles of the profession shows how sick the business got in both soul and spirit. Broadcast news became too rich, too insulated, too bloated—and ultimately corrupt.

The blue-collar pioneers of TV news didn't need diplomas or fancy theories to understand that their mission was simply to be purveyors of truth. They didn't muddle their north stars with abstract gibberish. They just rolled up their sleeves and hit the streets. They fearlessly went after politicians and CEOs. They served as effective checks on power.

I started this book with an anecdote about my father and how his worldview drew me to broadcast news.

Indulge me for just a moment as I share the sad final chapter of his story.

In early 2011, he was diagnosed with advanced heart disease and told that he needed a bypass operation.

My father, who was never comfortable living in truth, breezily dismissed the diagnosis: "Ach, these doctors. You do not understand. They just want to make money. I am fine."

Even though he and I were never particularly close, we had reached a détente—in part, because I finally understood that he would never change, so I decided to stop trying to police all the fabrications he had built his worldview on.

But this was a life-or-death matter and I just couldn't let it slide.

I pressured him to get a second opinion, which he surprisingly agreed to. "Ach, waste of time. You will see."

The second doctor was even more blunt, saying, "If you don't get this operation, you will have a massive heart attack."

But even that hard dose of reality didn't change his mind. He dug in his heels. He was not going to get the bypass, he was completely healthy, and these doctors were nothing more than shysters who wanted his money.

Alarmed by his intractability, I flew to Florida, where he had retired with my mom. I was determined to inundate him with so many irrefutable facts that he would have no choice but to give in.

I came armed with pages of research—studies proving that the surgery was effective and generally safe. I tried to guilt him, demanding to know how he could take the chance of leaving my mother a widow. I offered to go with him to get a third opinion.

I asked him if he enjoyed life, and when he answered yes, I asked him how he could voluntarily cut it short. After all, he was only seventy-five. He had good years ahead of him.

But none of this had the slightest effect on him. I was getting nowhere.

"You do not understand the way world works," he said, masking his denial with a false sense of worldliness. "I was doctor. I know how these people think."

I kept pushing, kept trying to open his eyes to the hard truth of his condition.

"Robbie, you are upsetting your father," my mother would implore. "Enough of this."

But I wouldn't and couldn't let it go.

"You are going to die soon," I blurted out to him one night.

He looked at me for a moment and then burst out laughing, just like he used to when a TV reporter would say something he found ridiculous back in our den in Boston.

"Why thank you," he said, still laughing. "That is very nice to say."

At that moment, I realized I had finally gotten my wish. I was the voice on the other side of the screen. A voice telling him the hard truths he refused to accept. A voice he mistrusted. A voice he found condescending. A voice he found easy to dismiss. A voice he mocked.

On the morning of February 13, 2012, my mom called me and simply said, "He's gone."

He had woken up that morning and suffered a massive fatal heart attack while making his morning coffee.

I often blame myself for not being a better son. For not being a better truth-teller. I should have been more compassionate, more empathetic. Maybe if I had met my father where he was in his denial, instead of aggressively hitting him over the head with a truth stick, I could have gotten through to him.

That is an important lesson for journalists, and it's one I have always struggled with. Truth-telling is essential, but it doesn't have to be cruel and callous. Sometimes, how you tell someone a hard truth is just as important as the crucial information you are trying to convey.

The history of African Americans is a tragic one. It's why millions of Americans had such a visceral reaction to the stories about police violence in the 2010s. They believed the argument that these weren't isolated incidents—that the shootings were a small piece of a bigger, more insidious picture—because it felt right. Because it confirmed their pre-conceived biases. Biases based on historical facts.

Legacy news needed to meet people where they were and *gently* tell them the truth about these cases. Yes, they risked upsetting their audiences. Yes, they were taking the chance that some viewers would turn on them, confusing the message with the messenger. But that is the job we all signed up for.

Journalism is a tough gig.

Truth can be cruel, difficult to hear, alienating, offensive, disappointing. It can hurt feelings and provoke anger and denial.

But in the end, lies can never bend reality. Life doesn't care about the stories we tell ourselves. Truth always wins in the end.

In a healthy and free society, a special group of honest and inquisitive people have the honor of serving as the impartial referees. These thick-skinned iconoclasts have a sacred duty to hold up a mirror to reality. When they shirk that duty—when they prioritize anything else over telling people the whole truth—they lose their way, and they lose the trust of the public.

And when that happens, everyone retreats to different rooms of the glass house, each living in their own siloed realities. That's when friendships break, families get ripped apart, and the nation divides itself in two.

American journalism didn't just break itself—it shattered the country. It might be wishful thinking on my part—maybe this is my blind spot, my refusal to live in the truth—but I firmly believe it's not too late to put the pieces back together again.

About the Author

Credit: Robert Toth

Rob Rosen is a veteran investigative journalist with more than thirty years of experience. He was the executive producer, creator, and showrunner of the investigative, true-crime series *Reasonable Doubt,* the creator of *The Infomercials that Sold Us*, and executive producer and director of *The Dead Files.* Rosen is a graduate of the Boston University College of Communication, and is a member of the DGA and SAG/AFTRA.